TWICE BITTEN

TWICE BITTEN

THE UNTOLD STORY OF HOLYFIELD–TYSON II

GEORGE WILLIS

MAINSTREAM
PUBLISHING

EDINBURGH AND LONDON

This edition, 2014

First published in Great Britain in 2013 by
MAINSTREAM PUBLISHING company
(EDINBURGH) LTD
7 Albany Street
Edinburgh EH1 3UG

ISBN 9781780576701

A catalogue record for this book is available
from the British Library

Printed in Great Britain by
CPI group (UK) Ltd, Croydon CR0 4YY

1 3 5 7 9 10 8 6 4 2

ACKNOWLEDGEMENTS

I HAVE TO THANK MATT Blank, the CEO of Showtime, for the idea of writing this book. It was during a press conference tour for the 2010 welterweight championship between Manny Pacquiao and Shane Mosley when Blank reviewed Showtime's long association with boxing and mentioned the Bite Fight. 'I'd love to read a book about that one,' he said.

I am forever grateful to Mike Murphey for taking me to the high-school football games he covered when I was still in junior high and instilling in me a love of journalism. I must also thank Joe Muench for giving me my first job at the *Las Cruces Sun-News* and my current sports editor at the *New York Post*, Chris Shaw, for continuing to draw out my best work.

This book would not be a reality without the support of literary agent Frank Weimann and his colleagues at the Literary Agency in New York. My gratitude also extends to my editor Ailsa Bathgate and the staff at Mainstream Publishing.

Having worked on this project for nearly two years I've conducted around a hundred interviews either formally or informally. The list of those I'd like to thank for their time and cooperation would be too lengthy to include here, but a few deserve mention, including the late Emanuel Steward, Marc Ratner, Steve Lott, Ken Hershman, Chris DeBlasio, Mario Costa, Joann Mignano, Ronnie Shields, Don King, Terry and

Tommy Lane, and finally Evander Holyfield, Mike Tyson and Kiki Tyson.

To my wife Teresa, thank you for your love and support. To my daughter, Taylor, you are the joy of my life; and to my mother, Gladys, thank you for being my guiding light.

CONTENTS

FOREWORD

TO HAVE COME FROM WHERE I was on 28 June 1997 to where I am now, I am only here because of the love and support I have from family and friends, in spite of believing I didn't deserve it. There are many things I am grateful for. However, there are many things that I look back on with regret. The notorious ear-biting incident that would become the pun of my life is one of those moments. I am sincerely appreciative that I had an opportunity to make amends for my actions and that Evander was gracious enough to forgive me. I have a great deal of respect for him and I'm glad our legacy as human beings doesn't have to be defined by this one disastrous moment.

When I look back on my second fight with Evander Holyfield, I still can't believe that I bit his ear. I mean, what was I thinking . . .? I wasn't. I just reacted, and badly at that. The world would never look at me the same.

When people called me 'the Baddest Man on the Planet', it was a role I embraced. I thought I deserved it because I worked hard to portray that image. I was taught by Cus D'Amato to believe I was the 'Baddest Man on the Planet'. My every waking moment was focused on being the best and believing I was the best. A lot of people didn't like my persona. They thought I was arrogant. I mastered the art of manipulation and intimidation. This is what being 'Mike Tyson' was all about. I was the greatest actor to ever enter the ring.

The first time I met Evander Holyfield had to have been about 1983 when we were in the amateurs. I heard about somebody beating Ricky Womack. I thought that was pretty interesting because Ricky Womack was a fierce competitor. The competitor in me wanted to know more about Evander Holyfield. I was a ferocious predator and needed to know more about what I believed would soon be my prey.

When we finally met, I respected him immediately. He was a quiet guy that seemed to have been raised in the Southern church circuit. But I knew he was a serious and focused fighter. I was highly competitive then. I couldn't wait to decimate him and continue on my reign towards becoming the Baddest Man on the Planet. I believed to be the best you had to beat the best, and Holyfield was considered one of the best during that time.

If we could have fought earlier in our careers as professionals, I think I would have done better. The first fight in 1990 got cancelled. But to be honest, my mind was so messed up I don't think I really would have done well. I was dealing with a great deal of emotional turmoil, and at that time I didn't have the tools or maturity to handle life's blows constructively.

When I learned about the death of Hector 'Macho' Camacho, one of my all-time favourite fighters, I was devastated. It saddened me that one of the most entertaining fighters to ever step into the ring had such a tragic ending. It made me grateful for the changes I had implemented in my life. I am more determined now than ever to stay focused on honouring myself and my family through my actions. I'm very blessed that I now have the opportunity to have another chance at a decent life. I am a happily married man, striving every day to be a better father and a better person all around. I have an amazing support team of people around me now and try to circumvent negative outcomes by staying away from dark people and places. I'm working on not allowing my past to define me as the person I am today. Some days are harder than others but I am constantly working on myself and working towards being the kind of person that makes my family proud.

Doing my one-man show *Mike Tyson: Undisputed Truth* has been a great blessing. It has allowed me a format to open up about the ups and downs in my life and it has given people an impactful look into what they thought they knew about me. My story is about victories and triumphs, mistakes and heartbreak. It's about owning up to what you do and never accepting being labelled something you're not. Through this journey into self-analysis, I am learning I like who I am these days and because of it I believe it makes me more likeable to others.

My continuous life assignment now is remembering gratitude and to live my life with dignity and continue being a good role model to my children. I am now in a place in my life where I recognise my mortality quickly approaching and want to be of service. I want to help underprivileged children and give them hope.

That's why I am dedicated to building my foundation, Mike Tyson Cares. It's something I've embarked on because I believe that everyone should have hope even if their situation appears hopeless. I owe these kids an opportunity because someone gave me one and I'd be nowhere if someone didn't believe in me. Cus D'Amato believed in me when I didn't believe in myself, and he made me believe that I had a purpose and could live out my dream. If only he had told me to be careful what I wished for. But I realise I am not defined by my mistakes. My legacy doesn't have to be defined by them either. I choose to continue growing as a human being and helping make children's lives better.

Mike Tyson
www.MikeTysonCares.org

1

THIRD TIME'S THE CHARM

IT'S THE FIGHT FANS THAT make a big fight. They hype it up with their words, finance it with their dollars and make it glitter with their wardrobes and own unique style. They debate who will win and defend their reasons why. They are passionate almost to a fault, understanding the ultimate thrill is to see their warrior render his opponent unconscious. Blood and bruises are expected if not applauded. That is the essence of the Sweet Science.

It doesn't matter if you're filthy rich or weekend rich, being part of a highly anticipated boxing event can be an orgasmic experience, especially when the coveted world heavyweight championship is on the line.

The Grand Garden Arena at the MGM Grand Hotel and Casino in Las Vegas has become the premier destination for such events. Since opening on 18 December 1993, it has been host to concerts, award shows, tractor pulls and beauty pageants. But in terms of sheer anticipation, excitement and energy, nothing had come close to the atmosphere that filled the building on 9 November 1996.

Close to 17,000 people – some covered in jewels, some wearing jeans – were all out of their seats, standing and cheering as Mike Tyson and Evander Holyfield traded punches in the centre of a boxing ring. For nine intense rounds, Holyfield, a huge underdog despite being a former heavyweight champion, had more than held his own against the heavily favoured Tyson, who was defending his WBA heavyweight championship. Tyson thought Holyfield would be easy work, but he was proving to be exactly what his nickname suggests, 'The Real Deal'.

The harder Tyson punched, the harder Holyfield punched back. That's why the crowd was standing. The roars that filled the arena were deafening.

At this point in his life, Tyson had already earned a fortune, lost a fortune and was now in the process of doing it all over again with little concern about who he faced in the ring. Holyfield was supposed to be another quick payday, a means to collect more cash to spend on houses, cars, women and jewels. 'I'm going to make $30 million Saturday night and sign for another $30 million on Monday,' Tyson had boasted during the press conference days before the fight.

This first fight between Evander Holyfield and Mike Tyson had been years in the making. It had been six years since their first fight was cancelled and twelve years since they had turned pro. Tyson was originally a 25–1 favourite when this fight was announced and a 6–1 favourite when the first bell rang. Holyfield, a two-time heavyweight champion, was viewed as washed up after three wars with Riddick Bowe, two of which Holyfield won, and a lacklustre showing against the former cruiserweight champion Bobby Czyz.

But instead of dominating Holyfield as many had expected, Tyson was getting battered by the underdog. By the end of the ninth round, Tyson was cut over his left eye, and his body and ego were being badly bruised by the determined Holyfield, who was expertly executing a simple game plan. 'When he hits me, I'm going to hit him back,' Holyfield had said.

That strategy, along with other psychological and technical warfare, had Holyfield winning the bout and ruining Tyson's post-prison comeback, which was being orchestrated by the flamboyant boxing promoter Don King.

Until that night, it had all gone exactly as King scripted it. Tyson's ex-wife Robin Givens was long gone and so too were his former managers Bill Cayton and Jim Jacobs. Also gone was his long-time trainer Kevin Rooney, who had moulded Tyson's fighting style since he was a troubled teenager living in the Catskills in upstate New York. King had Tyson all to himself now and his vision to maximise Tyson's earning potential was just getting started.

Three years in an Indiana prison after being convicted of raping Desiree Washington had soured Tyson's mood but elevated his street cred. Now he was idolised by gangsta rappers and the hip-hop generation. Iron Mike was also now known as the 'Baddest Man on the Planet'.

He could still knock people out, too. He had wiped out Peter McNeeley in one round of his celebrated comeback fight on 19 August 1995, and after knocking out Buster Mathis Jr in three rounds the following December, he recaptured the WBC championship by taking out a terrified Frank Bruno in three rounds.

One viable threat to Tyson's supremacy was avoided when Tyson gave up his WBC title instead of fighting mandatory challenger Lennox Lewis, a former Olympic champion from England, who was unbeaten. King was not about to risk his hold on the heavyweight championship and its future riches by having Tyson fight the 1988 gold medal winner at Seoul, Korea. At 6 ft 5 in., Lewis was 7 inches taller than Tyson and possessed an 84-inch long jab that could make it difficult for the stockier Tyson to get inside.

Instead of fighting Lewis, Tyson gave up his WBC belt the same night he knocked out a less imposing Bruce Seldon in one round on 7 September 1996, to capture the WBA heavyweight crown. Owning the WBA or WBC made no difference as long as Tyson had a title and looked invincible.

From the outside looking in, it seemed things couldn't be better for Tyson. But if he thought he was calling the shots on his career, he wasn't. He'd given up that right days before being released from prison when he signed an exclusive promotional agreement with Don King Productions, giving Don King the exclusive right to promote his bouts. King then used the agreement to negotiate exclusive deals with the Showtime Network, the MGM Grand and the Fox Network, deals that would make King a very rich man and Tyson not as rich as he thought.

Within three years, Tyson would file a $100 million lawsuit in a US District Court in New York, accusing King of diverting millions of the fighter's monies through accounting manipulations, improper deductions and reductions in Tyson's potential profit participation.

But Tyson was blind to all that when he stepped into the ring to face Holyfield for the first time. He was looking to replenish his bank account for his next spending spree. The $21.5 million King had given him the day he was released from prison was nearly gone. And the millions he had made for beating McNeeley, Mathis, Bruno and Seldon were being spent like sand through an hourglass.

Despite having won the heavyweight title two previous times, the thirty-four-year-old Holyfield was viewed as washed up for good reason. He had gone 4–3 in the last seven fights and looked awful in his most recent, a fifth-round TKO over Czyz. Many in the boxing media had suggested it was time for Holyfield to retire. His skills had seemingly diminished and the health of his heart was also in question.

The belief was Holyfield had waited too long to face Tyson. Yet, it was a fight that was inevitable since the day they met as youngsters trying to make the 1984 Olympic team. Holyfield would eventually settle for a bronze medal in Los Angeles and become celebrated because of the humble way he accepted being disqualified for hitting after the bell in his semi-final bout.

Tyson lost a box-off to Henry Tillman and didn't make the US squad. But he went on to captivate the sport with his knockout prowess as a professional. Dressed in black trunks, with black shoes, no socks and no robe, he became an instant sensation, revitalising the heavyweight division if not all of boxing.

'He took no prisoners and showed no mercy,' King said. 'He was there to seek and destroy. That's what Tyson was in that ring. He deserved the fanfare and became a phenomenon that was second to none.'

Tyson and Holyfield were initially scheduled to meet on 8 November 1991 in Las Vegas, with Holyfield defending the undisputed heavyweight championship he won from Buster Douglas and retained by beating George Foreman. Holyfield was supposed to earn $30 million and Tyson $15 million, the biggest payouts ever. But the fight never came off. Tyson was indicted for rape on 9 September 1991 and while awaiting trial would officially pull out of the fight a month later with a rib injury.

The much-anticipated Tyson–Holyfield rivalry was seemingly over before it began. Tyson would spend three years behind bars on a rape conviction he still disputes. With Tyson incarcerated, Holyfield would lose the heavyweight championship to Riddick Bowe, regain it again and lose it again. He was also diagnosed with a heart abnormality that threatened his career. But by 1996, it was time for the inevitable showdown, a bout that was appropriately nicknamed 'Finally'.

Holyfield knew he was fit enough in mind, body and spirit to challenge Tyson. But the Nevada Athletic Commission wasn't so sure. Before granting Holyfield a licence to fight, it ordered him to undergo a thorough physical and neurological examination at the Mayo Clinic in Rochester, Minnesota.

Even when doctors cleared him with an abnormally strong heart, there were doubts he had the skills to survive against Tyson. Despite being inactive for three years while serving his prison sentence, Tyson seemed more fierce and menacing than ever, knocking out four fighters in fewer than eight rounds after being released.

Holyfield's own trainers had their doubts as well, considering how bad he looked during his first few weeks of training in Houston, Texas. Gary Bell, an unbeaten heavyweight from

Brooklyn, was brought in to mimic Tyson's aggressive style.

Nicknamed 'Bring Da Pain', Bell was about three inches taller than the 5 ft 10 in. Tyson and didn't hold back while sparring with Holyfield. After one particularly violent session where Bell was the more dominant fighter, co-trainer Tommy Brooks was starting to believe Holyfield might be in over his head. Brooks had fought for the Air Force, coming up as an amateur during the same time Sugar Ray Leonard, Tommy Hearns, Aaron Pryor and the Spinks brothers Leon and Michael were just launching their careers. He eventually turned to training and joined Don Turner to be Holyfield's assistant trainer after he regained the heavyweight title in his second fight with Riddick Bowe. Brooks had seen the best of Holyfield, but he didn't like what he was seeing early in the Houston camp.

'I'm scratching my head thinking we're in a world of shit,' Brooks said. 'Everybody is saying we're sending this guy to the gas chamber and he's going to get murdered and blah, blah, blah. So one day I was sitting at the house in Houston and I told Evander, "You're not making the adjustments like we're looking for."'

Holyfield gave Brooks a half-grin and said confidently, 'Once you whip somebody's ass they ain't never going to forget that ass whipping.'

Holyfield was talking about a one-round sparring session he had with Tyson during training for the 1984 Olympics. Everyone on the team was intimidated by Tyson and wouldn't spar with him – everyone except for Holyfield. They were matched together for one round, which erupted into such a ferocious battle it prompted the Olympic coaches to halt the session before someone got hurt.

'He ain't ever forgot that and I ain't never forgot that,' Holyfield told Brooks. 'I'm not scared of him and he knows I'm not scared of him.'

Holyfield's lack of fear was evident in the days leading up to the fight, when Tyson and his entourage heckled him with taunts and threats. 'I want to hurt him,' Tyson said with a menacing grin. 'Whether it happens in thirty seconds or ten rounds, my objective is to hurt him.'

Though nearly all the boxing experts were picking Tyson to win easily, there were a few that thought Holyfield might be competitive, including famed Kronk trainer Emanuel Steward and Buster Douglas, who scored boxing's biggest upset by knocking out Tyson in Tokyo in 1990. 'Tyson is the stronger puncher, but Holyfield is the better boxer and the media isn't giving him enough credit,' Douglas said. 'It won't be a short fight. It's going to be an exciting fight. Evander is going to fool a lot of people.'

Ron Borges, then with the *Boston Globe*, was the only sports writer predicting a Holyfield victory. But amid the pessimism about Holyfield's chances was a late groundswell of support from those willing to risk money on the fight. Several huge bets for Holyfield were wagered just before the bout, three of $100,000 or more and one of $15,000 by Brooks, who had pooled together money from family members. Holyfield's trainer, who once thought his fighter was 'in a world of shit', was now confident of victory. 'Once we arrived in Las Vegas, I saw that little swag on him,' Brooks said. 'I knew we were in the house now.'

The game plan Holyfield and his trainers worked on for weeks in Houston was not complicated. First and foremost, Holyfield could not show any signs of intimidation or fear. Second, when Tyson punched him, he had to punch him back just as hard if not harder. Third, Holyfield would stay low, keeping Tyson from getting inside and unleashing the powerful uppercuts that had produced many of his 39 knockouts to that point. 'Don't let Mike get lower than us,' Brooks had told Holyfield repeatedly during his training camp. 'When he gets low, you've got to get low right with him and beat him to the punch.' And perhaps most importantly, Holyfield had to force Tyson to fight backing up. That meant imposing his will on Tyson.

That strategy was put to an immediate test soon after Gerald and Eddie Levert finished the national anthem and referee Mitch Halpern had given his last-minute instructions. As the bell sounded to begin round one, Tyson went to the centre of the ring and behind a lazy left jab fired a thunderous overhand right that landed flush on Holyfield's cheek. Bam!

It was a punch that would have finished many of Tyson's previous opponents, and even Holyfield jumped back from its force. He bounced off the ropes before quickly gathering himself and putting his gloves up as Tyson came in for further assault.

A clinch – the first of many during the fight – forced the slender Halpern to step in and separate the heavyweight boxers. It gave Holyfield additional time to recuperate before he announced his presence by firing his own right hand that hit a ducking Tyson on the top of the head. It was the start of a fiercely contested opening round, with Tyson throwing straight right hands to the head and uppercuts to the body, and Holyfield countering with his own combinations.

By the end of the round, Holyfield was working his game plan. He matched Tyson punch for punch and stayed as low as his opponent. And when they clinched, Holyfield began walking Tyson back toward the ropes or pushing him off to show he was the stronger fighter.

If Tyson didn't initially know he was in for a long battle, he knew it at the end of the first round. Tyson hit Holyfield with a right hand–left hook combination just after the bell, and Holyfield answered with a message-sending straight left of his own.

The first round had gone about as well as could be expected for Holyfield. He had taken Tyson's best punch, shown him he wasn't intimidated and was making him fight backing up.

'All you got to do is stay calm and it's you,' Turner told Holyfield in the corner. 'You see everything. You're the bully in here. He ain't the bully.'

It was clear Holyfield had the more experienced corner. By the time Tyson and Holyfield met, Tyson had split with Rooney, who trained him at the beginning of his pro career until he became the youngest heavyweight champion by beating Trevor Berbick at age 20.

But less than three years later, amidst the turmoil of his marriage to Robin Givens and the expanding influence of Don King, Tyson fired Rooney after his 91-second victory over Michael Spinks. For his fight with Holyfield, Tyson was trained by Jay Bright, one of the friends he grew up with at Cus D'Amato's home in the Catskills. Bright had little experience training in big-time fights, but Tyson was searching for someone he could trust, while King was looking for someone he could control. With Bright as Tyson's trainer and John Horne and Rory Holloway serving as co-managers, Tyson was in charge of Tyson.

He had controlled his own training camp, running when he wanted to, goofing off and partying when he wanted. It mattered little in his first four fights after leaving prison, as he easily defeated what Brooks called 'tomato cans'. But now he was fighting Holyfield, and his corner had no clue how to offer the kind of advice needed to guide a boxer through a tough fight.

'They were space cases,' Brooks said simply. 'It seemed like they weren't working as a unit. Everybody was for themselves.'

All the psychological posturing before the bout turned into a collision of physical forces in the centre of the ring. With both fighters determined to stay lower than the other, they each dived in to punch, often winding up in clinches, forcing Halpern to work as hard as the boxers.

There were ten clinches in the first round and eight in the second, with Halpern shouting orders to 'work out of it', before having to force his way between Tyson and Holyfield and demand they 'step back'. At times he was ignored, especially in the third round when Tyson began hanging on after Holyfield landed a jarring body punch to the ribs. Holyfield wasn't eager to release Tyson's arms either, fearing he'd catch a left hook to the head.

Halfway through the third round, Halpern had had enough. He called for time and scolded the two fighters. 'When I say break, you step back. I'm not messing round in here,' Halpern barked.

The fight resumed, but the tone had been set. Holyfield was standing his ground, taking all of Tyson's punches and doing damage with his own. He began walking Tyson backward whenever they were tied up and stepping back only when needing space to deliver a quick combination.

At the end of the fourth round, Tyson's corner tried to diminish any frustration by offering false assurance. 'You got him right where you want him,' said Stacey McKinley, one of his trainers. 'Keep wearing him down. Just like a pro.'

By the sixth round, the action was getting even more rugged as Tyson and Holyfield pulled and tugged each other. Their heads and cheeks clashed as they battled to get lower than the other. Early in the sixth, as Tyson moved in to deliver a punch, Holyfield moved in to counter. Holyfield's head hit Tyson above the left eye, causing a cut. Halpern immediately called time, informing the judges of the 'accidental head butt' as ringside doctor Flip Homansky came to the apron to inspect the injury.

'Both guys led with their heads,' Halpern said after the bout. 'That's their styles and that's how they fought. It wasn't a dirty thing. They just would lay their heads on each other. There wasn't any intentional butting there at all.'

Tyson seemed enraged at seeing his own blood for the first time in his career. When the fight resumed, he launched a fierce attack, firing combinations at Holyfield's head and body. But again Holyfield didn't flinch. He met force with force, digging uppercuts and rights that halted Tyson's assault.

By the end of the round, Tyson began to stagger. Instinct told him to keep moving forwards and that was to his detriment. With 50 seconds left in the round, as Tyson stumbled in to throw a punch from a crouch, Holyfield rocked him with an uppercut to the upper chest. The power of the punch sent Tyson tumbling back onto the canvas for the first knockdown of the bout.

By the time Halpern counted to eight, Tyson was back on

his feet, showing no emotion. He finished the round, but the sell-out crowd sensed an upset and began chanting 'Ho-ly-field . . . Ho-ly-field.'

Tyson wasn't as bothered by the knockdowns as much as he was the clashing of heads. After a vicious collision in the seventh, Tyson backed off and Halpern warned Holyfield to watch his head, though it was Tyson who was the aggressor. The clashing of heads would be central to their rivalry, with Tyson complaining it was intentional. Jim Thomas, Holyfield's long-time adviser, has a different view.

'Everybody Mike ever fought went backwards, so Mike thinks that space in front of him is his,' Thomas said. 'But Evander doesn't think that. Every time Mike went forward, Evander went forward, and Mike's view is "you're head butting me because you're not getting your head out of the way". Evander's thinking "you're head butting me because you're not getting your head out of the way".'

With each passing round, Holyfield's confidence began to grow, as did Tyson's frustration. The punches that had finished so many of Tyson's opponents were showing no signs of hurting Holyfield.

By the end of the ninth round, Holyfield and his corner began to sense victory. 'You've got three more rounds,' Turner told him, as he poured water from a bottle over the fighter's sweaty bald head. 'Three more rounds,' he repeated.

'Three more rounds and you'll be the new champ,' Brooks added.

The menacing look Tyson had entered the ring with less than an hour earlier was gone. He had a cut on his left eyebrow. His legs were starting to buckle, he was breathing heavily and his punches were losing power.

Faint chants of 'Let's go, Mike' were drowned out in the tenth round by Holyfield's thunderous fists. If there was any doubt of the outcome it ended in the closing seconds of the round. A right hand as hard as anything Holyfield had thrown all night blasted into Tyson's face, sending him stumbling into the ropes.

Holyfield raced in for the kill. Left hook, right hook, left hook, right hook: they all landed flush on a defenceless Tyson.

After 15 unanswered punches, only the bell caused Holyfield to stop. As Tyson walked slowly back to his corner, he glanced back at Holyfield as if wondering how this was happening. Slumped on his stool, Tyson was clearly a beaten man. Exhausted and battered, he came out for the 11th looking finished. It wasn't long before he was.

Thirty-seven seconds into the 11th round, after Holyfield had fired eleven unanswered punches that started with three hard left jabs and finished with a straight right hand that backed Tyson into the ropes, Halpern leaped in to stop the fight, waving his right hand high in the air before clutching Tyson to protect him from further damage. There was no argument from Tyson.

Joy flooded the Holyfield corner. He had joined Muhammad Ali, becoming only the second man to capture the heavyweight title three times. Instantly the ring was swamped with a mass of humanity. As Holyfield was lifted in the air in triumph, Tyson was back on his stool having the cut over his left eye attended to by Ira Trocki, a plastic surgeon King had hired from Atlantic City, New Jersey.

Tyson would say he didn't remember much beyond the first time the fighters clashed heads. 'After the end of the first round, I don't know what the hell happened,' Tyson said. 'He was shellacking me with some hard punches, but he wasn't hurting me. But he kept me hitting me. I just couldn't get it together. If he was a little slower, I would have gotten it together, but the punches were hitting me too consistently.'

Jimmy Lennon Jr, whose father introduced some of the biggest fights in boxing history, was ready to announce his own moment of history. 'Ladies and gentlemen we have the time – 37 seconds in round number 11, our referee Mitch Halpern stops the contest. He's the winner by way of technical knockout, in a stunning upset, the new WBA heavyweight champion of the world, Evander "The Read Deal" Ho-ly-field.'

Afterwards, Holyfield, a devout Christian, credited God for

his victory. 'My God is the only true God and everything must bow to God,' Holyfield told Showtime's Ferdie Pacheco. 'I was led by the spirit of God. Like I told everybody, whatever God led me to do that's what I would do. It wasn't so much nothing that I did. Everybody knew that I was washed up. But with God I'm not washed up.'

Halpern did not second-guess himself about stopping the fight. 'If [Tyson] had taken any more punishment, it would have been unjust, so I stopped it,' he said, adding, 'some of those punches were hitting his gloves. But bottom line before I stopped it, he was hurt and he was about to get knocked down, so I didn't want him to get hurt.'

Tyson was humble after the bout. The threats, the taunts and the gangsta attitude were gone. 'Man, I just want to shake your hand,' he told Holyfield at the post-fight press conference. 'Man, I just want to touch you. I just commend you. Thank you very much. I have the greatest respect for you.'

In defeat, Tyson had earned his own measure of respect. 'He was talking all the trash about what he was going to do, but he took his ass whipping like a man,' Brooks said. 'That's one thing I can say about him that I can appreciate. Whatever Mike does, he's willing to pay the freight for it good, bad, indifferent, ugly, pretty . . . he's willing to pay the freight for it. That's what I like about Mike.'

Brooks also liked winning his $15,000 bet on Holyfield, who at the time was a 15–1 underdog. The payout was $250,000, enough to send 20 family members on a trip to Italy.

Having watched the heavyweight championship slip through his grasp, King was already talking about a rematch. Tyson had been scheduled to face Michael Moorer on 16 March at the MGM, but now the only way for Tyson to regain his credibility and earning power was to fight Holyfield again.

'It could be like Ali–Frazier,' King said after the fight.

Many in boxing trumpeted the outcome of Tyson–Holyfield I as shocking. It paled in comparison to what would happen in Holyfield–Tyson II.

2

YOU'LL BE CHAMP SOMEDAY

WHEN EVANDER HOLYFIELD AND MIKE Tyson met for their first fight in 1996, the bout was hyped as a battle between contrasting characters. Tyson was the hero of the gangsta rap and hip-hop generation. He put life to the lyrics of the street. He was anti-establishment and anti-order, a machine intent on destruction. Militant and menacing, he was the personification of 'bad ass', casting an image that empowered some and disgusted others. He was 'Iron Mike' 24/7.

Holyfield, meanwhile, was the Bible-talking Southerner, the humble warrior who had earned the respect of his country by not casting blame when he was robbed of a gold medal at the 1984 Olympics. He had grown into the consummate professional, who never cussed or complained and pursued his profession with nobility and honour.

Tyson was all about intimidation, while Holyfield was all about competition. One was a Christian; the other a felon turned Muslim. The clash of cultures helped hype their two fights into the highest-grossing boxing events in history at that time.

What few recognised is that Tyson and Evander had plenty in common. They both had the surname of men who weren't their natural fathers. They both were raised by single-parent mothers. They both endured extreme poverty. They both were motivated by older white men who told them they could someday be champion of the world, and they would both lose their mentors before those prophecies were fulfilled.

It was Constantine 'Cus' D'Amato who predicted greatness from Tyson after he first watched the then twelve year old spar with Bobby Stewart, a former National Golden Gloves champion who was working as a counsellor at Tryon School For Boys in Johnstown, New York, about a two-hour ride from Manhattan. Tyson had been sent there after becoming a habitual juvenile delinquent. A life of crime seemed to be his destiny.

Born 30 June 1966 at Cumberland Hospital in Forest Greene, Michael Gerard Tyson was the youngest of Lorna Smith's three children. They were all fathered by Jimmy Kirkpatrick, Smith's long-time boyfriend following a brief marriage to Percel Tyson. All three children – Rodney was born in 1961 and Denise in 1964 – carried the Tyson name.

After the relationship with Kirkpatrick ended, she moved her family from Williamsburg to East New York and finally Brownsville, where they lived in a six-room apartment at 178 Amboy Street. It was an area of abandoned buildings, sweatshops, unpaved streets, dirt lots, crime and poverty.

Though big for his age, Tyson spoke with a lisp. That along with his dirty clothes and the glasses he briefly wore made him a target of constant teasing from neighbourhood bullies. Insecure and timid, Tyson was too humiliated to retaliate.

His escape was to nurture his coop of pigeons atop an abandoned building, an activity that took him away from the teasing and the taunting and the poverty. But his space of tranquillity was invaded one day when a neighbourhood thug ripped the head off one of his cherished pigeons. An enraged Tyson beat up the assailant, gaining revenge with every swing of his fist. Seeing his battered foe gave him a sense of power and self-assurance. Instead of being intimidated, he became the intimidator.

Aged just nine, Tyson quickly learned that being humble equated to weakness and those that showed weakness came under constant attack. Those who instilled fear got respect. It was the code of Brownsville.

Bored with school, he became a habitual truant in the second grade and eventually stopped going to school altogether. The lure of the streets was far more exciting. There was no right or wrong. He took what he wanted, when he wanted. He spent his days stealing fruit, doughnuts and the handbags of elderly women who thought he was helping them with their groceries.

At age ten, he began drinking cheap liquor and smoking cigarettes. He picked pockets and joined a gang of punk thugs called 'The Jolly Stompers', who took pride in being criminals. Tyson's image as a hellion not only protected him but also his siblings and his mother. No one would dare mess with the Tysons or they'd face the wrath of Mike.

Tyson was arrested close to 40 times before he turned 12. On several occasions he was sent to Spofford Juvenile Center, a medium-security youth detention centre in the Hunts Point section of the Bronx. Since many of his hoodlum friends were always in Spofford, it was more like a frat house than a reformatory. The only positive impression made on Tyson there was the day when Muhammad Ali came to visit. The loud-talking, confident champion who had been stripped of the heavyweight title for not entering the draft was everything Tyson wanted to be: admired, respected and confident.

When Tyson's behaviour in and out of Spofford didn't change, he was ordered to Tryon, a state-run juvenile facility opened in 1966 by Governor Nelson Rockefeller. Tryon housed about 300 troubled boys, more than half of them diagnosed with some form of mental illness. He arrived there in a state-owned van with shackles on his legs and handcuffs locking his wrists.

Early on, Tyson remained unruly, acting out, clashing with teachers, counsellors and the other juvenile delinquents. Then he learned about the boxing programme run by Stewart and remembered the visit from Ali. Tyson asked one of the staff members, 'How can I meet Stewart?'

A 1974 National Golden Gloves champion, Stewart was a red-headed, blue-eyed native of Amsterdam, New York, who went 13–3 as a pro before retiring. He had been hired by the state to run a boxing programme at Tryon, which mainly served as a way for the boys to release some of their aggression.

Stewart was in no hurry to appease Tyson. He had encountered plenty of kids who thought they wanted to box only to quit the first time they got hit or had to wake up at dawn to train. Stewart ignored Tyson for days. Then one night after Tyson had fallen asleep in his room, Stewart loudly banged on his door. 'What the hell do you want?' Stewart yelled.

Caught off guard, Tyson replied, 'I want to be a fighter.'

'So do the rest of these guys,' Stewart said. 'But they haven't got the balls to be a fighter.'

Stewart told the cocky youngster if he straightened up his act and improved in the classroom, he might show him how to fight. In two weeks, Tyson had stopped challenging teachers and improved his reading level.

Stewart decided to put him in the ring but was wary that at 5 ft 8 in. and nearly 200 lb Tyson might hurt the smaller boys in the programme. He would spar with Tyson himself.

Fuelled by desire but short on experience, the flailing Tyson was no match for Stewart, who didn't hold back in landing a barrage of punches intended to test Tyson's commitment. He eventually dropped the 12 year old with a body punch.

When Tyson showed up the next day and the day after that, Stewart knew the boy was serious. They would train every day and spar every other day, as Tyson absorbed every ounce of teaching like a sponge. Everything Stewart showed him, Tyson would practise at the gym during the day and in his room at night. The staff at Tryon would sometimes hear Tyson in his room past midnight, making the sounds of someone throwing punches and shuffling around.

Stewart sensed something special in Tyson and knew boxing had brought some structure to his tumultuous life. The best way to keep him out of trouble was to keep him involved in the sport. Knowing Tyson would leave Tryon someday soon, Stewart wanted to see if D'Amato had any interest in grooming him into a more skilled boxer.

The 70-year-old D'Amato was a fight manager and trainer who operated a small boxing gym atop a police station in downtown Catskill, New York. It was a meagre existence for someone with such a rich boxing background. D'Amato was born in the Bronx in 1908 and was a boxing coach in the US Army in the mid 1930s. In 1939, he opened the Empire Boxing Club at Gramercy Gym on 14th Street in Union Square. It was there he first honed the skills of heavyweight champion Floyd Patterson and light heavyweight champion José Torres.

D'Amato was a maverick, blind in one eye and paranoid about mobsters and potential repercussions for refusing to do business with the once-powerful International Boxing Club of New York. D'Amato had spurned the IBC, which sought control of the match-making process, by refusing to match his fighters with any connected to the corrupt promotional corporation. His concerns were justified in 1959, when the IBC was forced to dissolve. But D'Amato was already comfortable in his role of a nonconformist.

He moved to Catskill in 1962 to work in relative obscurity, away from the Mob and away from the IRS, which hounded him for unpaid taxes and forced him to declare bankruptcy. He opened a gym above a police station in downtown Catskill. It became a sanctuary for troubled kids. He also housed as many as eight youngsters in his home, a three-storey, seven-bedroom, English-style house four miles from Catskill, just off the Hudson River.

He lived there with Camille Ewald, his common-law wife. Stewart figured if D'Amato liked what he saw in Tyson, he might take him in and prevent a return to a life of crime and destruction in Brownsville.

Stewart trained and sparred with Tyson, showing him enough to get him to the point where he might be able to impress D'Amato. Finally, it was time for the audition. When Stewart and Tyson walked through the door, D'Amato and his chief trainer Teddy Atlas were already in the gym. 'We let him spar with Stewart because it was a special project and we understood it as such,' Atlas says more than 40 years later. 'We were going to take a look at what he could do, being that he wasn't a normal 12 year old. We wanted to see what his make-up was and how he would act when he was in the ring.'

There was little conversation as Stewart and Tyson put on gloves and began to spar just as they had at Tryon. It took all of Stewart's experience and skill to hold off the ferocious Tyson, who had Stewart wincing from his body blows. In the second round, blood began to flow from Tyson's nose, but he kept up his relentless assault, trying desperately to impress his onlookers. By the end of the second round, Atlas had seen enough. 'OK, that's it. That's enough,' Atlas shouted, ending the session.

Tyson, unsure whether he'd done enough to impress, asked for another round. 'We always go three rounds,' he pleaded.

Atlas wiped the blood from Tyson's nose and ordered him to get out of the ring, setting a tone of authority for the future. 'The responsible thing was not to let him box two or three more rounds with a bloody nose, because I didn't need to do that,' Atlas said. 'It wasn't the right thing to do and I didn't need to see more. I saw he was physically strong and I saw that he was raw and I saw from an emotional standpoint he could force himself to behave the way we needed him to behave when we wanted him to. I also needed to make clear to him who the boss was because I knew we would be training him.'

Stewart wasn't sure what D'Amato was thinking until the old man wrapped his arm around the camp counsellor as they headed for the door. 'This boy is going to be the heavyweight champion of the world someday if he maintains interest and desire in the game,' D'Amato said. Tyson would hear those same words from D'Amato's mouth when he was released into his custody and moved into his home on his 14th birthday.

Some called it a halfway house for juvenile delinquents. But for Tyson it was a safe haven, a chance for a better life, a chance to become a fighter. 'You work hard and you'll be the heavyweight champion of the world,' D'Amato told him over and over. It took a while for Tyson to believe him.

Holyfield would hear those same words predicting his future as a champion. It came from an older white man who saw promise in him when he was a young boy unsure of himself and what his destiny would be. Evander Holyfield was born on 19 October 1962, the last of Annie Laura Holyfield's nine children.

She was born Annie Laura Riggen in 1928 in Atlanta. She married Joseph Holyfield when she was 15 but kept his last name when they separated in 1953. After the end of the marriage, she moved her family to Atmore, Alabama, to take care of her mother. It was there she met Isom Coley, a lumberjack who was described as a strong, gentle man. They never married but conceived Evander in 1962, while her name was still Holyfield. Isom Coley left the home before Evander was born. Father and son would not meet until Evander was 21 years old.

Annie Laura served as mother, father and counsellor to her children. A devout Christian, she used the teachings of the Bible to instil in them the importance of honesty, humility and integrity.

But Evander was far from a model child. Like any young boy he was overloaded with energy and curiosity that would push him to test the limits of what he could get away with. He got his share of beatings from his mother but was always made to understand their purpose.

The Holyfields moved back to Atlanta when Evander was four, joining extended family members to the point where there were fourteen under one roof. To escape the congestion he spent much of time playing outside with his brother Bernard and other neighbourhood children. He was as content as a child could be. But his curiosity was piqued one day when a friend left in the middle of a game, saying he was going to 'the Boys Club'.

Eventually, Evander learned it was a place where young boys gathered to play baseball, football and basketball. They also swam, played ping-pong and pool, and did arts and crafts.

Instructors supervised the kids and neither violence nor bad language was tolerated. It took some convincing and begging, but Mama Holyfield eventually gave her approval for Evander and his brother Bernard to take the bus to the Warren Memorial Boys Club.

Initially, Evander wanted to be a football player and star for his hometown Atlanta Falcons. And though he was just 65 lb when he joined the Boys Club, he had a fierce determination to compete and succeed. Growing up without a father, he was driven by the insecurities that come with having to prove he was just as athletic, just as talented and just as resourceful as those that had fathers. And there was the element of racism in the South that taught young black kids at an early age they needed to perform far and above their white counterparts to achieve any kind of affirmation or recognition.

Evander and his brother were enthralled by the Boys Club and got involved in all it had to offer. The only place off-limits was a fenced-off part of the gym where no one was allowed without permission.

Being curious, Evander wanted to know what went on there. He could see leather bags hanging from the ceiling and smaller bags hanging from round wooden circles of wood. He learned it was the boxing area, where boys went about their work in a more serious fashion than those in the other parts of the club.

If Evander got too close to the fence and looked for too long, he was told to step back or move on. The lack of access added to the intrigue. After football practice, Evander would stop by and stand at an acceptable distance to watch the boxers train. A white man about 50 years old seemed to be in charge. Evander would learn his name was Carter Morgan.

Early one day, Evander got to the club and went to the boxing area where he waited for Morgan to arrive. 'Can I go in there?' he asked politely.

'No,' Morgan said, hardly acknowledging the boy.

A week later, he tried again without getting Morgan's approval. But even as a child, when Holyfield set a goal, he couldn't be discouraged. Day after day he persisted, bugging Morgan to give him a chance. Eventually, Morgan consented to letting him hit the heavy bag. Just once.

Evander squared back and hit the bag, instantly feeling a shooting pain through his wrist, arm and elbow. The bag hardly budged. He tried not to react, but Morgan saw his discomfort and told him, 'If you wanna be a fighter, you gotta be tough.'

Despite the difficult introduction to the sport, Evander was determined to gain Morgan's approval to be part of the boxing group. He showed up every day and hung around the fence until Morgan finally let him in and began showing him the proper technique to hit a heavy bag.

Not long afterwards, Evander began to spar with other kids his age and showed enough promise for Morgan to let him box for real against other clubs. When his arm was raised in victory, it was the best feeling he had ever experienced.

Mama Holyfield had her concerns about Evander being involved in boxing. But she liked the influence Morgan was having on her child. Evander was excited, he was focused and he was accountable.

As he grew into his high-school years, it was becoming clear a career as a professional football player wasn't going to happen. But there was boxing and there was Morgan, who kept him active in the ring and motivated.

Coach Carter, as Evander called him, wasn't a man to give out compliments easily. They came few and far between, which gave them added meaning.

After a particularly difficult fight against an opponent who forced Evander to battle toe-to-toe to earn the victory, Coach Carter pulled him aside. Evander sensed something different in his mentor and was unsure if maybe he had done something wrong. It was quite the opposite.

His coach, who had once kept him away from the boxing ring, looked him in the eye and told him, 'One of these days you're going to be the champion of the world.'

The young Holyfield was stunned, unsure if his coach was

serious or just trying to be nice. That was something the boys might tell each other. But he had never heard those words from his coach. 'I believed him and my mama believed him,' Holyfield says all these years later. 'The only challenge is if you don't quit. Everybody reaches their goal if they don't quit.'

Suddenly, the dream of one day playing for the Falcons had given way to a new dream of becoming a world champion.

The young Holyfield soaked in everything Coach Carter showed him and told him. They were words of instruction or encouragement. Morgan, like D'Amato, wasn't concerned about being politically correct.

'When you get in the ring, move your head,' he told Holyfield. 'You hit and don't get hit. Don't act like them white boys. Them white boys act like a big part of boxing is taking a shot. You don't take them shots. That's why I like you black kids. You black kids don't like getting hit in the face. You get your head down. Ya'll ain't too proud to get that head down.'

He would quiz Holyfield at tournaments as they scanned the competition. 'Who do you think is tougher?' he would ask Holyfield.

The student would point to a rugged-looking kid with battle scars on his face. Morgan would promptly correct him. 'He's got knots because he gets hit all the time,' the coach said. 'Anybody who gets hit all the time can be beat. The pretty ones, the ones that are smiling, those are the one that are tough, because that shows they don't get hit. All the good fighters look good because they hit and they don't get hit.'

While Carter Morgan taught Holyfield everything about boxing, D'Amato spent more time talking to Tyson than training him. Training was left to Teddy Atlas, who, like Tyson, had been a troubled youth who had spent time in Rikers prison but found his way to D'Amato's home in the Catskills and eventually gave up his career as a fighter to train the wannabe boxers at D'Amato's gym.

Atlas knew the techniques to teach: how to slip punches, how to punch in calculated combinations, how to use a left jab to set up a straight right, how to move your head with gloves up in a U-shaped motion. D'Amato was more of a manager and mentor.

Initially sceptical about why a white man would be so interested in a black kid, Tyson eventually became mesmerised by everything D'Amato had to say. They talked about fear and how important it was to control your emotions in the ring. Though Tyson projected a confident, defiant and unruly exterior, D'Amato knew it masked a distrustful, insecure young man still wearing the scars of the taunts and intimidation that haunted his young life.

'That was something that was always going to be in the wings,' Atlas said. 'It was part of his personality, part of his temperament and part of his weakness that he wasn't as sure of himself as his body would suggest. As strong as he was physically, in other areas from an emotional standpoint, from a discipline standpoint, it was always going to be a work in progress. It was always going to be something to be paid attention to.'

Tyson's propensity for trouble continued even after he moved into D'Amato's home. He had the discipline to get up at the crack of dawn and run with the other fighters in the house, but he had no interest in attending school and soon began acting out at Catskill High School, where he beat up classmates and threatened teachers. D'Amato eventually had to hire a private tutor for Tyson to appease the juvenile court system. But it was D'Amato's tutoring as a boxing sage that interested Tyson the most.

'When I was a young kid in high school, Cus used to call me out of high school to spar with professionals,' Tyson said. 'I'd be in class, flunking a test, and all of a sudden they would say, "You have an emergency at home. You need to go home right away." But it would be for me to go and train with Frank Bruno or Carlos De Léon. I was sparring with them when I was a kid at age 15.'

D'Amato saw Tyson as his next world champion and seemed to dismiss his other antisocial behaviour. It would lead to a rift with Atlas, who wanted to suspend Tyson from the gym for acting out in class. But D'Amato, who had demanded discipline from his other fighters, overlooked many of Tyson's transgressions. 'Cus wanted to have one more champion, and that became more important than anything else,' Atlas said.

It came to a head when Atlas learned that Tyson had lewdly propositioned his wife's 12-year-old sister. In his autobiography, *Atlas*, Teddy Atlas details how he borrowed a .38 revolver and waited for Tyson to arrive at the gym. Just as Tyson entered the building, Atlas put the gun to his head and threatened to kill him. He fired a shot over Tyson's head to show he was serious.

When D'Amato got word of the confrontation, he fired Atlas. Kevin Rooney, another ex-fighter from D'Amato's stable, became Tyson's primary trainer.

Tyson had won his power struggle with Atlas, but it sent a destructive message: a message that said Mike Tyson, the future champion of the world, could do as he pleased. His success in boxing was giving him an inflated sense of power, power that he was too fragile and emotionally immature to handle.

In the midst of it all, Tyson was dealing with the loss of his mother. As much as he longed for his mother's love, she never came to visit him during his stay at Tryon, nor did she visit him in the Catskills. She never even met D'Amato in person. They had spoken over the telephone only a few times when Tyson hadn't returned from one of his trips to Brownsville and D'Amato was inquiring about his whereabouts. But Tyson's contact with his mother was minimal. She died of inoperable cancer at age 52 when Tyson was 16.

D'Amato soon became Tyson's legal guardian and, left with no real mother or father, the heartbroken teenager asked Camille if he could call her 'Mother'. She agreed, but Tyson would never really shake off the feeling of being abandoned.

If there was one clear difference between Holyfield and Tyson it was the influence and wisdom Holyfield gained from an involved and protective mother. If Carter Morgan taught Holyfield what to expect in a boxing ring, Annie Laura Holyfield made sure she taught her son what to expect in life.

When Evander turned 14, he became interested in girls and dating. His mother wanted to keep him committed to boxing. 'My big thing was at 14 and 15, you want to date, you want to go out with girls,' Holyfield said. 'You want to go out with your buddies. But my mama wouldn't let me do it. She told me, "You ain't going to prom. You doing this [boxing]." By me having to make those kinds of decisions at that age, let me know what the priority was.'

In fact, Annie Laura Holyfield spent a lot of her time preaching about the pitfalls women could create. 'My mama would say every time a man doesn't reach a goal there's some woman that stopped him,' Holyfield said. He's 50 now but says the word 'mama' as if he was still in grade school. 'She'd say, "Son, they'll tell you that they love you. They'll tell you anything. When they tell you that they love you, son, it means they're trying to stop you."'

That wasn't all. She sat him down and looked him in the eye.

'Once a girl tells you they love you, everything changes,' she told him. 'You could be talking to everybody. But once she says she loves you, she doesn't want you talking to nobody. She wants to be first. She wants to be before anything you do. Eventually, they want to be more important than your mama. They want to be the most important person in your life. She wants to stop you from what you're doing and you want to stop her from what she's been doing. So now how are you going to take care of each other?'

She also taught him there's no crying in boxing.

'Because I was the youngest of nine and because I started crying all the time, my mama would tell me to be quiet,' Holyfield said. 'If I wanted to cry, I had to mask my pain. You couldn't cry. You couldn't show your feelings. My mama said, "You don't wear your feelings on your sleeve. Somebody will poke at them all the time. So don't let nobody know you're hurt. If you don't tell nobody, you don't have to worry about God telling them."'

She also taught him about winning.

'My brothers were faster than me. My sisters were faster than me,' Holyfield said. 'I would say, "They don't never let me win." But my mama would say, "They're not supposed to let you win. In life, nobody's going to let you win. If you want to win, you have to run faster."'

It was Holyfield's mother who wouldn't let him quit boxing when he wanted to give up the sport after losing his first fight at age 11 to a kid named Cecil Collins. Holyfield was shattered by the defeat and came home to tell his mother he was quitting.

His mother would have none of it. 'You go back there and beat that boy,' she said. 'You don't quit until you do what you set out to do.'

Holyfield went back and fought Collins again. And lost again. 'Go back and fight him again,' his mother insisted.

When they met a third time, Holyfield won and was thrilled with his accomplishment. He couldn't wait to race home and tell his mother. 'Good,' she said. 'Now you can quit.'

The young Evander was stunned. The last thing he wanted to do was quit. He was proud of himself, proud of what he had accomplished. He loved the feeling and wanted to experience the thrill of victory more often. 'Don't you feel good having finished what you started?' she asked her son. It was a life lesson he carries with him to this day.

Were Tyson and Holyfield different? Yes, they were. But in many ways they were the same: both shaped from their fatherless childhood experiences; both nurtured by caring mentors; both finding boxing as their destiny and both driven to fulfil their mentors' prophecies to become a champion one day.

3

FIGHTING FOR GOLD

THE RIVALRY BETWEEN THE COUNTRY boy from Georgia and the street thief from Brownsville took root during the lead-up to the 1984 Olympic Games in Los Angeles.

It was part of Cus D'Amato's master plan for Tyson to win the gold medal and stand atop a podium the way Olympic heroes Muhammad Ali, Floyd Patterson, Joe Frazier and George Foreman had done in the past. Olympic gold would be as valuable as winning a professional world title, if not more so. The status that came with winning such a prize endured a lifetime.

Sugar Ray Leonard had been the most recent example, capturing the heart of the nation while winning gold at the 1976 Olympics in Montreal. He went on to become a world champion and multi-millionaire by the time the '84 Olympics arrived.

D'Amato knew that winning the gold on American soil would mean instant celebrity for Tyson, creating the ideal platform from which to launch a lucrative professional career. It was the logical next step in becoming the youngest heavyweight champion in the history of boxing.

This was also the heyday of amateur boxing in the United States, when fighting against international competition and in the Olympics could take a kid like Paul Gonzales from a ghetto in East Los Angeles and allow him to meet five US presidents and ride in a ticker-tape parade up Broadway in New York City.

This was an era when amateur boxing was a staple of Saturday-afternoon television viewing, with Howard Cosell broadcasting from ringside for ABC's *Wide World of Sports*.

The Los Angeles Games would be the first Olympics for the United States team in eight years, as they had boycotted the 1980 Games in Moscow. President Jimmy Carter called for the boycott in retaliation after the Soviets sent troops to Afghanistan in December 1979. Fifty-four other countries supported the boycott, denying thousands of amateur athletes their Olympic dreams over a political issue. Twenty-one years after the boycott, the United States would launch its own invasion of Afghanistan.

The boycott didn't dull interest in amateur boxing in the United States. That was thanks in large part to the indelible performance of the 1976 US boxing team in Montreal.

There had been singular boxing stars in the previous Olympics: Floyd Patterson winning gold in the 165-lb division in 1952 at Helsinki, Finland; Cassius Clay (later Muhammad Ali) capturing the 178-lb light heavyweight crown at the 1960 Games in Rome; Joe Frazier winning the heavyweight title in 1964 in Tokyo; and George Foreman waving the American flag after claiming gold in the heavyweight division at the historic 1968 Games in Mexico City.

The 1976 group was memorable because it was considered the best team from top to bottom. Howard Davis Jr, Ray Leonard, Leo Randolph and the Spinks brothers Michael and Leon, won a then record five gold medals. Each of the boxers was endearing in his own way: Leonard with his boyish charm, the Spinks brothers with their rugged East St Louis upbringing, and Davis fighting for gold one week after his thirty-seven-year-old mother died of a heart attack.

Inspired by the last words he heard from his mother – 'You better bring home the gold medal' – Davis won all five of his fights and was voted the most outstanding boxer of the tournament, winning the Val Barker Award.

Leonard would become an instant favourite with his flashy

smile and flurry of punches. He punctuated his Olympics with a victory over Cuban knockout artist Andrés Aldama to capture gold. He initially vowed to give up boxing only to become one of the most popular fighters ever. Both of the Spinks brothers won gold, with Leon defeating Sixto Soria of Cuba and Michael beating Rufat Riskiev of the Soviet Union in their respective finals.

The legacy of the '76 team only heightened expectations for '84. Yet any notion of duplicating that level of excitement in Los Angeles seemed doomed early on. In retaliation for the Carter-led US boycott of the 1980 Games in Moscow, the Soviet Union announced on 8 May 1984 that it would boycott the '84 Games. The Cubans and East Germans followed suit.

It eliminated, among others, a strong Cuban boxing team that had dominated the 1983 Pan American Games in Caracas, Venezuela, capturing eight gold medals and two silvers.

The US boxers were disappointed. They knew first-hand the Cubans had plenty of talent, having competed against them at the '83 Pan Am Games and various other international tournaments. Unlike the American teams that had to be rebuilt constantly as boxers turned pro, the Cubans remained in their 'amateur' programs for multiple Olympics.

Adolfo Horta, the famed featherweight, won gold at the '83 Pan Am Games and had also captured silver three years earlier at the '80 Olympics. Pablo Romero, another Cuban, would box on the Cuban Amateur team from 1982 to 1989. Included on his record were two gold medals at the World Championships and a victory over Evander Holyfield in the finals of the light heavyweight division in the '83 Pan Games.

Emanuel Steward, the late famed Kronk trainer, worked with several American amateurs in preparation for the '76 and '84 Games. He viewed the Cubans as professional fighters in a sport for amateurs. 'They were seasoned guys with 230 fights,' Steward said almost three decades later. 'That's why I never thought much of them. I thought they were just professional fighters taking advantage of our kids.'

Yet the '84 US boxers didn't fear the Cubans despite their success and were looking forward to competing against them at the Olympics. 'Everybody on our team had fought the Cubans and it was back and forth,' said Jerry Page, who would make the '84 US team as a 139-pounder. 'There was never a dominant situation. With the scene and the atmosphere with the Olympics being in Los Angeles, they would have been in trouble.'

Though the Cubans and Russians weren't going to the Olympics, the goals of each of the young American boxers invited to the National Training Center in Colorado Springs that summer didn't change. 'We were all there to do the same thing,' said Gonzales, the 106-lb light flyweight from East Los Angeles. 'We were trying to make the Olympic team. We were all competitive and we were all going for the same goal.'

A 17-year-old Tyson and a 21-year-old Holyfield were among those invited to train at the state-of-the-art facility in Colorado Springs. Holyfield earned his invite by capturing a silver medal at the 1983 Pan Am Games, while Tyson qualified by winning the 1983 National Golden Gloves Championships in St Louis. That's where the country boy from Georgia and the city kid from Brooklyn met for the first time.

Tyson was in Missouri competing in the heavyweight division, while Holyfield was a light heavyweight. They neither became fast friends nor enemies at that tournament. But from the onset there was competitive chemistry between them.

Tyson won all five of his bouts, four by knockout. Holyfield knocked out all five of his opponents to gain some measure of satisfaction, though Tyson was named 'the Outstanding Boxer'. It wouldn't be the last time Holyfield obsessed about beating Tyson.

When Holyfield and Tyson arrived at the Training Center in Colorado Springs, they were among the elite amateur boxers in the country but not necessarily considered the elite of the elite. That level belonged to welterweight Mark Breland of Brooklyn, a five-time National Golden Gloves champion and the sport's most decorated amateur boxer. There was super heavyweight Tyrell Biggs of Philadelphia, who won gold at the 1982 World Championships; Pernell Whitaker, a 132-pounder from Norfolk, Virginia; Frank Tate, a 156-pounder from Detroit; Ricky Womack of Detroit, the favourite in Holyfield's 178-lb light heavyweight division; and the highly-touted Gonzales.

The process of making the Olympic team would be gruelling. The boxers were to spend six weeks in Colorado Springs, with the Olympic Trials set for June 1984 in Fort Worth, Texas. Following the trials, the final roster would be determined by a box-off a few weeks later in Las Vegas. The divisions were so competitive that only Breland seemed to be a sure thing.

'Only 12 guys would make the Olympic team, but there were about 60 guys who could have made it,' said Page, who entered the trials as a virtual unknown 139-pounder from Detroit. 'That's how competitive the amateur boxing programme was back then. There were so many guys that were capable. Guys like Mike Tyson.'

Steward was in his heyday as the founder of Kronk Gym in Detroit and working with Tate, Briggs, Tillman, Womack and Breland. He recalled Cus D'Amato wanting Tyson to compete in the super heavyweight division, where his speed would overpower the heavier boxers. But D'Amato had no pull with the US Olympic Committee, who preferred the more experienced Biggs, who had won gold two years earlier at the World Championships in Munich and a bronze at the 1983 Pan Am Games. Tyson would compete as a 201-lb heavyweight.

D'Amato along with future co-managers Jimmy Jacobs and Bill Cayton viewed the trials as a formality for Tyson. He was already one of the most feared amateurs in the nation. On 12 August 1983, four days before the 1983 US National Championship, Tyson had destroyed his first two opponents by knockout. The first was beaten in the first round, while his next opponent was hit so hard in the second round he was unconscious for nearly ten minutes. His opposition for the finals claimed he had an injury and didn't show up for the fight. 'As he progressed, people were so intimidated by him until it was ridiculous,' Breland recalled. 'They were scared to death.'

By the time Tyson got to Colorado Springs, there was plenty of curiosity about the hard-punching knockout machine from New York who had a man's body and child-like voice. He was already different from the others because he had a professional management team in place with Jacobs and Cayton ready to take over as managers. Using what D'Amato taught him, and refined by Teddy Atlas and then Kevin Rooney, Tyson already had a pro style where punches were thrown not to score points but do damage.

But his reputation hardly intimidated the other would-be Olympians in camp. Tyson might have come from the tough streets of Brownsville, Brooklyn, and he might have been built like a small tank, but Gonzales was a gang member in an East LA barrio at age eight; Tillman was a one-time gang member from Compton, California; Page grew up in the toughest ghetto in Columbus, Ohio; and Womack was from the tough streets of Detroit.

Several of the fighters had already met Tyson, including Gonzales, who was impressed Tyson knew his boxing background. 'The guy knew my story,' Gonzales said. 'He knew my ranking. He knew all about my boxing and what I'd done as an amateur. So I took him down the street and bought him an ice cream.'

No one paid homage to Tyson. Respect had to be earned. 'At that stage you hear about different guys, but because of your own mentality and your own swag, you're not really about being a fan of anybody,' Page said.

Tyson kept to himself mostly, as did Holyfield, who wasn't always easy to read. Most of the fighters had come from tough urban cities like East Los Angeles, Columbus, Philadelphia, Detroit and Brooklyn. Holyfield was from the South, though no one was eager to test him because of the snarl that seemed permanently etched on his face. It was the kind of look that put others on the defensive, unsure whether Holyfield was simply in a bad mood or looking for conflict.

'He always had this look like he wanted to fight,' Gonzales said. 'I remember Pernell looked at him and said, "I don't know if I should smile at you or fight you." He's just looking at you with his eyes and just staring right through you. You would assume that he wants to fight you. But that's just the way Holy is.'

Sometimes the snarl wasn't meant to be friendly. Having so many fighters housed together for such a long time was a recipe for some intense showdowns. Two of the most memorable involved Tyson and Holyfield.

The first occurred when Pat Nappi, the head coach of the US Olympic boxing team, wanted someone to spar with Tyson, who was brutalising his other sparring partners. Though competing in a lower weight class, Holyfield volunteered.

According to onlookers, their battle was so ferocious that Nappi had to stop the sparring after the first round. Twelve years later, as Holyfield prepared to face Tyson for the first time as a pro, he would refer back to that sparring session, telling a confidant, 'I whipped his ass. He ain't ever forgot that and I ain't ever forgot that.'

Tyson doesn't recall much from the sparring session, only that, 'I think he hurt his arm. He wasn't feeling well.'

Their second showdown wasn't physical but was just as intense. It happened over a pool table. Tyson had control of the table until he scratched while trying to make the eight ball. He wasn't happy, believing that he hadn't really lost the match. Tyson was reluctant to yield to the next player: Holyfield.

Holding a cue stick, Tyson dug out the cue ball and stood as if he wasn't going anywhere. That prompted Holyfield to grab his own cue stick and stare at Tyson with the Holyfield snarl.

The stand-off may have lasted five seconds but it seemed like five minutes of not knowing whether the two chiselled athletes were going to brawl right then and there. 'Fuck it,' Tyson said, throwing his cue stick and the cue ball on the table before heading back to his room.

Today, Tyson says he has no recollection of their showdown over a pool table. 'I don't know nothing about that,' he said. But Holyfield felt he'd scored a huge psychological victory. 'I'm not scared of him and he knows I'm not scared of him,' Holyfield said to himself. Even then, Holyfield was confident he could take Tyson in the ring.

The truth is, Tyson viewed Holyfield more as a friend than an adversary. He respected that he had beaten Womack and they even rolled a few games of dice together during their down time.

Tyson easily reached the finals of the trials in Fort Worth, where he was matched against Tillman, the former gang member from Compton. Most in attendance were expecting Tyson to knock out the 23-year-old Tillman, an experienced amateur with an awkward style who was looking to make his first Olympics.

Tyson looked well on his way to doing just that when he knocked Tillman down in the first round with a vicious body attack along the ropes. Tillman got up and somehow survived the round as a confident Tyson headed back to his corner.

But the second round didn't go as easily. The taller Tillman fought more intelligently in the second round, punching behind a long left jab and refusing to let himself get caught along the ropes.

Tillman kept his jab persistent and stiff, peppering Tyson's face and making it difficult to get inside. Tillman stayed on his toes as he punched, circling to his left. Tyson made the mistake of robotically following Tillman around the ring, occasionally lunging forward with a hard hook that failed to fully connect to the body or head.

At the end of the second round, Rooney was scolding Tyson. 'Get him into a corner. Get him against the ropes. You've got to have a big round. You've got to pour it on him.'

From ringside, Cosell muttered, 'Easier said than done.'

Tyson came out for the third round a fireball of aggression, charging at Tillman and trying to back him into a corner. Tyson swung wildly with left and right hooks, desperately trying to connect with anything hard. But Tillman survived the initial assault, squeezed out of the corner and got back on his toes, circling, dancing, even running away from Tyson when necessary.

Tyson again became hypnotised by Tillman's foot movement, holding his gloves under his chin and trailing Tillman around the ring. The slugger couldn't solve the boxer. Tyson lost the last two rounds of the three-round fight.

Tyson hugged Tillman and raised the victor's hand when the unanimous decision was rendered. He would leave the ring beaten and dejected. But it didn't end his Olympic dreams.

They would meet in the box-off on 7 July 1984 at Caesars Palace, where Tyson could still land a spot on the Olympic team with a victory. Wearing a blue tank top, with trunks that had red and white stripes with blue trim, Tyson planned to cut off the ring on the elusive Tillman and make him a more stationary target.

But Tyson got caught fighting Tillman's fight again. It was as if Tyson wanted to show off his boxing skills. He bounced around the ring like Tillman and tossed out his own jabs, much to the frustration of those wanting more action. 'These fighters are hardly setting a high mark in excitement,' Cosell said in sarcastic fashion.

Tyson tried to force the action in the second round, but Tillman wouldn't comply, bouncing away whenever Tyson threatened his space. The third round was Tyson's last chance to beat Tillman; his last chance to make the Olympic team; his last chance of having any hope of winning a gold medal that would be the springboard to a professional career.

With 1:30 left, Tyson landed a hard right hand to Tillman's head, his best punch of the fight. But if it hurt Tillman, he didn't show it. He continued to dance to his left, keeping Tyson at a distance with his jab and quick combinations.

Tyson tried again to be the aggressor, which would have earned him points in professional boxing. But amateur bouts are scored only on punches landed and neither fighter had an obvious edge. Just before the bell, Tyson landed another hard right that rocked Tillman backward, a final punch that gave Tyson hope he had won the fight.

As he headed back to his corner, Tyson lifted his two hands in the air in a sign of victory. He had fared better than he did in the first fight. He thought he had done enough to win.

Standing in the centre of the ring, Tyson couldn't believe what he was hearing when the decision was read: 'The winner in the heavyweight division and an established member of the 1984 Olympic team, from Los Angeles, California, in the red corner, Henry Tillman.'

Tillman actually attempted to console Tyson, seemingly almost apologetic that he'd won. Tyson wanted none of it. He stomped around the ring in a mini-tantrum, disappointment flooding his body. 'I thought I won the fight,' Tyson says nearly 30 years later. 'But everything happens for a reason. Nothing is coincidental. Maybe if I won that gold medal, I wouldn't have trained as hard as a pro and felt I was entitled to things.'

Holyfield was not the clear-cut favourite to represent the United States in the light heavyweight division at Los Angeles. Womack had been the number-one-ranked light heavyweight in the country before Holyfield beat him in the second fight of a box-off to earn a spot in the '83 Pan Am Games in Caracas.

Many figured Womack would avenge that defeat at the Olympic trials. He was a slick boxer from Detroit, trained by Steward at the famous Kronk Gym. He became a favourite of Cosell after knocking out the Cuban medal favourite Pablo Romero earlier in the year on *Wide World of Sports*. A gold medal match-up between the two was highly anticipated at Los Angeles before the Soviet–Cuban boycott was announced.

Despite earning a silver medal at the Pan Am Games, Holyfield was generally viewed as an outsider. His biggest supporters were within the hierarchy of the USA Amateur Boxing Federation, which is now USA Boxing. Loring Baker was the first president of the USA Amateur Boxing Federation, serving from 1980 to 1984. He was also from Georgia. The Olympics would be the most significant event of his presidency, having sat out the boycott in 1980.

Baker, along with Buddy and Bo Davis, leaders of amateur boxing in Georgia, had pushed hard for Holyfield to be invited to the trials for the Pan Am Games. They weren't shy about their desire for Holyfield to make the Olympic team.

To do that, Holyfield would have to get past Womack, who was an excellent fighter when he was in shape and focused. Outside the ring, Womack could be unpredictable, if not dangerous.

But Womack was focused and determined at the trials in Fort Worth, beating Holyfield in what might have been his best performance as an amateur. Holyfield's Olympic dreams were on the brink of ruin. His last chance to make it to Los Angeles would be to beat Womack on consecutive days at a box-off a month later in Las Vegas.

Holyfield managed to win two decisions that Steward questioned. 'Somebody on the Olympic Committee wanted someone from Georgia on the Olympic team,' Steward said, perhaps pointing at Baker, who died in 2004.

Losing to Holyfield was the first major setback in what would be a life of unfulfilled potential for Womack. He turned pro after not making the Olympic team, but after just ten pro fights was arrested in 1985 for armed robbery of a video store where a customer was shot over three videos and $110. He would serve 15 years in prison. Upon his release in 2000 he tried to resume his pro boxing career and fought four times, winning all four fights. But two months after his final bout, which improved his record to 13–0–1, Womack killed himself in January 2002 with a self-inflicted gunshot wound after battering his wife to near death.

'Sometimes some people can't help what they do,' Steward would say years later of Womack. 'It's just in their DNA.'

After beating Womack for a second time and earning his Olympic spot, Holyfield watched to see how Tyson did against

Tillman. Holyfield may have also wanted to gloat a bit since Womack and Tyson had been roommates.

Excited by his own outcome, Holyfield quietly rooted for Tyson to beat Tillman. He was already comparing himself to the smallish heavyweight, watching how he handled bigger guys and seeing what he would do differently.

When Tyson lost to Tillman, Holyfield was disappointed. He thought that would be the last he'd see of Tyson until after the Olympics. But behind the scenes, D'Amato hadn't given up on Tyson making the American squad.

He knew if for some reason Tillman or Biggs couldn't fight because of injury or illness when the Olympics arrived, Tyson could step in. That possibility was enough for Tyson to be named as an alternate and join the Olympic squad during its training sessions in Gonzales, Texas.

He didn't stay long. D'Amato told Tyson not to hold back during sparring in the hope that he might crack a rib or cause another injury to create an opening. Nappi and the USA coaching staff sensed Tyson's motives and sent him home before the team left for Los Angeles.

Not qualifying for Los Angeles denied Tyson of being part of what many consider the greatest US boxing team in Olympic history. Certainly it is the most decorated, earning nine gold medals, one silver and a bronze.

The gold medal winners at the competition held at the Memorial Sports Arena included the local kid, Gonzales, who swept through his four opponents before winning his final match in a walkover to capture the 106-lb title. Steve McCrory of Detroit won in the 112-lb division; Philadelphia's Meldrick Taylor won at 125 lbs; Whitaker of Norfolk, Virginia, breezed through the 132-lb division, while Page (139), Breland (147), Tate (156), Tillman (201) and Biggs (201-plus) also took gold.

Yet it was Holyfield who emerged as the most memorable boxer of the Olympics. He looked headed for his own golden podium when he knocked out his first three opponents to get to the semi-final round where he would face Kevin Barry of New Zealand.

Holyfield dominated the first round, hurting Barry with quick combinations to the head and body. The plan was to throw punches in rapid succession to keep Barry on the defensive. Holyfield kept up his assault in the second round, as Barry desperately tried to clinch and hold in order to slow his punches. Referee Gligorije Novicic of Yugoslavia repeatedly warned Barry about the holding but didn't deduct any points.

Holyfield's intention was to win every fight by knockout and not let the judges become a factor. That was his goal against Barry. With only seconds left in the round, Barry was trying to hold again when Holyfield fired a quick combination. It started with a right hook to the body, followed by a crushing left hook to the jaw that floored Barry.

It looked like a clean punch to everyone in the Sports Arena and a worldwide television audience. But after declaring a woozy Barry unable to continue, Novicic went over to Holyfield to tell him he had been disqualified. Amid the roars of the crowd, Novicic apparently had yelled 'Stop!' just before Holyfield delivered the knockout punch.

It took several seconds for everyone in the Arena, including Holyfield, to realise what was going on. The disqualification became official when Novicic raised Barry's hand as the public address announcer said, 'The winner by disqualification . . . Kevin Barry.'

Barry seemed almost embarrassed. Immediately he dropped Novicic's hand and grabbed Holyfield's, raising it high in the air to show who he thought had truly won.

Novicic's work was widely ridiculed, especially by the American press. The actions of a Yugoslavian referee had cleared the way for a Yugoslavian boxer to win gold. Anton Josipovic was slated to meet the Holyfield–Barry winner in the finals. But now Holyfield had been disqualified and Barry couldn't fight because of the rule prohibiting boxers from fighting for at least four weeks after being incapacitated. Josipovic would show his support for Holyfield by inviting him up to the top tier during the medal ceremony and raising his hand in the air.

Holyfield had every reason to be angry. He'd been robbed of a chance to win a gold medal and all the adulation that comes with it. But instead of pouting, he showed up on the day of the finals to support his teammates. Standing in front of the locker room door of the US team, Holyfield wished each boxer good luck as they headed to the ring for their gold medal match.

Holyfield may have settled for the bronze medal, but the injustice he received and the class with which he handled the adversity made him the best-known boxer of the Olympics. Gonzales would win the Val Barker Award as the most outstanding boxer of the 1984 Games and would later be part of an Olympic contingent that met with President Ronald Reagan and were later feted in a ticker-tape parade up the Canyon of Heroes in New York. But what happened to Holyfield captured the heart of America.

'There was no doubt I was cheated,' Holyfield would say 28 years later. 'But if you look at it, if I wouldn't have been cheated, I wouldn't have been as popular. You talking about a guy who worked eight hours [a day] to make $8,000 year and all of sudden because I got cheated and Howard Cosell was telling everybody how I got cheated and how good my attitude was, I'm the one that got the big million-dollar contract. As a kid, I was mad when it happened, but now that I look at it as an adult who would I be if I was just one of the gold-medal winners?'

The Olympics had turned Holyfield from a virtual unknown into a national hero. The platform couldn't have better for starting his professional career. Meanwhile, Tyson would turn pro without as much fanfare, but their goals were the same: to become champion of the world.

4

BECOMING THE REAL DEAL

NOT WINNING A GOLD MEDAL didn't hurt Holyfield's appeal when it came to promoters trying to sign him to a professional contract. The way he handled himself in the aftermath of his disqualification in Los Angeles made him as popular if not more so than his teammates who had won gold.

It was time to turn pro, and Holyfield needed someone to help him start his career. The logical choice was Ken Sanders, an Atlanta car dealer who befriended Holyfield when he entered his showroom looking to buy a car. Sanders, who had an interest in boxing, co-signed the loan for Holyfield to buy a car and gave him $300 a month to support him during the lead up to the Olympics. Sanders had earned Holyfield's trust enough to help select a promotional company that would match him against the right fighters and maximise his earning power.

The choice eventually came down to two potential suitors. One was Josephine Abercrombie, a wealthy Houston-based heiress who had amassed a $100 million fortune in Texas ranch land, oil wells, cattle and breeding thoroughbreds. Five times divorced and the mother of two grown sons, she wanted to add boxing to her list of endeavours and had plenty of money to entice fighters like Holyfield.

Born in Kingston, Jamaica, in 1926, Abercrombie was a lady of privilege and culture with an extensive list of civic and philanthropic contributions to her credit. But she also was an athlete, becoming a skilled equestrienne by the time she was a teenager and later a champion show rider of gaited horses.

She also had a soft spot for boxing and boxers. An only child, she had been introduced to the sport by her father, oilman James Smither Abercrombie, who would take her to prizefights. She remained primarily a fan until 1982, when she watched the heavyweight championship fight between Larry Holmes and Gerry Cooney on closed circuit. The build-up of the fight and the interest it generated convinced her to take a shot at managing and promoting fighters. She set her sights and wallet on signing a few of the 1984 Olympians, including Holyfield. What she lacked in experience, she made up for in cash, offering Holyfield nearly $500,000 to sign with her.

The other contender was Main Events, a New Jersey-based promotional company headed by Lou Duva and his son Dan. Born on 28 May 1922 in New York City to Italian immigrants, Lou Duva was one of seven children. His family moved to Paterson, New Jersey, when he was four years old. He once said he had to quit school when he was young because of pneumonia. 'Not because I had it, because I couldn't spell it,' he joked.

He became a boxing trainer in the US Army at Camp Hood and though he returned to New Jersey to establish a successful trucking business, the lure of boxing never left him. He eventually started his own Garden City Gym and in the 1960s became friends with Rocky Marciano. His son Dan was born in 1951 and after earning his degree from Seton Hall Law School joined his father and formed Main Events in 1978.

With Lou serving as the head trainer for his stable of boxers and Dan handling the business end, Main Events made its mark by developing several fighters into world champions, such as Rocky Lockridge, Bobby Czyz and Livingstone Bramble. Also in their stable were members of the 1980 US team that boycotted Moscow, including Johnny Bumphus, Tony Tucker and Tony Ayala Jr.

In 1981, Main Events proved its ability to produce a mega

fight when it promoted the first bout between Sugar Ray Leonard and Thomas Hearns, which generated $40 million, becoming the largest-grossing non-heavyweight bout at the time.

Main Events already had targeted selected members of the '84 Olympic team, signing Mark Breland, Pernell Whitaker, Tyrell Biggs and Meldrick Taylor to multi-year contracts. Holyfield's dilemma was that Main Events was offering him roughly half the signing bonus Abercrombie was offering.

Dan Duva's final pitch to Holyfield was direct. 'If you think that you're not going to be the heavyweight champion of the world, you should take the money. But if you think you're going to be the heavyweight champion of the world, then you need to come with us, because we have a track record and she doesn't.'

Ultimately, that made sense to Holyfield. He was confident he would fulfil Carter Morgan's prediction he would be a champion someday. After conferring with Sanders, Holyfield signed with Main Events. 'I don't want to be that woman's toy,' Holyfield told Dan Duva.

With Holyfield, Breland, Biggs, Whitaker and Taylor under contract, Main Events signed an exclusive deal to televise the Olympians together on the ABC television network and also the USA Network. The Olympians made their pro debut together on 15 November 1984 at Madison Square Garden. It was called 'The Night of Gold' and was televised on prime-time television on ABC.

Bill Cosby was sitting ringside, an interesting occurrence since the boxing card was being televised opposite the very popular *Cosby Show* on NBC. 'You're going to blow us out of the water and you know it,' Dan Duva told a smiling Cosby.

All the Olympians easily won their debuts except for Holyfield, who found himself in a toe-to-toe slugfest with Lionel 'The Boiler' Byarm, a Philadelphia cruiserweight who wasn't impressed with Holyfield's Olympic credentials. Byarm was 9–1–2 with four knockouts at the time – hardly the stiff most prospects face in their pro debuts these days.

Trying to steal the spotlight, Byarm went after Holyfield with full force, pressing him on the ropes and delivering a barrage of non-stop punches as the Garden crowd roared its approval. Neither fighter went down, but Holyfield did enough to earn a unanimous decision.

While the fight was tougher than expected, Holyfield had proven he could survive six rounds. As an amateur, he could barely go three rounds without tiring at the end. It's one reason he fought so hard to accumulate 75 knockouts as an amateur.

Lou Duva and his co-trainer George Benton looked at Holyfield's chiselled body and figured it had to be more of a mental problem than anything physical. Benton, a former middleweight contender from Philadelphia in the 1950s and '60s, became a trainer after his career ended when he was shot in the back. Studying under the legendary Eddie Futch, Benton was in Joe Frazier's corner for his third fight with Muhammad Ali, 'The Thrilla in Manila'. He also helped train Leon Spinks when he upset Ali in 1979. When he joined Main Events, he was already one of the most respected and smartest trainers in boxing.

Unbeknownst to Holyfield, Benton came up with a plan to trick him into believing he was gaining more stamina. Benton adjusted the timer to where Holyfield would spar eight to ten two-minute rounds instead of three-minute rounds. The tactic paid quick dividends in the Byarm fight as Holyfield finished strong despite fighting twice as long as he ever had as an amateur.

Nonetheless, Dan Duva wasn't exactly sure what he had in Holyfield. He saw plenty of potential and talent, but a fighter's true worth is measured by his heart. That's something that can't be tested until he becomes desperate in the ring and a choice must be made to either quit or stand and fight.

Holyfield had shown courage against Byarm, but it wasn't until his eighth pro fight against Anthony Davis on 21 December 1985 that Dan Duva became convinced. Davis, a thirty year old from Las Vegas, was 17–3 with six knockouts at the time of the fight. In the third round of their scheduled ten-rounder in Virginia Beach, Virginia, Davis landed a devastating overhand right that had Holyfield nearly out on his feet. Davis closed in for the finish, but a dazed Holyfield was saved by the bell.

When the fourth round began, Holyfield was after quick redemption. He attacked Davis with a ferocity that nearly knocked off the side of his nose. Referee Al Rothenberg was forced to stop the fight at 1:31 of the round.

Duva, sitting at ringside, was now certain he had something special in Holyfield. He turned to his wife Kathy and said, 'He's the one! He's the one.'

'Everybody gets hit,' he told her. 'Everybody gets hurt. It's what you do when you get hit. Now we know what he's going to do. Did you see how he came back at that guy? It was like he wanted to kill him.'

Convinced Holyfield was ready to move up to a higher level of completion, Dan Duva began charting a course to create a world champion. Fighting once a month beginning in March of 1986, Holyfield scored three consecutive knockouts, stopping Chisanda Mutti of Zambia in three rounds, Jesse Shelby of Roswell, New Mexico, in three rounds and Terry Mims of Cleveland in five rounds.

In just his 12th pro fight, Holyfield was ready to challenge Dwight Muhammad Qawi for the WBA cruiserweight championship. Holyfield had proven to be a fast learner under the guidance of Benton, who may not have won a world championship as a boxer but was eventually voted into the International Boxing Hall of Fame in 2001 as a trainer before dying on 19 September 2011 from pneumonia.

Benton worked with all the boxers in the Main Events stable, but his primary focus with Holyfield was to improve his defence. As an amateur and early in his pro career, Holyfield's offence was his defence. He was confident he could eventually overpower any of his opponents by throwing a volume of punches, which was one reason he would tire so quickly.

'You can't go in there and throw punches for 12 rounds and

expect not to get hit,' Benton told Holyfield during one of their early conversations. 'You've got to have a good defence to go with your offence.'

Benton taught Holyfield how to deflect punches with his gloves and avoid getting hit flush by rolling his shoulders. 'Until George taught him defence, Evander was just an ordinary guy,' said Ronnie Shields, a former featherweight who had modest success as a pro before joining Duva's staff at Main Events as a trainer in 1988. 'George really took his time with Evander and taught him defence. The defence Benton taught him made Evander an elite fighter. George did a great job as far as teaching Evander defence and how to handle himself inside the ring. It gave him the confidence that he could go in there with anybody.'

To further address Holyfield's stamina issues, Lou Duva brought in Tim Hallmark, a Houston-based physical therapist who had been recommended by an orthopaedist who had treated one of Duva's other fighters. Hallmark had worked with all kinds of athletes. He had been a director of sports medicine at an athletic club and an athletic director at a country club. He had worked with business clients, amateur athletes, professional athletes and Olympic athletes in just about every sport.

Duva told Hallmark about Holyfield's stamina problems and the upcoming fight with Qawi. 'Evander's got a conditioning problem,' Duva said. 'He seems to get tired fast. We're concerned if this fight goes the distance, which we believe it will, he could have a lot of trouble.'

After doing an extensive one-on-one consultation with Holyfield that included everything from filling out a questionnaire to going through a sparring session, Hallmark learned Holyfield's recovery rate was 'not good at all'.

Hallmark developed a training programme unlike anything other boxers were doing. He worked him out in a swimming pool with a flotation device under his legs and over his shoulders to keep him upright as he threw punches as fast as he could. The pressure of the water would make Holyfield's heart rate shoot up.

They didn't do long distance running or jump rope. Instead, Hallmark identified drills that focused on the specific work tasks needed in the ring. He made Holyfield run short sprints, nothing over a mile. He introduced him to natural supplements, weightlifting and the benefits of a chiropractor. Their workouts would last for up to two hours in the afternoon after Holyfield had already gone through a boxing workout in the morning. And Hallmark did all the drills with Holyfield. The twice-a-day workouts lasted six weeks.

'He and I connected real quickly because the first thing we did before we put on shirts or shoes is we prayed about whatever we were going to do,' Hallmark said. 'I learned years ago that when you pray about things and get God involved, things can go better. He totally was on board for that.'

Holyfield might have been on board, but he wasn't totally convinced this new approach was necessary. He didn't like getting his hair wet in the pool, and at times he thought Hallmark pushed him too hard.

'It bothered me because regardless of whatever I did, he'd take it to another level,' Holyfield said. 'I'd think, "When is it going to stop?" But he would do it with me and I'd always do it a little faster. There was always a thought in my mind that he's trying to make me quit. Me living in the South and Tim happening to be a white guy, things would pop in my head about how people do black people and try to make you feel like you ain't nothing. But I had this thing about you can't make me quit. I don't quit.'

If Holyfield didn't immediately notice the results, his trainers did. 'When Tim came in, that's when everything changed for Evander,' Shields said. 'His stamina really picked up and he started to believe in himself. He just needed someone to help him understand that conditioning was as important as training to his boxing. A lot of guys, all they did was run. But when Tim came in, he introduced Evander to a whole new world of cardio. It really changed his whole life.'

The teachings of Benton and the conditioning of Hallmark

would be tested against Qawi at the Omni in Atlanta. Nicknamed 'the Camden Buzzsaw', Qawi was a strong, rugged fighter, who picked up boxing while serving a five-year sentence in the New Jersey State Penitentiary in Rahway for armed robbery. Qawi was only 5 ft 5½ in., but he was built like a tree trunk with a hard round head, thick shoulders and powerful legs. He was a skilled body punch, who could get inside but remained hard to hit because of his constant head movement. Some compared him to Joe Frazier because he often fought in a crouch. But Qawi viewed himself to be more of a counter-puncher. 'I didn't take a whole lot of punches,' Qawi said. 'I was strategic coming in. I would look at things and set things up.'

Despite the absence of an amateur background, he earned success as a pro, capturing the WBC light heavyweight title in 1981 when he stopped Matthew Saad Muhammad in the tenth round. He successfully defended the crown three times before losing to Michael Spinks in 1983.

He would move up to cruiserweight and claim the WBA belt by beating Piet Crous in 1985. Three fights later, he was 26–2–1 and defending his title against Holyfield.

Heading into the bout, Qawi had called Holyfield 'mediocre' and was fully aware of the stamina problems the Olympic hero had battled early in his career. He guessed there was no way Holyfield, who had not gone past eight rounds in his previous eleven fights, could go fifteen gruelling rounds with the Camden Buzzsaw.

Qawi's game plan was to apply constant pressure on the young challenger and make him fight every second of every round, anticipating Holyfield would be gassed by the middle of the fight. 'I figured he was tailor-made for me,' Qawi said.

The strategy seemed to be working when they met on 12 July 1986, a hot humid night that turned the Omni into a sauna. Qawi, formerly known as Dwight Braxton, knew he was facing adversity by fighting Holyfield in his home town. But after the adversity of surviving a prison sentence, he wasn't concerned.

His plan to pressure Holyfield turned the fight into a brawl, with Holyfield using a seven-inch reach advantage to fire hooks and combinations at the oncoming Qawi.

The inside fighting was brutal in the third round, with Qawi getting the better of it. By the fifth round, Holyfield was starting to show some fatigue. He began backing up more than he'd done earlier in the fight, as Qawi's bodywork looked to be taking a toll. But by the eighth round, Holyfield was standing his ground and connecting with hard punches that got through Qawi's hands-high defence. It became a rugged give-and-take for the rest of the fight, with Holyfield finishing strong. Combined, the two boxers had thrown more than 2,300 punches in the fight.

The scorecards showed the closeness of the bout. Harold Lederman, who would later become an 'unofficial' judge for HBO, saw Holyfield winning 144–140; while Gordon Volkman had it 143–141 for Qawi. Judge Elias Quintana had the widest margin, 147–138, making Holyfield the new WBA cruiserweight champion.

'It was a 15-round war,' Lederman said. 'It was two guys killing each other. It was a sensational fight: back and forth and back and forth. I thought Evander did enough to win. I was glad I was the deciding vote in the fight.'

In becoming the first of the '84 Olympians to win a world title, Holyfield was elated with the victory. But the toll his body took in the battle began to show when he was overcome by cramps and collapsed in the shower. By the time he was arrived at the hospital, Holyfield was suffering from severe dehydration. He had lost 15 lbs during the fight and there was real concern his kidneys might shut down.

Nearly 30 years later, Qawi says he was surprised about Holyfield's performance that night. He wonders how someone who suffered from stamina problems could suddenly go 15 hard rounds and finish strong.

'With Holyfield, I didn't expect him to go the distance with the pace I was going to set for him by pressing him,' Qawi said. 'I knew the pressure should have broken him down. I watched him spar about six months before the fight and he couldn't go six rounds without breathing hard.

'And then he comes back a few months later and goes the distance like that. I was surprised by that. I knew he was faster and younger. But I figured I'd hit him in the body and stay in his face and press him, press him, press him.

'In the fifth round, it was working as planned. He was getting tired and I was taking his power away, and then all of a sudden he got a second wind. He got a burst of energy and was more energetic in the second half of the fight than he was in the first. That still puzzles me today.'

Qawi has no real proof, only what his gut tells him. 'I just think he got something extra from somewhere,' Qawi said. 'Maybe he drank something and had a black bottle in the corner. I'm an athlete. I've been around. I know you can get a second wind. But you don't get a second wind like that.'

Qawi was admonished several times by referee Vincent Rainone for throwing low blows. But Qawi would complain Holyfield got away with his own questionable tactics. 'He kept pulling me by my head, pulling me down, trying to keep me off balance,' Qawi said. 'No one said nothing. But they kept interrupting me and breaking up my fight. I was very disturbed by how the referee would distract me. They never once reprimanded him for pulling my head and throwing me off.'

Qawi would get a chance for revenge 17 months later when they met in a rematch on 5 December 1987 at the Convention Center in Atlantic City. Holyfield was now 16–0, while Qawi had gone 2–1 since that night at the Omni. But by then Qawi was in the throes of alcohol addiction, drinking after his training sessions. He became indifferent towards the fight after learning Holyfield would make $1 million while he was to get $75,000.

'I had some family things going on at the time and my head was messed up,' Qawi said. 'I wasn't training right. I was just going in there trying to knock him out as fast as I could.'

Instead, it was Qawi who got stopped. With 1:12 left in the fourth round, Holyfield unleashed a three-punch combination that dropped Qawi on the seat of his pants. He quickly popped back up and ringside announcers called it 'a flash knockdown', guessing Qawi wasn't badly hurt. But after Qawi missed with a looping right hand, Holyfield stoned him with a short right hook. Qawi was down again and rolled onto his stomach, where he stayed until he was counted out by referee Randy Neumann.

'The politics of it, I let it get to me,' Qawi said. 'Usually I was mentally tough enough. I had some other things in my camp that wasn't up and up. That fight I wasn't myself.'

Qawi would fight 11 more years, finishing his career as a heavyweight. In 2004, he was elected to the International Boxing Hall of Fame with a career record of 41–11–1 with 25 knockouts. He now serves as an addiction counsellor in Atlantic County, New Jersey. 'It's more rewarding than a million dollars,' he said.

Four months after beating Qawi for the second time, Holyfield became the undisputed cruiserweight champion by capturing the WBA, WBC and IBF belts with an eighth-round technical knockout over Carlos De Leon in Las Vegas. Holyfield had to spend ten minutes sparring in a steam room to make the 190-lb limit for the fight and afterwards the Duvas announced that he was moving up to the heavyweight division being ruled by Mike Tyson.

The Duvas thought it would be ideal for Holyfield to beef up to 220 lb before entertaining any thoughts of fighting Tyson. But Hallmark had other ideas. Holyfield might have been muscular from the waist up, but his legs were smaller in proportion. Hallmark thought 210–215 would be a better target, telling Holyfield, 'If you get too big, too strong, too fast, you'll lose your hand speed and your ability to recover between rounds. If you lose any one of those two things, you're not the same fighter.'

Having already benefited from Hallmark's work, Holyfield agreed. Even 215 lb was a hefty jump from the 177½ lb he weighed for his pro debut four years earlier as a skinny light heavyweight. But to stand up to Tyson and the other heavyweights, Holyfield would need to get at least that big.

Hallmark reworked his training programme to incorporate kinesiology and cardiovascular conditioning designed to maintain Holyfield's explosiveness and stamina while adding muscle to his body. The programme consisted of a two-hour early-morning strength-training session three times a week using free weights and resistance machines. Hallmark used the heavy weights not only to build muscle but to enhance explosive movements.

Holyfield also ate four to five times a day, beginning with a high-protein breakfast and complex carbohydrates before and after his morning workout sessions. After a mid-morning rest, Holyfield then worked with Benton and Shields on his boxing skills. For an early lunch, he had another high-protein meal that included complex carbs and vegetables. Later in the afternoon, he would return for conditioning and cardio work.

'We had our arguments,' Hallmark said, 'and there were times that he thought I pushed him too hard. But he'd look at me and realise I was doing it and that I wasn't a clipboard trainer. The more he understood about how he trained, the more he knew he had a cutting edge and was doing something other guys weren't doing.'

Three months after becoming boxing's first undisputed cruiserweight champion, where he fought at 190 lb, Holyfield debuted for the first time as a heavyweight against James 'Quick' Tillis, who had lost a WBA heavyweight championship fight to Mike Weaver in 1981. He also was competitive against Mike Tyson in 1986, winning as many as four rounds before losing a ten-round decision.

Holyfield weighed in at 202 lb and looked sharp, dominating the 6 ft 1in., 210-lb Tillis, who quit on his stool after the fifth round. By December, Holyfield was up to 210 lb when he met former WBC heavyweight champion Pinklon Thomas in Atlantic City. Though Thomas, who weighed 222, hadn't fought in more than a year, his trainer Angelo Dundee predicted he would win by knockout. But Thomas looked slow and uninterested, and Dundee stopped the fight after seven rounds.

A much tougher test loomed on 11 March 1989 against 'Dynamite' Michael Dokes at Caesars Palace in Las Vegas. Unlike Tillis and Thomas, the 30-year-old Dokes wasn't a fading heavyweight past his prime. At 37–1–2 with 23 knockouts, he was a former WBA heavyweight champion who had won 11 straight fights and seemed past the troubles that landed him in a rehabilitation centre after being charged with cocaine trafficking. The WBC Continental Americas heavyweight title would be at stake, but more importantly the winner would be viewed as a credible opponent for Tyson, the reigning heavyweight champion.

The game plan devised by Benton was to keep constant pressure on Dokes, a boxer puncher with a good jab. The Holyfield camp thought Dokes lacked one-punch knockout power and wasn't concerned about a toe-to-toe battle. 'The plan was to make Dokes fight like he's never fought before,' Shields said. 'We didn't want to let Dokes get comfortable. If Dokes got comfortable, then he's really hard to fight. But if you don't let him get comfortable and put the pressure on him and make him fight when he doesn't want to fight, that's how Evander had to beat him.'

Holyfield had been a 9–1 betting favourite when the fight was first announced, but the odds dropped to 3½–1 by the first bell. Dokes entered the ring at 225 lb to Holyfield's 208. Unbeaten in 20 fights with 16 knockouts, Holyfield wasted little time implementing the game plan and Dokes didn't back down. What developed was what was easily the heavyweight fight of the year and in many eyes the heavyweight fight of the decade.

It began at a furious pace, with Dokes digging shots to Holyfield's body, including a low blow that drew a warning from referee Richard Steele. Holyfield countered with a low blow late in the first round that doubled over Dokes and caused a brief stoppage in the fight. Steele warned Holyfield, but neither fighter showed any signs of holding back.

Their torrid pace continued in the second round, with Holyfield landing hard hooks to Dokes's head. They often stood with their heads positioned cheek-to-cheek on each other's shoulders.

With Duva shouting from the corner, 'Get that respect. Get that respect,' Holyfield tagged Dokes with a left–right combination to the head. But Dokes got the better of things in the third round when he switched from focusing on the body to targeting Holyfield's head. It put Holyfield briefly on the defensive. 'You've got no business getting hit with those punches,' Benton told Holyfield between rounds. 'Go to the body.'

Holyfield did just that but in the fifth round exposed his chin to a crushing right hand from Dokes that backed him into the ropes. It was Dokes's best punch of the fight to that point. Intent on re-establishing himself, Holyfield pressed the action in the sixth and Dokes responded with another low blow that prompted Steele to take away a point. By the end of the round, Dokes had a cut above his left eye, the first blood drawn in the fight.

By the seventh, Dokes began to show some attrition. His legs looked unsteady as Holyfield kept up his relentless pace. In the corner, Benton's early anxiety about the pace of the fight had morphed into a confidence that went beyond the present.

'This guy is going to be the heavyweight champion of the world,' Benton told Shields. 'There's no doubt in my mind. Nobody is going to be able to handle the stuff that he's dishing out, and nobody is going to be in the shape this guy is in.'

The eighth round was classic, with Dokes starting strong and staggering Holyfield with a series of combinations to the head. But Holyfield used his heart and courage to inflict his own damage in the second half of the round. The furious action had the crowd on its feet roaring its approval.

The tenth round started out competitive, but Holyfield landed a sweeping left uppercut that Dokes never saw. It caught him flush on the chin, causing Dokes to stagger backwards. As

Holyfield closed in, Dokes tried to defend himself. But Holyfield caught him with a left hook that shot his head backward. Only the ropes kept Dokes upright. Steele had seen enough, jumping in to stop the fight just as Dokes slumped to the canvas.

'Nobody had really hurt Dokes,' Shields said. 'We knew it would take an accumulation of punches. The plan was to pour it on late in the fight and that's what Evander did.'

Holyfield would fight twice more in 1989, scoring a second-round TKO over Adilson Rodrigues of Brazil in July and an eighth-round stoppage of the previously unbeaten Alex Stewart in November.

While working his way up the heavyweight rankings, Holyfield was obsessed with getting a shot at Tyson. 'He talked about fighting Mike Tyson from the very first time I started working with him,' Shields said. 'Mike was knocking everybody out, and Evander would say, "They're fighting him wrong. Everybody's running from him. You can't run from him. You've got to go to stay in there with him. Otherwise, he'll eat you alive."'

Holyfield (23–0 with 19 knockouts) was among the top-ranked heavyweights in the world. It became impossible for Tyson and his promoter Don King to avoid him, or Tyson would face being stripped of his titles. An agreement was reached for Holyfield to face Tyson in June of 1990. The only potential obstacle was that Tyson had a title defence scheduled in Tokyo against James Buster Douglas. That seemed to be only a formality, since the unbeaten Tyson was a heavy favourite, but as the Real Deal would learn, nothing was a formality when it came to landing a fight with Mike Tyson.

5

SHARPENING IRON MIKE

UNLIKE HOLYFIELD, WHO HAD TO search for a management team to guide his professional career following the Olympics, Tyson was already committed to the men who shared the goal of developing him into the youngest and richest heavyweight champion in the history of boxing.

D'Amato, Jimmy Jacobs and Bill Cayton had been plotting Tyson's pro career since the day he arrived at D'Amato's home in the Catskills. All three were long-time friends and partners in D'Amato's plan to find one great fighter to make a last run at heavyweight-championship glory.

D'Amato believed Tyson was that guy. Jacobs and Cayton had to be convinced. It wasn't unusual for D'Amato to get excited about a prospect. Hundreds of fighters had passed through his gym and D'Amato's confidence in his ability to turn a troubled kid into a champion made him see potential in many of them.

But Jacobs and Cayton had enough faith in D'Amato to use their fortune from their fight film business Big Fights, Inc. to finance much of the expenses needed for Tyson's training. Sparring partners costing up to $2,000 had to be paid and there was the cost of travelling to various national tournaments. Jacobs and Cayton were covering all that as well as providing D'Amato with a stipend to maintain his home.

Born in 1930 in St Louis and raised in California, Jacobs

first came into prominence as one of the nation's best handball players. He won his first national championship in 1955 and was the best at his sport for more than a decade. He also had a passion for boxing and was a collector of vintage fight films featuring legends like Jack Johnson, James Corbett and James Jeffries. As a handball player, he could identify with being a boxer. He knew what it felt like to be alone in the arena, and the nakedness of wondering if you had trained as diligently as your opponent. He knew how the fear of failure could paralyse an athlete before the competition even began and what it took mentally to overcome it. To Jacobs, handball players and boxers were kindred spirits.

Jacobs met D'Amato and Cayton when he moved to New York in the mid 1960s to promote his then fledging fight film business. Cayton, born 1918 in Brooklyn, also was a collector of fight films, and it wasn't long before they decided to become partners, combining their film inventory to create sports programming for television. It proved to be a lucrative partnership that earned them millions.

But their interest in boxing wasn't limited to collecting fight films. Jacobs and Cayton wanted to manage fighters, an idea that grew when they met D'Amato during the normal course of being part of the New York fight scene.

D'Amato took an instant liking to Jacobs. He appreciated the younger man's knowledge of boxing history. Most of all he liked the way Jacobs handled himself. He had a quiet confidence that showed no ego despite his success as a handball player. He was personable and unflappable. When Jacobs was under pressure, he wouldn't show it. That's what D'Amato taught his fighters to do.

Steve Lott, who met Jacobs on the handball circuit and later worked as Tyson's camp manager, described their relationship this way. 'Cus liked Jimmy because he was a professional,' Lott said. 'A professional can be calm in a burning building and that's what Jim was and that's what Cus was.'

Cayton's value was more on the business side. He got his

first taste of boxing in the 1940s through his role as president of Cayton Advertising, when he saw boxing on television and recognised it as a viable format to market products. Soon he was buying film rights to develop his own sports programming. But his strength was public relations and marketing. He could be stern, calculating and aloof.

With D'Amato handling the boxing end, Jacobs shaking hands and schmoozing whoever needed to be schmoozed, and Cayton handling the business and marketing needs, the trio had all aspects of Tyson's career covered.

This was not their first boxing endeavour together. They had had success guiding the careers of Puerto Rican fighters Wilfred Benítez and Edwin Rosario. Benítez won world titles as a light welterweight, welterweight and light middleweight. But he lost his belts in high-profile fights against Sugar Ray Leonard and Thomas 'Hit Man' Hearns. Rosario also became a multiple world champion, winning titles as a lightweight and junior welterweight. But he also lost key fights against the flashy Hector Camacho and the great Mexican champion Julio César Chávez.

Failure to win the kinds of fights that turn boxers into legends had left Jacobs and Cayton feeling unfulfilled. Tyson presented the chance to rule the boxing landscape, to do something that had never been done before – win a heavyweight championship at a younger age than anyone in the history of boxing.

D'Amato was out to break his own record. On 30 November 1956 at Chicago Stadium, Floyd Patterson knocked out a 39-year-old Archie Moore in the fifth round to claim the heavyweight title vacated by the retirement of Rocky Marciano. Patterson's age was 21 years and 10 months, making him the youngest heavyweight champion in boxing history. If Tyson was going to eclipse that record he would have to win a crown within three years of turning pro.

The initial plan was to capitalise on the gold medal Tyson was expected to win at the 1984 Olympics. He would become a national star and be sought after by the television networks the way Holyfield was. But losing to Tillman in the Olympic trials had derailed those plans. It proved to be a blessing in disguise.

While Holyfield made his pro debut on the 'Night of Gold' televised by ABC television at a packed Madison Square Garden, Tyson climbed through the ropes on 6 March 1985 to face Hector Mercedes at the Plaza Convention Centre in Albany.

Mercedes was no threat. Born in Puerto Rico, he was winless in three fights and would go on to win only one of eleven fights in his brief pro career. With fewer than 2,500 in attendance, Mercedes lasted just 1:47 as Tyson won his pro debut by TKO.

Kevin Rooney worked as Tyson's trainer that night. But afterwards, Rooney put on gloves and fought in the main event, earning an eight-round decision over Garland Wright. Having fought Alexis Arguello and other quality competition, Rooney still harboured dreams of making something of his own boxing career as a welterweight. But two fights later, he lost by TKO to Mike Picciotti of Ridley Park, Pennysylvania, in the fourth round and suffered a bad cut over his eye. 'Cus didn't want me to fight any more,' Rooney said. 'I talked to Jimmy and he didn't want me to fight any more either. They just wanted me to concentrate on training Tyson.'

Beginning his pro career in relative obscurity proved ideal for Tyson. He wasn't ready emotionally or physically for the spotlight winning the Olympics would have brought. He'd compiled a 24–3 record as an amateur but wasn't comfortable with everything involved with being a prizefighter. He was still emotionally fragile and needed to learn how to handle himself in public and with the media. That would take time and be a fight-by-fight process.

D'Amato remained convinced that if Tyson stayed on the straight and narrow, dedicated himself to boxing and developed emotionally he could become a devastating heavyweight in the mould of Jack Dempsey, Joe Louis, Joe Frazier and Marciano. But few others outside Catskill agreed.

The critics had plenty to work with. Listed at 5 ft 10 in., he was too small; he didn't make the Olympics; his peek-a-boo style was outdated; he didn't have a deep enough amateur background; his personality was too volatile. 'I just never thought he was big enough physically,' said Hall of Fame trainer Emanuel Steward.

Fighting out of the spotlight in upstate New York was the perfect setting to keep Tyson away from the negativity until D'Amato could build up his confidence and work on his character. 'Cus knew Mike needed work inside the ring and outside the ring,' Lott said. 'He needed the physical and emotional experience of driving to the arena, going into the locker room, getting his hands taped, hitting the pads, walking to the ring, hearing his name announced and hearing the bell ring. He needed to experience the fear of looking bad and the fear of losing or being embarrassed and understanding that's OK. Great champions can control all those things. But the only way to do it was to do it often.'

To aid in Tyson's emotional development and build his confidence D'Amato hired a hypnotist to work with the boxer before each fight. While in a hypnotic trance, Tyson was told what he would see as he entered the ring – the crowd, the media, the referee, the opponent – and that he would thrive in that environment.

D'Amato also knew he had to keep Tyson busy to limit the possibility of him getting into trouble or taking extended visits back to Brooklyn, where he would revert back to his old habits. With D'Amato's age and Tyson's unpredictability, there was no room for idle time. Tyson fought 19 times in his first 13 months as a professional. He won all 19 fights by knockout, including 12 in the first round.

All of the opponents had been carefully selected so they didn't pose a real threat. Most were tall and slow with primitive defensive skills. Most were intimidated before they even got in the ring. 'They froze because they were worried they were being thrown in with a carnivore,' said Ross Greenburg, an executive producer for HBO during that time.

Tyson's first real competitive test was supposed to be against Donnie Long on 9 October 1985 at Trump Plaza in Atlantic City. Long was a 27 year old from Youngstown, Ohio, who had amassed a record of 15–3 with 10 knockouts. Nicknamed 'The Master of Disaster', he had regained his confidence by winning his last two fights by early knockouts after going 1–3 in his previous four. Tyson was 8–0 having turned pro just seven months earlier.

Long came out stiff-legged with his hands up but separated, exposing his chin. Early in the first round, he threw a lazy left jab that Tyson ducked under and came up firing a powerful left hook. It landed flush on Long's chin, knocking him into the ropes and down to the canvas.

Long struggled to his feet, only to be dropped again moments later by a Tyson uppercut. Long got up to give it one more try but a vicious left hook by Tyson finished him at 1:28 of the first round.

Over the next four weeks, Tyson added to his list of first-round knockouts by stopping Robert Colay and Sterling Benjamin to improve to 11–0 with 11 knockouts.

On 4 November 1985, three days after Tyson's fight with Benjamin, D'Amato died of interstitial pneumonia at Mount Sinai Hospital in New York City. He was 77.

Tyson knew D'Amato was hospitalised and had been struggling to breathe. But he was devastated to learn of his death. He'd lost his mentor, his best friend, the person who had given him confidence and purpose; the man who had rescued him from a life of destruction and put him on the path to greatness.

'I think I pretty much went insane when Cus died,' Tyson says 30 years later. 'I became so focused on that mission that we had, I was so locked on that mission, I was just gone. I didn't really care about anything else. Even if I died, I had to complete this mission.'

It was natural for Tyson to wonder about his future, but, understanding his age and his health, D'Amato had frequent talks with Rooney, Jacobs and Cayton on how to develop Tyson in case he wasn't around. He told them the right kind of opponent to match him against, how often he should fight and how to handle him during his moments of fear and doubt. It was a blueprint they were determined to follow.

'Me and Cus had such a weird relationship,' Tyson said. 'It was about conquer and conquest. I just wanted to kick some ass brutally in the ring.'

Tyson served as a pallbearer at D'Amato's funeral, where he was laid to rest under a tombstone that read: 'A boy comes to me with a spark of interest, I feed the spark and it becomes a flame, I feed the flame and it becomes a fire, I feed the fire and it becomes a roaring blaze.'

The boxing world was on fire with talk of Tyson. Nine days after D'Amato's death, he stopped Eddie Richardson in the first round of a bout in Houston, Texas. Three more KOs, two in the first and one in the second round, improved his record to 15–0 with 15 knockouts and brought a close to 1985.

On 6 January 1986, or about six months before Holyfield would win the cruiserweight title from Dwight Muhammad Qawi, Tyson was featured on the cover of *Sports Illustrated*. One headline read: 'Kid Dynamite'. The other: 'Mike Tyson, The Next Great Heavyweight – And He's Only 19'. The accompanying article told readers about how Tyson had been discovered by Bobby Stewart, taken out of reform school, mentored by the now deceased D'Amato and displayed an uncanny knack for knocking people out.

Jacobs and Cayton were already launching their own campaign to fan the hype about Tyson. They developed a videotape of his knockouts and sent copies to the top boxing writers and television executives around the country. Among those on the list was Ross Greenburg, the HBO executive. The videotape came with a note: 'Rising young heavyweight you should get a look at, Kisses, Jim.'

Greenburg was intrigued enough to go to Troy, New York, where Tyson met Jesse Ferguson on 16 February 1986. It would be Tyson's debut on ABC television, part of a four-fight deal

Cayton negotiated with the network for $1 million. Ferguson, 28, was a respectable 14–1 with 10 knockouts.

It was important for Tyson to look impressive, and he was up to the challenge. He charged Ferguson back into the ropes and began to land a series of crushing body punches that had Ferguson doubling over as he tried to cover up.

Occasionally, Ferguson would work his way to the middle of the ring and try to box. But Tyson would inevitably land a body shot that would send him into retreat. By the fourth round, Ferguson was fighting to survive. His main tactic was grabbing Tyson around the arms and holding him. But Tyson was too slippery. In the fifth, Tyson launched a vicious right to the kidney followed by an uppercut that crushed Ferguson's nose, dropping him to the canvas.

Ferguson got up at nine. But he took a brutal beating before the round ended. Tyson came out to finish him in the sixth, but Ferguson grabbed and held Tyson, refusing to break when referee Luis Rivera commanded. At 1:19 of the round, Rivera had seen enough and disqualified Ferguson for his blatant holding. It went down as a TKO, keeping Tyson's knockout streak intact.

Afterwards, Tyson told reporters, 'I tried to punch him and drive the bone of his nose back into his brain.'

Jacobs would tell Tyson to tone down such rhetoric. But Greenburg liked what he saw and heard. The next day he told Seth Abraham, the president of HBO Sports, 'Not only is he dynamite in the ring, I've never seen anybody so charismatic.'

Abraham was hearing the same thing from Larry Merchant, HBO's top boxing analyst and someone seldom prone to hyperbole. Before the Ferguson fight, Jacobs invited Merchant to his office at Big Fights, Inc., to view the videotape of Tyson. 'I was so impressed that I took the reel to Seth Abraham and asked him to look at it and suggested Tyson might be a fighter we would follow on HBO, something we'd never done before,' Merchant said, 'and that was to isolate a young fighter and show his development.'

Soon after, HBO signed Tyson to a three-fight deal that averaged $450,000 per fight.

Two fights after dispatching Ferguson, Tyson faced another important test against veteran heavyweight James 'Quick' Tillis. At 31–8 with 24 knockouts, Tillis was a seasoned veteran. The 'Fighting Cowboy' from Oklahoma had lost a close 15-round decision to Mike Weaver for the WBA heavyweight championship in 1981 and had been in the ring with some of the best in the heavyweight division. Outpointing Earnie Shavers over ten rounds in 1982 was his signature win, but by the time he met Tyson he was regarded as a former contender on the downside of his career. He was coming off three straight losses by decision to Tyrell Biggs, Gerrie Coetzee and Marvis Frazier. He also had the reputation of fatiguing toward the end of his fights.

What few knew was that before his fight with Tyson, Tillis visited a nutritionist who told him his diet of sugary fruit juices, rice, cheese grits, oatmeal and other heavy food was the reason he was fading during his fights. After implementing a healthier diet, Tillis said he 'felt like a million dollars. I had a slim body.' He weighed 207¾ lb for Tyson, nearly seven pounds lighter than his fight four months earlier against Biggs, where he said he was so tired 'my throat was barely opening and closing'.

Still, Tyson was a heavy favourite fighting in front of a partisan crowd of 8,000 at the Civic Center in Glen Falls, New York and millions of viewers watching on ABC television.

Knowing the bout would get massive exposure, Lott began discussing what Tyson would wear for the fight and he broached the subject with Jimmy Jacobs's wife Loraine. 'I like when he wears black,' she told Lott, who liked the idea of putting Mike in black trunks and black shoes to mimic those worn by legendary boxers like Jack Dempsey and Joe Louis.

The only problem was Lott couldn't locate a pair of low-cut black boxing shoes. He had to get creative. 'I found a pair of white low-cut shoes, so I painted them black,' Lott said. 'The colour sometimes rubbed off on Mike's feet.'

Lott also found a small American flag to put on the trunks,

figuring it would make Tyson even more appealing. 'The press in general and the public in general, if they see a fighter no matter if he's black, red or green, if they see him wearing an American flag it's tough to say anything negative about him,' Lott reasoned.

Entering the ring with black trunks, black shoes and no robe, Tyson had the look of a warrior. It thrilled the sell-out crowd. Most came expecting to see Tyson record his 20th win and 20th straight knockout. What they saw was him go the distance for the first time in his career.

Tillis grew up idolising Muhammad Ali and patterned his boxing style after him. He fought behind a long left jab and his legs were as much of a weapon as his fists. He used movement and quickness to frustrate his opponents. He darted in and out to avoid punches. In contrast to Tyson's all-back apparel, Tillis wore white trunks with white tassels dangling from his white boots.

From the opening bell, Tillis bounced on his toes and moved easily around the ring, using his footwork and stiff jab to keep Tyson from charging. 'I was moving in and out, and side to side,' Tillis said. 'I had legs like a kid. My legs were my defence. If you stand in front of him, he'll murder you.'

The sold-out crowd came expecting Tyson to be the destroyer he'd been in his previous fights. They were accustomed to quick finishes. But when Tyson was able to get in close, he was passive, especially after catching a couple of hard right uppercuts from Tillis. The ferocious body punching Tyson had displayed in his previous 19 fights wasn't as evident against Tillis. He didn't let his hands go in buzz-saw fashion. He often settled for one or two punches and waited for referee Joe Cortez to separate them from a clinch.

The fight's only knockdown came in the fourth round, when Tillis swung wildly with a left hand and Tyson countered with a left hook. But Tillis was more off-balance than hurt. Tyson never solved how to handle Tillis, who took all of his best punches. As the final bell sounded to end the ten-round bout,

Tillis was trading toe-to-toe with Tyson, who didn't look like the next great heavyweight. He looked mediocre.

He won a unanimous decision 6–4, 6–4 and 8–2, but the end of the knockout streak and lacklustre showing took much of the shine off Tyson, leaving some in the media calling him a myth.

'Everyone knows I won that fight,' Tillis says all these years later. 'But I knew I had to knock him out to win in New York. He was tough, though.'

The only positive coming out of the Tillis fight was that Tyson had gone ten rounds for the first time in his career. It was something he would have to do in his next fight against Mitch 'Blood' Green at Madison Square Garden.

The heavyweight championship was split among three different boxers at the time. Michael Spinks owned the IBF Championship, Tim Witherspoon was the WBA champion, while Trevor Berbick had the WBC belt. It still wasn't clear if Tyson belonged in their class, but HBO was ready to see if he was.

His fight with Green would be the first of the three-fight deal with HBO. It was part of a package that, including deals with ABC, would earn Tyson over $2 million for eight fights, an unprecedented amount for a non-champion. It would also be the first Tyson fight where Don King served as the primary promoter, though he had no long-term ties to the boxer.

Jacobs and Cayton were wary of King but had done business with him during fights with Benítez and Rosario, and needed the HBO exposure on the cards he promoted. They were careful never to do any long-term deals with promoters, preferring to work with them on a fight-to-fight basis. But King also had a stronghold on the heavyweight division, having signed most of the top contenders and champions to his company, Don King Productions. If Tyson was ever going to win a title, he'd likely have to face a Don King fighter.

Though Tyson had blind faith in Jacobs and Cayton, he wasn't oblivious to the politics of boxing. As early as age 19, he was showing signs of paranoia and not knowing whom to trust.

'Everybody always wants something,' he told reporters before his fight with Green. 'Just as hard as you work in the gym there's always people trying to separate you from your money.'

Green was unimpressed with the hoopla surrounding Tyson. A former gang leader in the Bronx, he had asked to fight Tyson figuring he could make an instant name for himself. He entered the ring 16–1–1 with ten knockouts, the only loss being a twelve-round decision to Berbick nine months earlier.

With the Garden crowd in a buzz, Tyson entered the ring with his now traditional black trunks and black shoes. He also had a snarl on his face, something he'd picked up after watching several fight films of Sonny Liston. During his time living with D'Amato and with access to the library owned by Cayton and Jacobs, Tyson was constantly engrossed in the boxing films at his disposal. He would study each fighter's technique and figure out how to beat him.

Randy Gordon, a former editor-in-chief of *The Ring* magazine and one-time commissioner of the New York State Athletic Commission, recalls visiting with Tyson, who started to cry while watching a film of a young Sonny Liston. Gordon asked Tyson what was wrong.

'I could never beat him no matter what I do,' Tyson said. 'There's nothing I can possibly do to beat him. I can't figure out in my mind how to beat him.'

With other fighters, Tyson would be animated while watching the film. He'd stand on his feet mimicking punches. 'But when he saw Liston, he froze,' Gordon said. 'He never thought he could beat Sonny Liston. He watched tape of Jack Johnson and he watched tape of Joe Louis. He watched a tape of Ali and said it would have been a fun fight. But when he watched Liston, he just knew in his mind he could not beat Sonny Liston.'

Green was no Liston. The fight went the full ten rounds, but Tyson dominated the bout, winning all but one round on two judges' scorecards and winning eight of ten rounds on the other's.

Green had white trunks, white shoes and white tassels like

Tillis and tried to use his jab and 6 ft 5 in. height to keep Tyson at bay. But Tyson was more assertive than he was against Tillis, constantly getting into Green's body and pounding him with hooks to the ribs and uppercuts to the chin. Green was in survival mode early and spent most of the fight holding. Tyson seemed to relish going the distance and finishing stronger. 'I used a great deal of discipline in there not knocking him out,' Tyson said after the fight.

The marketing of Tyson was back at full steam. Three weeks later, he added to his list of first-round knockouts by stopping Reggie Gross at Madison Square Garden. Gross made the mistake of trying to mix it up with Tyson. Midway through the first round, he tried to swarm Tyson with a flurry of two-fisted punches, leaving his chin exposed. Bobbing and weaving to avoid Gross's assault, Tyson timed a perfectly executed left hook that blasted into Gross's chin. The force of the punch dropped him flat on his back.

Gross rolled over and struggled to his feet at the count of six. But Tyson attacked and floored Gross with another left hook, prompting the referee Johnny LoBianco to stop the fight.

Two more knockout wins over William Hosea and Lorenzo Boyd followed before Tyson met Marvis Frazier on 26 July 1986, in Glen Falls. The son of former heavyweight champion Joe Frazier, Marvis was 16–1 with seven knockouts, his only loss to former heavyweight champion Larry Holmes via a first-round knockout. Tyson was 24–0 with 22 knockouts. It would be his final fight in upstate New York. Again, he entered with his version of the Liston snarl.

Frazier's fighting style was just like his father's. The intent was to apply pressure, come forward and stay close. It was tailor-made for Tyson. The old adage is to box a puncher and punch a boxer. You don't punch with a puncher. Soon after the bell sounded, Frazier had his back to the ropes and his gloves up trying to defend himself as Tyson closed in.

The first uppercut Tyson threw landed flush underneath Frazier's chin. Frazier was hurt. The second uppercut knocked

Frazier out as he slumped down in his corner. Before referee Joe Cortez could come to Frazier's rescue, Tyson landed one last right hook. The fight lasted only 30 seconds. 'I knew deep down in my blood I was going to stop him in the first round,' Tyson said after the fight.

While Tyson was becoming the hottest fighter in boxing, HBO was launching a heavyweight unification series meant to decide the first undisputed champion since Leon Spinks defeated Muhammad Ali in 1978. Tyson was not initially in the tournament because Jacobs and Cayton weren't sure he was ready for the elite competition he would face or the media scrutiny that would build along the way. They were also wary of Don King, who promoted almost all the other boxers in the tournament. But the legitimacy of the tournament would be questioned without Tyson being involved.

That became evident when IBF champion Michael Spinks was set to defend against Steffen Tangstad on 6 September 1986 at the Las Vegas Hilton. With ticket sales lagging, Jacobs and Cayton were approached about putting Tyson on the undercard against Alfonzo Ratliff, a 30-year-old former cruiserweight. Jacobs and Cayton decided it would be good exposure with little risk. Tickets sold out within two hours after it was announced Tyson was added to the card. It would be Tyson's first fight in Las Vegas.

Tyson was such a heavy favourite, the only betting offered was an over-under on whether the fight would go five rounds. It lasted only two rounds, as the over-matched Ratliff was dropped by a short left hook. Ratliff got up, but it was only a question of time. A right hook followed by a left to the body and a left to the head ended the bout.

After dispatching Ratliff, Tyson officially entered the unification series with his first fight against Trevor Berbick for his World Boxing Council heavyweight championship. It was the chance to fulfil the prophecy laid out by D'Amato when he predicted Tyson would become the youngest heavyweight champion of the world.

His shot at the title had arrived. Yet the marketing of Tyson was not complete. He needed a nickname. He'd been known simply as Mike Tyson. The public relations department of the Hilton came up with the moniker 'Iron Mike Tyson'. Jacobs and Cayton thought it fitted the packaging of their fighter.

There were some in the media who still questioned Tyson's ability to be a great heavyweight. But few could question the job Jacobs and Cayton did in marketing their fighter. They'd carefully selected low-risk opponents. They fought him frequently to quickly build an impressive record. They coached him on what to say during interviews. They sent videos of his most spectacular knockouts to selected media. They turned the story of Cus and the troubled kid into folklore. They dressed him in black trunks and black shoes, and they covered up whatever indiscretions he might have committed that would harm his appeal.

'Nothing behind the scenes happened by accident,' Lott said. 'Everything was calculated.'

Berbick, 33, was 31–4 with 1 draw and 23 knockouts. He had won the WBC title on 22 March 1986, when as a 6–1 underdog he earned a unanimous decision over Pinklon Thomas in the first round of the unification series at the Riviera Hotel in Las Vegas. Until then he was best known for beating an ageing Muhammad Ali in his final fight in 1981.

Despite holding a title, Berbick was considered among a group of mediocre heavyweights. He could have walked in the middle of Times Square and no one would have known who he was.

A native of Port Antonio, Jamaica, Berbick represented his country at the 1976 Olympics in Montreal after just 11 amateur bouts and had built a respectable résumé as a pro, beating former WBA heavyweight champion John Tate and fringe contender Greg Page, in addition to losing a tough 15-round decision in 1981 to then WBC champion Larry Holmes.

For his fight against Tyson, Berbick would have the legendary Angelo Dundee in his corner. Dundee insisted he had the perfect game plan to beat Tyson. 'You don't stay in front of Tyson, you stay at an angle because his punches come from the outside,' Dundee told reporters days before the fight. 'And you keep your hands up. But the whole trick is angles.'

To underscore his confidence, Dundee added, 'If he's the same Trevor Berbick who fought Pinklon Thomas, he'll do a number on Tyson.'

A sell-out crowd of 8,800 filled the Las Vegas Hilton on 22 November 1986. Among those in attendance were Ali, Larry Holmes and George Foreman.

At age 20 years, 4 months and 22 days, Tyson climbed into the ring prepared and confident. Berbick looked nervous. His game plan to outbox Tyson and frustrate him with angles must have left his thinking as soon as the bell sounded. Berbick came out and stood right in front of Tyson, eager to exchange blows in the centre of the ring. It was a flawed strategy.

Tyson began to score at will late in the first round, repeatedly landing hooks to Berbick's head and jaw. As the bell sounded to end the round, a wobbly Berbick looked at Tyson and stuck out his tongue. Then he staggered to his stool like a drunken sailor.

Dundee tried to revive Berbick with an ice pack and cold water. But it didn't help. Moments into the second round, Tyson launched a vicious assault, connecting with seven unanswered punches that sent Berbick to the canvas for the first time.

Berbick bounced right up and took a standing eight count from referee Mills Lane. Hurt, dazed and overmatched, Berbick tried to survive the round by holding Tyson's arm at every clinch. But his luck ran out just before the bell when a short left hook to Berbick's temple sent him flat on his back.

This time when Berbick tried to bounce up his legs betrayed him. He stumbled into the ropes and into the ringside cameramen. He tried to get up again only to topple forward. He rolled over and tried to get up again, finally collapsing into the arms of Lane, who stopped the fight.

Six years after moving into D'Amato's home, Mike Tyson

became the youngest heavyweight champion of the world. 'Do you think Cus would have liked that?' Tyson asked Jacobs in the centre of a crowded ring.

In the midst of the celebrations, Don King, who was Berbick's promoter of record, lifted Tyson in the air after the WBC belt was placed around his waist. The picture went worldwide, much to the chagrin of Jacobs and Cayton.

'It was my best fight,' Tyson said afterwards. 'I was so intense. I was out for blood. I refused to be beat. I couldn't be denied.'

Having fulfilled Cus's dream of becoming the youngest heavyweight champion, Tyson had two more goals to chase. One was to become the undisputed heavyweight champion of the world by holding all the three major belts. The other was to break Rocky Marciano's unbeaten record of 49–0.

The unification series offered a clear path to unifying the titles within a reasonable amount of time, something that might not have happened had Tyson not been in the tournament. With the WBC title secured, his next bout was against WBA champion James 'Bonecrusher' Smith, another King fighter of merit.

Smith had won his title with a first-round knockout of Tim Witherspoon three months earlier at Madison Square Garden. At 6 ft 4 in. tall and weighing 233 lb, Bonecrusher fitted the build of most of Tyson's previous opponents. But at 33 years old with a spotty record of 19–5 with 14 knockouts, Smith was a sizeable underdog to Tyson, then 28–0 with 26 KOs.

Fighting in the same ring at the Las Vegas Hilton where he had won the WBC title, Tyson's performance wasn't nearly as exciting. He would win easily, but the fight was a dud. Smith fought to survive, holding, clinching and reluctant to exchange. Tyson complied. Clearly ahead on the scorecards for the little aggression he did show, he grew passive in the fight. He didn't attack Smith's body with consistency, kept his combinations at a minimum and seemed content to win on points. He fought like he was bored.

His performance did nothing to excite the media and audience that had grown accustomed to spectacular knockouts. 'Every fight wasn't necessarily measured against the opponent,' HBO's Larry Merchant said. 'It was Tyson against Tyson and how did he look compared to the last time.'

Still, Tyson had added the WBA belt to his collection. The only major belt left was the IBF, then owned by Michael Spinks. Yet there were those who were sceptical of how long Tyson could continue his reign of terror. Whether it was his fighting style or unpredictability outside the ring, there were people who weren't completely convinced he would be able to sustain a run with all of his issues. They included Muhammad Ali, who whispered to Merchant after Tyson's win over Berbick, 'How long is he going to be able to keep this up?'

Little did anyone know, the life of Iron Mike Tyson was about to become as volatile outside the ring as it was inside it.

6

HEAVY LIES THE CROWN

AFTER DEFEATING BONECRUSHER SMITH, TYSON'S next fight was supposed to be against Michael Spinks, the IBF champion, for the undisputed heavyweight championship. That would have been the natural progression for HBO's unification series. But Spinks's promoter, Butch Lewis, wanted no part of that fight. Lewis, a former used-car salesman, had worked for Bob Arum at Top Rank before breaking out to start his own promotional company and knew Spinks was his meal ticket to riches.

He had no intention of fighting Tyson in the series. For starters, he wasn't sure Spinks, a blown-up light heavyweight, could beat Tyson. Second, if that fight ever happened, he wanted it to be worth far more money than the contract for the HBO Unification series was offering. Much to the anger of HBO and Jacobs, Lewis pulled Spinks out of the series.

Instead of facing Tyson, Lewis matched Spinks against Gerry Cooney in a closed-circuit pay-per-view bout. Cooney had fought just three times and seven competitive rounds in the five years since losing to Larry Holmes in their much ballyhooed heavyweight championship showdown in 1982. But he remained a big name and a big draw with an impressive record of 28–1 with 24 knockouts.

When the fight was announced, the IBF stripped Spinks of his title, keeping the belt within the unification series and within Tyson's grasp. That was fine with Lewis. Spinks would earn $4 million for an impressive fifth-round technical knockout over Cooney on 15 June 1987, in Atlantic City.

With public sentiment starting to view Spinks as the true heavyweight champion, Jacobs and Cayton knew they would eventually have deal with Lewis for Tyson to be recognised as the undisputed champion. But they were in no hurry to make that match. There was money to be made in other fights.

HBO was offering Tyson a seven-fight deal worth $26.5 million. He had been good for business and drawn added subscribers to the premium network. 'The ratings went through the roof,' Greenburg said of Tyson's impact. 'Every fight was a major event. We were doing like a 27 rating and 46 shares on his fights on HBO. It was probably the zenith of HBO boxing history.'

With Spinks out of the picture, Tyson signed to defend his WBC and WBA titles against Pinklon Thomas, another Don King fighter. The press conference to announce the bout was notable because it was the first time Tyson made public his budding relationship with a young actress named Robin Givens.

Tyson pursued Givens after seeing her on the ABC television show 'Head of the Class'. He was smitten with the actress and arranged an introduction through John Horne, one of his friends from Albany, who was now based in Los Angeles. Givens was the kind of woman Tyson once thought was beyond his grasp. She was educated, confident, successful and beautiful. But Tyson had already learned as heavyweight champion that women were at his disposal. They were eager to please him even if his tactics were often crude.

Few in the Tyson camp initially viewed Givens as a threat. She was just another girl. Even if Tyson was serious about her, it was viewed as a good thing. Perhaps he'd settle down a bit instead of going through a parade of faceless women. Besides, Rooney, Jacobs and Cayton were preoccupied with trying to get through the heavyweight unification series, sign a new deal with HBO and work on a mega-fight with Spinks. There was a sense of urgency to their planning. Time was of the essence.

Jimmy Jacobs had known since 1981 he suffered from chronic lymphocytic leukemia, a cancer that would likely shorten his life. Virtually no one in boxing aside from Cayton knew about his condition, certainly not Tyson.

No one would have suspected Jacobs was sick. He maintained the athletic build of his handball days and always presented a personable and confident exterior. His attitude was positive and his negotiations could be tough but fair. There was no sign his time was running out.

Pinklon Thomas proved to be just another name in Tyson's growing list of knockout victims. He lasted just six rounds on 30 May 1987 in Las Vegas.

The next step was to become the first undisputed heavyweight champion since Leon Spinks upset Muhammad Ali in 1978. That was the goal on 1 August when Tyson faced Tony Tucker, who had claimed Spinks's vacated IBF title by beating James 'Buster' Douglas two months earlier. It wouldn't be the last time Douglas would fight for a title.

Tucker, a 28 year old from Grand Rapids, Michigan, was like most of the previous boxers Tyson had faced: tall with long arms. He was 6 ft 5 in. with an 82-inch reach and an unblemished record of 34–0 with 29 knockouts.

Fighting again at the Las Vegas Hilton, Tyson was a 10–1 favourite going in. But Tucker, dressed in red trunks and red shoes, had a good first round, landing a hard left uppercut that momentarily stopped Tyson's early charge. It was a hard solid punch, but Tyson shook it off and continued his pursuit.

Knowing what was at stake and with HBO televising the bout, Tyson seemed intent on scoring an early knockout. He went headhunting with hard wild hooks as Rooney shouted from the corner, 'Go back to the body.' But Tucker was a smart boxer who had won a gold medal at the 1979 Pan American Games. He neutralised Tyson's aggression by grabbing his arms and forcing a clinch whenever Tyson got inside.

As the rounds went on, Tucker gained confidence in his survival. His lateral movement and accurate punching proved a tough puzzle for Tyson to solve. Between rounds, Rooney told Tyson he needed to box more and use combinations to the body and head. It was shaping up to be a fight that would go the duration.

Tyson didn't get frustrated. He won rounds with his aggression and by landing more punches than Tucker, who did more holding than punching. The crowd at times grew restless with the clinching. In an effort to appease the fans, Tucker tried to do his version of the Ali Shuffle in the 11th round. But it didn't impress Tyson, who kept up the pressure.

In the end, the judges gave Tyson a clear unanimous decision: 119–111, 118–113 and 116–112, making him the undisputed heavyweight champion at age 21.

Tyson wasn't thrilled with his performance, despite owning all three major belts and a crown King gave him at the press conference following the fight. 'I'm a perfectionist,' he said. 'I want to be perfect.'

If not perfect, Tyson was clearly the best heavyweight on the planet. His path of destruction continued with a seventh-round pounding of former Olympian Tyrell Biggs in Atlantic City followed by a fourth-round knockout of former heavyweight champion Larry Holmes on 22 January 1988.

Jacobs was at the Holmes fight, but it was becoming evident something wasn't right. He was pale and weak. To protect their respective interests in Tyson, Cayton and Jacobs had drawn up new contracts stating that in the event of Jacobs's death, Cayton would take over as the manager of record. Tyson had signed the contracts that February not knowing the man he trusted with his career could die at any time, immediately making Cayton his manager.

Tyson was too distracted by his pursuit of Givens to worry about contracts or Jacobs. He went to Los Angeles after the Holmes fight to meet with Givens. It was on that trip that Givens told Tyson she was pregnant. Within days they were married.

Everything seemed perfect in Tyson's life. He'd married

someone of a social status he thought was beyond his means. He was making commercials for Kodak, Pepsi, Nintendo and the New York City Police Department. He was the hottest thing in boxing, with nearly $24 million in career earnings.

A fight against Tony Tubbs set for 21 March in Tokyo seemed yet another in a list of match-ups where Tyson would dominate and enhance his international appeal. When he left for the fight, he had no idea Jacobs was in the hospital preparing to undergo radical chemotherapy treatment and would not be at ringside for the first time in his career.

Cayton assumed the role of Tyson's primary manager in Japan while Givens played the honeymooning wife. Tyson did his part by knocking out Tubbs in the second round, much to the delight of the Japanese crowd at the Tokyo Dome.

The first real sign of turmoil came on the plane flight back to the United States when Givens walked up to where Cayton was seated and demanded to see the contracts he had with Tyson. Cayton was defensive, not knowing exactly what to say. For one, he didn't want to risk revealing Jacobs was in the hospital. Second, he viewed Givens as an outsider who had no right to question his management of Tyson.

Stonewalled by Cayton, Givens went to Tyson, ordering him to tell Cayton to let her see how much money he and Jacobs were making. Tyson was caught in the middle between trying to be a dutiful husband and a trusting fighter who believed in the men in charge of his career. He went to Cayton and the two decided they would address the issue at a later date. Soon that would be the least of their concerns.

Two days after Tyson defeated Tubbs, Jacobs died of pneumonia. Leukemia had ravaged his body to the point where it couldn't fight the infection. He was 58.

One moment Tyson was celebrating his victory over Tubbs. The next he was a pallbearer carrying the casket of another friend. The funeral was in Los Angeles, where Jacobs was buried next to his mother.

If Tyson lost a father figure when D'Amato died, he lost a

brother in Jacobs. They watched fight films together and shared their inner thoughts. They sometimes kissed, even on the lips, immediately after fights. There was nothing Tyson wouldn't do for Jacobs and he was filled with so many questions when Jacobs died. How did he die? Why did he die? How long had he been sick? Why wasn't he told so he could at least say goodbye?

Finding the answers to those questions began to strip away the inner confidence that had transformed Tyson from street thug to champion. He became suspicious and insecure. What else had Jacobs and Cayton kept from him? Did they only care about him because of the money? Did they even care about him at all?

'I call it the dark side of love – betrayal – and that's what it was,' Tyson said. 'It's the dark side of love. It's not a pretty picture.'

Betrayal was a familiar, ugly feeling for Tyson. One that he was about to experience more of as Don King and Givens began to battle over his trust and fortune. If there was a point in life where Tyson's life and career began to unravel, this was it.

Losing D'Amato was devastating to Tyson. But in Jacobs he still had someone he thought he could trust. Tyson knew to his core that Jacobs had his best interests at heart. He trusted every decision he made as his manager, even signing the contract extension just before Jacobs's death that would ensure Cayton would immediately become Tyson's manager should anything happen to Jacobs.

But the circumstances surrounding Jacobs's death and the friction between Cayton and Givens caused Tyson to question everything around him. He had virtually no relationship with Cayton, the hardened businessman who was now posturing as the mastermind behind the marketing of Tyson. And his marriage to Givens was rocky from the beginning.

Two days before the Tubbs fight, Tyson told Lott, 'Robin's driving me crazy.' Caught between loving his wife and being loyal to a manager he didn't really trust, Tyson was taking the first steps toward a meltdown.

'Once Jacobs died there was really no tie to Cus for Tyson,' Greenburg said. 'Rooney at that point was still around, but from a business standpoint Tyson never really had a relationship with Cayton. He only had a relationship with Cus and then with Jimmy.

'People are under the misconception that things changed once Cus died, but that's not true. Things started to unravel when Jimmy died. That's when King saw the opening and went after Tyson.'

King, Givens and her mother Ruth Roper were at first allies in their mutual goal of loosening Cayton's grip as Tyson's manager. The women wanted to remove Cayton from power, while King wanted to sign the fighter to an exclusive promotional contract that would ensure his control of boxing's money-making machine.

Their target was the contract extension Tyson signed less than two months before Jacobs's death, authorising Cayton to become his manager in the event of Jacobs's demise. The contract also made provisions for the spouses of Cayton and Jacobs to receive a portion of Tyson's earnings in the event either Jacobs or Cayton died. The timing of the contract and Jacobs's death seemed too coincidental to not be premeditated.

By the time Tyson's inevitable showdown with Michael Spinks arrived, everything around him was in turmoil. Givens and her mother Ruth Roper had purchased a $4 million home in Bernardsville, N.J., paying the asking price in cash.

Rooney and Lott weren't exactly silent bystanders. They had become agitated by Givens's intrusion into Mike's career, while Givens and King viewed them as loyalists to Cayton.

Two weeks before the Spinks fight, Givens blamed Lott for allowing Tyson to be interviewed by *People* magazine without her consent and wanted him fired. 'She screamed at me "you motherfucker" and called me every word in the book,' Lott said. 'Later when I saw Mike, he told me, "Steve man, she probably scared you, right?" I said, "Yeah." He said, "I felt the same way the first time she talked to me like that."'

Tyson and Givens were having their share of problems. An argument between the newlyweds on 8 May 1988, while driving into New York City, resulted in Tyson crashing his $150,000 Bentley. A day later, King bought Tyson a Rolls-Royce to replace the Bentley.

Accusations of misappropriations, mistrust and mistreatment were being exchanged through the news media, creating a feeding frenzy over the soap opera erupting around Tyson. The New York tabloids were in full 'he said, she said' mode, with reporters aligning themselves with either the women, King or Cayton.

'It was a really shitty time,' Tyson recalls. 'I was married and having a shitty time with my marriage and I was having a shitty time with my managers who were ripping me off, too.'

In the midst of this chaos, Tyson arrived at the Convention Hall on the Boardwalk in Atlantic City on 27 June 1988 to take on Michael Spinks in the most anticipated heavyweight fight since Ali vs. Foreman in Zaire. Tyson was a 3–1 favourite, though there were plenty of boxing experts who thought the taller awkward Spinks could give Tyson trouble.

Spinks was 31–0 with 21 knockouts, a former Olympic gold medallist, an undisputed light heavyweight champion and former IBF heavyweight champion. He was trained by the 77-year-old legend Eddie Futch, who had forgotten more about boxing than most people ever knew.

At 6 ft 1 in., 212¼ lb, Spinks was lighter than Tyson, who was 218¼ lb. In compiling a record of 34–0 with 30 knockouts, Tyson had averaged just 3.5 rounds in his 34 pro fights.

A celebrity-packed crowd filled the Convention Hall while millions tuned in on closed-circuit, the pay-per-view system that guaranteed this would be the richest fight in boxing history, with Spinks guaranteed $13.5 million and Tyson $20 million.

Spinks's promoter Butch Lewis, known for wearing a white suit with a white bow tie and no shirt, had brilliantly orchestrated a rich deal for his fighter and himself. A Philadelphia native, Lewis had skilfully guided Michael Spinks to the point where he became the first light heavyweight champion to win a heavyweight crown.

But Lewis entered the ring for Tyson–Spinks sensing doom. Minutes earlier he had gone to Tyson's dressing-room looking to agitate the opponent. Instead he saw Tyson punching holes in the wall. 'Mike Tyson was at the best he could be that night,' Lewis would say.

As the announcer made his pre-fight introductions, an attorney representing Tyson and Givens handed Cayton an envelope. It contained notice of a legal complaint charging that Tyson had been fraudulently induced to sign the contracts automatically appointing Cayton as his manager. The action was reported on air by HBO.

As the bell sounded, Tyson practically skipped to the middle of the ring as if delighted to finally be in an element he could control. There was no wife, no mother-in-law, no managers, no promoters fighting for money. There was no one telling him what he should do, feel or think. It was just him and Spinks getting ready to fight, and Tyson had been fighting all of his life.

He went on the attack immediately, throwing a hard right hand that sent Spinks into retreat. During their first clinch, Tyson threw a left elbow at Spinks, drawing a warning from referee Frank Cappuccino.

Tyson didn't flinch. He went right back after Spinks, staggering him with a right hand to the head. Seconds later, Tyson fired two punches. First a left uppercut to the chin followed by a right hook to the body. Spinks went down on his right knee for the first time as pro.

By the time Cappuccino reached the count of three, Spinks was on his feet, shaking his head as if to say he was all right. Three seconds later, he wasn't. As Spinks tried to throw a right hand, Tyson blocked the punch with his left and fired a right cross that caught Spinks flush on the chin.

Spinks dropped back flat on his back, his head bouncing hard off the canvas. He lay there with his eyes open and glazed. As

Cappuccino counted, Spinks tried to get up only to roll into the ropes. It had taken 91 seconds for Tyson to knock out Spinks.

Tyson walked around the ring with his arms extended at his side and the palm of his gloves facing upwards in a look of invincibility. Rooney was the first to jump into his arms and grab him in a bear hug. King tried to join the celebration but couldn't break the lock Rooney had on Tyson.

Most in the Convention Hall were shocked the bout ended so abruptly, but not HBO's Larry Merchant. 'I thought the fight would last 90 seconds and it lasted 91,' Merchant said. 'I said on the air I'd be surprised if it lasted a half of a round. I have the highest admiration for Spinks. I did at the time. I think he's one of the best light heavyweights ever. But he was an old former light heavyweight fighting a young dynamic heavyweight. I didn't see any way he could cope with Tyson.'

It would be Spinks's last fight. Tyson talked of retiring after the bout. He was angry at the media for its portrayal of his personal life and distrustful of King and Cayton. Little did anyone know, but the Spinks fight would be the crowning moment of Tyson's career.

'That's the best he ever was,' Rooney said years later. 'He should have been better. The goal was to break Marciano's record of 49–0 and Mike was 37–0. Maybe we could have continued on. But first Cus died then Jimmy died and that's when everything got whacked out.'

Soon after the Spinks fight, Cayton settled the impending lawsuit by Givens and Roper by cutting his manager's fee from 33 per cent to 20 per cent and agreeing Tyson had final say in all matters concerning his boxing career. But the settlement hardly ended the power struggle.

Cayton was desperately trying to keep his title as Tyson's manager, while King was manoeuvring to be his exclusive promoter. Donald Trump was even in the mix, trying to ensure Tyson's upcoming bouts, including a potential bout with Evander Holyfield, would be fought in Atlantic City. The common priority they shared was to keep Tyson fighting in the ring and filling their pockets and purses with millions.

What they didn't envision was Tyson injuring himself fighting in a parking lot for free. While leaving Dapper Dan's, a clothing store in Harlem, on 23 August 1988, Tyson ran into his old nemesis Mitch 'Blood' Green. It was 4 a.m. The two exchanged words. A fight erupted. Green wound up with a busted lip and a swollen eye. Tyson suffered a hairline fracture in his hand, delaying a scheduled fight with British heavyweight champ Frank Bruno in Wembley.

It wasn't the last out-of-the-ring injury he would suffer. On 4 September, while visiting Camille Ewald at D'Amato's home in Catskill, Tyson made headlines again when he drove his BMW 750il into a tree. He was knocked unconscious and suffered injuries to his chest and head. Givens rushed to his side and made a scene as Tyson was transported to Columbia-Greene Medical Center in Hudson, New York. While he lay on a gurney, Givens stepped over him to shove away reporters. 'Give him a break,' she yelled.

Later that month, on Friday, 30 September, Tyson and Givens sat down with Barbara Walters to tape an interview for ABC's *20/20* programme in their New Jersey home. As a stoic Tyson sat by her side, Givens emasculated the heavyweight champion. 'He gets out of control, um, throwing, screaming . . .' Givens said.

'Does he hit you,' Walters asked Givens, as if Tyson wasn't there.

'He shakes, he pushes, he swings. Sometimes I think he's trying to scare me. There were times when I thought I could handle it. And just recently I've become afraid. I mean very, very much afraid.'

Givens called their marriage 'pure hell' and labelled Tyson a manic-depressive. In subsequent interviews she would accuse Tyson of choking her and throwing a telephone at her. Just over a week after the infamous *20/20* interview, Givens filed for divorce citing 'irreconcilable differences'.

Later it was revealed Tyson had been taking the medications Thorazine and Lithium prescribed by Dr Henry Curtis, a psychiatrist Givens and Roper had persuaded him to see. 'Robin was brilliant,' Lott said. 'She knew if she could put Mike on the Barbara Walters show and Mike believed he was manic-depressive and a wife beater when they broke up and she took all the money, who was going to side with Mike?'

It didn't quite work out that way. Givens tried to reach a financial settlement close to $10 million. But Tyson refused, believing she had spent an estimated $5 million during their eight-month marriage. Eventually, she agreed to a divorce without compensation.

'The one thing I remember about Robin Givens,' said *New York Times* Pulitzer-prize-winning columnist Dave Anderson, 'was I never saw her smile. Not once.'

At the most vulnerable point of his career, Tyson turned to King for help. Acting as a friend and confidant Tyson could trust, King helped Tyson seal his bank accounts from Givens and invited him to his home outside Cleveland. King also formed an alliance with Tyson's two friends from Albany, John Horne and Rory Holloway. They had little knowledge of the boxing business, but they had Tyson's trust, which was true of few others.

The longer Tyson stayed around King, the more he became distrustful of Rooney and Lott. Tyson was made aware of every negative comment Rooney made about King or Givens, while Lott's distrust of both had been well documented.

Rooney didn't deny talking about Givens, saying simply, 'Robin said Mike was hitting her in the face and in the body. I was saying if Mike Tyson was hitting Robin Givens in the face and the head, she'd be dead.'

Tyson found such remarks disloyal and fired Rooney. Lott was out soon after the Spinks fight. With Cayton minimised, Givens and Roper gone, and the last links to D'Amato removed, King was Tyson's only confidant.

D'Amato and Jacobs had always warned Tyson to be wary

of King. But Tyson was lost and needed a lifebuoy. King had worked as the promoter on most of his HBO fights. He had become a familiar face and a familiar voice. He had softened Tyson with cars and cash, and echoed Tyson's complaints against Cayton and Givens. He had Horne and Holloway in place to monitor Tyson almost hourly and bonded with Tyson as rich black men who came from the streets. It was enough to get Tyson to sign a four-year agreement naming King as his exclusive promoter.

Lott saw it as all part of a master plan. 'Don surrounded Mike with guys to keep Mike away from Bill and put Mike back into a street mentality,' Lott said. 'Mike was a bad kid from Brooklyn and it took Cus D'Amato six years to turn him around. The result was success from 1985 to 1988. But Don knew that if you surrounded him with enough jerks, he'd put him back into a street mentality. He knew that because he was from the streets.'

King insists getting Tyson to sign the agreement was not some sort of diabolical scheme. 'I never stole him,' King said. 'Not only that, Jacobs told me to help him out with [Tyson] and Bill Cayton went along. Jim did everything he could to encourage me to try to help them take him to the next level after they'd taken him as far as they could, and I did that.'

Concerning the negative press he received during that time, King said, 'They take the errors and the falsities and make truths out of them because they hear them so much and repeat them so much they become believable and they convince the masses. But I never took none of these guys from anybody. They come to me after they've been screwed or something happened to them.'

By the time Tyson met Bruno on 25 February 1989, at the Hilton Hotel in Las Vegas, his divorce from Givens was complete, and King had replaced Rooney and Lott with Aaron Snowell, a trainer of little note, and Jay Bright, a friend of Tyson who had lived in D'Amato's home in the Catskills.

Bruno was 27 years old with an impressive record of 32–2

with 31 knockouts. Though he hadn't fought in 16 months, he would be cheered on by about 5,000 British fans who had made to trip to Las Vegas to support the Englishman. A muscled 228 lb, Bruno showed no fear, glaring at Tyson during the pre-fight instructors. But it was false bravado. Seconds into the fight, Bruno was down after absorbing a Tyson right hand.

Bruno survived the round by holding Tyson around the neck with his left hand and hitting him with his right, a foul that eventually forced referee Richard Steele to deduct a point from the challenger.

Bruno didn't seem to mind the deduction. He was in survival mode. He used his size, his jab and his strength to keep Tyson from landing anything clean. But he began tiring in the fifth, and Tyson hurt him with a short left hook and battered him against the ropes with a series of hooks and uppercuts before Steele stepped in to stop the fight.

In his post-fight interview, Tyson boasted: 'How dare they challenge me with their primitive skills? They're just as good as dead.'

It was a comment that would have drawn a quick rebuke from Jacobs. But King loved that kind of talk. 'He was there to seek and destroy,' King said. 'That's the type of attitude he came to the ring with. There was no pretence. The opponent could see that was his attitude. He was there to destroy and show no mercy.'

Tyson bought into his invincible image and it became cemented when he stopped Carl 'The Truth' Williams in the first round on 21 July 1989, in Atlantic City. King had started calling Tyson 'The Baddest Man on the Planet,' which sounded nice to Tyson.

He certainly felt that way. It's why he had little regard for his next opponent: James 'Buster' Douglas.

7

ON AGAIN, OFF AGAIN

EVANDER HOLYFIELD HAD TARGETED MIKE Tyson since he became the youngest-ever heavyweight champion. It bordered on an obsession, but it was an obsession born mainly out of respect and an inner confidence that he could beat the so-called 'Baddest Man on the Planet'.

The respect came from their days at the Olympic training centre after the two lost their first bouts at the Olympic trials and trained together in the losers division. 'Tyson was the only person in the gym who out-worked me,' Holyfield said. 'Both of us were on the losing squad, trying to make the Olympic team. But I've never seen anybody work harder than Tyson. Not ever. I've never seen anybody who was an expert in all the things that he could do. To see him hit a speed bag, to see him hit hand pads, to see him hit the heavy bag or jump rope – everything he was doing was like a show.'

The admiration for Tyson's training skills, however, didn't create any doubts he could beat Tyson. The memory of their brief but volatile sparring session at the Olympic trials and their stare-down over the pool table had never left Holyfield. 'The Baddest Man in the Planet' didn't look so bad to him.

So Holyfield was ecstatic when an agreement was reached for Tyson to defend his heavyweight championship against him on 18 June 1990 in Atlantic City. Having knocked out all six of his opponents since moving up from cruiserweight to heavyweight, Holyfield had established himself as the no. 1 contender in the heavyweight division, making him the mandatory challenger in the WBA and the WBC.

Don King was reluctant to make the fight with Holyfield, mainly because he had no options on the fighter. Holding options on the opponent was a way for King to protect himself by guaranteeing the winner of the fight would remain under his promotional banner. If Holyfield won without King having options, all the hard work of gaining Tyson's allegiance would be at risk. Ultimately, however, the financial windfall from such a fight proved too tempting for King to resist.

Casino owner Donald Trump paid $12.5 million, the largest site fee in the history of boxing, to secure the much-anticipated bout. Tyson was to make at least $22 million while Holyfield was guaranteed $12 million. It would be called 'The Brawl For It All'.

'I've never seen him so pumped in my life,' Ronnie Shields said of Holyfield. 'Evander got up for every fight. But when he signed to fight Mike Tyson, he said, "This is the fight that's going to put me where I need to be."'

Tyson still had to get past Buster Douglas. But that seemed a foregone conclusion. While Tyson was preparing for Douglas, Holyfield began preparing for Tyson. George Benton sketched out a game plan to take advantage of Tyson's peek-a-boo style. He wanted Holyfield to work on throwing a hard, jarring uppercut. 'That's the punch that's going to kill him,' Benton told Shields.

Benton had a basic philosophy when it came to preparing a game plan. A fighter's best punch was his weakest defence. 'Mike's best punch is an uppercut, and that's the punch that he's going to get hit with,' Benton said.

Holyfield went to Tokyo to witness Tyson's fight with Douglas first hand even though he thought it wouldn't last very long. He had two reasons for making the trip. He had seen all of Tyson's fights in person, on television or on film. But he also knew Tyson had undergone changes to his management and training team, and wanted to see how he looked since all the turmoil had erupted in his life. Also, Holyfield was asked to be on hand to start the promotion of his chance at Tyson once Douglas was vanquished.

But Holyfield wasn't in Tokyo long before he got an uneasy feeling Tyson might be in trouble. 'This guy's got nothing to lose and everything to gain,' Holyfield said of Douglas. 'He's probably killing himself in the gym and Mike's out having a good time.'

Indeed, Tyson couldn't have hit Douglas any harder than the blows life was dealing him. James 'Buster' Douglas was the son of Billy 'Dynamite' Douglas, who had a modest career as a middleweight and then a light heavyweight in the 1970s. Buster Douglas had wanted to be a pro basketball player until he dropped out of Sinclair Community College in Dayton, Ohio. He focused on boxing and turned pro in 1981. By the time he was matched against Tyson, Douglas was 29–4–1 with 19 knockouts and ranked no. 2 by the IBF. But he wasn't a highly touted prospect.

Three of his defeats had come by knockout, including being stopped by Tony Tucker in the tenth round of their 1987 fight for the IBF heavyweight championship the same night Tyson defeated Pinklon Thomas. Douglas's chin was viewed as suspect, as was his will to fight through adversity. He was on the verge of beating Tucker when he suddenly quit fighting in the tenth round, forcing referee Mills Lane to stop the fight.

Tyson was to make a quick $6 million for the fight, while Douglas would earn $1.3 million, which was far and beyond anything he had made to that date. But money was the least of Douglas's concerns.

A few months before the fight, Douglas's wife Bertha left him after nearly three years of marriage. They had been together since 1982. That personal trauma would have been enough for any fighter to lose the will to battle. But that feeling of abandonment was compounded when his mother, Lula Pearl, died 23 days before the fight from a sudden stroke after battling severe hypertension. She was 47.

On top of it all, Douglas was suffering from a nasty cold. It was customary for HBO executives to visit the boxers the night before each bout to gather any last-minute notes or impressions. When they knocked on Douglas's door, the fighter looked like he'd already gone 12 rounds. 'It was the worst cold I'd ever seen a fighter have 24 hours before a fight,' said HBO's Ross Greenburg. 'We literally thought this was going to be another 90-second fight, which would have been a disaster.'

Few knew Tyson was ripe for an upset. His training leading up to the fight had been sporadic at best. During his fight with Tubbs in Tokyo, Tyson was still under the watchful eyes of Rooney and Cayton. Now he was his own boss, and not a very dedicated one. Rumours were rampant he was spending more time visiting nightclubs and chasing females. There were days when he skipped training altogether. Other days he wasn't fully committed or focused. During a sparring session less than three weeks before the fight, Greg Page, a former heavyweight champion, floored Tyson with a right hand.

'He certainly hadn't trained as he had in the Cus D'Amato–Rooney days,' Greenburg said. 'He had his buddies with him, who never really trained fighters. He probably trained himself.'

The 63,000-seat Tokyo Dome was barely half full for the fight, which started at 9 a.m. local time to appease American television. Tyson, 37–0 with 33 knockouts, came into the fight weighing 220½ lb, which was two pounds more than when he knocked out Spinks. From all outward signs, he was prepared to do battle. 'Tyson once again is in great shape,' Jim Lampley told the HBO viewing audience.

Douglas, 29, was 6 ft 4 in. and 231½ lb. His most significant advantage appeared to be his 83-inch reach. But Tyson had a history of knocking out taller fighters with a longer reach. He merely got inside their punches, wrecked their bodies with vicious hooks and blinded them with his devastating hand speed. Douglas bounced on his toes throughout his introduction by Jimmy Lennon Jr. He looked calm and focused. Tyson, meanwhile, stalked around the ring, pacing back and forth without emotion or expression. When they came together in the centre of the ring, Tyson tried to give Douglas the evil stare. But Douglas paid no attention.

He channelled his grief and feelings of isolation and ridicule into one of the most historic performances in sports history. Any notion Douglas was there simply for a pay cheque was dispelled early. He showed good movement from the opening bell. Wearing white trunks and white shoes with red and white tassels, Douglas worked behind his long left jab. When Tyson tried to dart in, Douglas either bounced back or tied up the champion. Midway through the first round, Douglas sent a message. As Tyson tried to pressure him on the ropes, Douglas fired two short, hard right hooks that stopped Tyson's aggression. Douglas followed with another right and a hard left. He was standing his ground and fighting back.

Producing the fight for HBO, Greenburg bellowed into Lampley's earpiece, 'Wow, I think we have a fight.'

It was clear Tyson was sluggish and not really bobbing and weaving. His defensive skills had always been underappreciated. But his head didn't move from side to side with the rhythm of earlier fights. He became a sitting duck.

By the end of the round, Douglas was consistently landing his left jab and right hand. He easily won the opening round. 'It's probably the best round I've ever seen him fight,' Merchant told the viewing audience.

Douglas was even better in the second round, landing a four-punch combination to Tyson's head. At the end of their first six minutes of action, Douglas had landed fifty-two punches to just sixteen for Tyson.

Working Tyson's corner again were Snowell and Bright, whose lack of preparation would factor mightily in the fight. They offered no real instruction. 'Close the gap, Mike, you're not inside enough,' Snowell said.

Tyson tried to be aggressive in the third round, but his lunging hooks missed their target as Douglas countered with a stream of jabs and combinations. By the end of the round,

Tyson was beginning to look frustrated, and his corner was concerned.

So was Holyfield, who was watching the fight from ringside. Wearing a dark suit with blue tie, his expression looked like someone seeing $12 million starting to disappear. A fighter knows when another fighter isn't ready, and Holyfield saw it that night in Tyson. 'Buster had nothing to lose,' Holyfield would say later. 'His wife left him and his mama died. There wasn't nothing else Tyson could do to hurt him.'

In the fifth round, a right cross behind a strong left jab caused Tyson's legs to buckle. The hard right hands from Douglas were beginning to inflict damage. Tyson's left eye began to swell.

His incompetent corner was not prepared for such a battle. They lacked the proper tools to deal with the swelling. It's common for corner men to use a chilled enswell or ice bag to treat swelling between rounds. But the only thing at Snowell's disposal was a latex glove filled with water and tied by a string. He pressed it on Tyson's battered eye after the fifth round. Some at ringside thought Snowell was using a condom.

'Mike Tyson is anything but the dynamic terror we're used to seeing,' Merchant said on air. 'Buster Douglas has neutralised him, frustrated him, beaten him to the punch.'

But just as Douglas appeared to be dominating Tyson and landing every punch he threw, Tyson countered with a vicious bone-jarring right uppercut that dropped Douglas with five seconds left in the eighth round.

As referee Octavio Meyran counted, Douglas leaned up on his right elbow. 'Seven . . . eight . . . nine,' Meyran yelled. Before he reached ten, Douglas got to his feet. Meyran didn't clean Douglas's gloves, didn't ask him if he was OK to continue. The referee, who had worked the 'No Mas' fight between Sugar Ray Leonard and Roberto Duran in 1980, simply called for action to resume and the bell instantly sounded to end the round.

When the ninth round began, Tyson tried for the finish. He

came out headhunting. But Douglas stood his ground. He fired a three-punch combination that stopped Tyson's assault. By the end of the ninth, Douglas was the aggressor, batting and bullying Tyson along the ropes.

Tyson opened the tenth by landing a hard right hand. Douglas immediately put Tyson in a clinch and walked him back into the corner. It was almost as if Tyson was surrendering. The end of his unbeaten record began with a hard right uppercut from Douglas that sent Tyson backward. Douglas followed with a right cross, a left hook, a right hand and a final left hook. Tyson flopped on his back, down on the canvas for the first time in his career.

As Meyran counted, a delirious Tyson rolled onto his knees and drunkenly searched for his mouthpiece, which had fallen out. He grabbed it with his right glove and put only the end of it in his mouth.

Just as Meyran reached the count of ten and was signalling the end of the fight, Tyson stood up and leaned into Meyran's arms. 'Mike Tyson has been knocked out,' Lampley screamed in disbelief.

As pandemonium filled the ring, lost in the moment was Meyran's long embrace of Tyson. Jacobs wasn't there to comfort him. Givens was gone, so were Rooney and Lott. King and Cayton had their own business interests. The only one there to comfort Tyson was the referee, the only one who really cared about him as a human being.

'I would be willing to say it's the greatest upset in boxing history,' Merchant said at the time. More than 20 years later his opinion hasn't changed.

'A pressure aggressive fighter like Tyson is always vulnerable,' Merchant said. 'But it takes someone with a lot of skill and poise to neutralise that explosive force, and nobody knew that it would be Buster Douglas. There were boxing people already offering blueprints on how to fight Mike Tyson. The question was who was going to be able to execute the blueprint? I think Douglas with his athletic background and his skill and other things going on his life turned out to be the right man at the right time.'

History generally views that fight as a fluke. Douglas had a career night against an over-confident and under-trained Tyson. That might be extreme.

'People have suggested Mike Tyson wasn't in shape, etc.,' Merchant added. 'Nobody suggested that before the fight. I don't think he was in bad shape. Did he overlook Douglas? Probably. Why wouldn't he? He was blowing everybody over. But all things said, Tyson fought a tough, hard fight in which he took an awful lot of punishment, and that beat him.'

Douglas was now the undisputed heavyweight champion, while Tyson was relegated to being one of several contenders. Holyfield left Japan bitterly disappointed. Not only did he lose $12 million and his chance to fight for the title, he'd lost his dream of being the first to defeat Tyson. After arriving back in the States, he told Ronnie Shields, 'That fight's going to come back to me. I don't know when. But when it does, I'm going to knock Mike out.'

Behind the scenes, King was trying to get Douglas's victory over Tyson overturned, saying Meyran had given a slow ten-count when Douglas was knocked down in the eighth. His pleas were ignored. 'It's not ten seconds. It's a ten-count,' respected referee Mills Lane would clarify.

What needed to be determined was the opponent for Douglas's first title defence. As the mandatory challenger, Holyfield was next in line. Looking to bring a big fight to his casino, Mirage owner Steve Wynn won a purse bid by offering Douglas more than $19 million to defend his title against Holyfield, who would make $8 million. The fight was set for 25 October 1990.

'I'm looking to fight Buster at his best,' Holyfield said during the press conference announcing the bout. 'If Buster's not at his best, then that's on Buster.'

Holyfield was going to make sure *he* was at his best. He prepared himself physically and mentally to win the undisputed heavyweight championship of the world. Benton, as was his role, devised the game plan for beating Douglas. 'You've got to land the right hand over his left jab,' Benton told Holyfield. 'You've got to get in there and you have to be quicker. If you stay on the outside, he's going to pick you apart. So we've got to move in and when he throws his left hand, you've got to be right over the top right away.'

Meanwhile, Douglas was hardly the motivated machine he had been against Tyson. In the eight months since his historic upset win, Douglas had enjoyed the spoils of being the heavyweight champion. He enjoyed the adulation and the celebrity. He also enjoyed the food.

The Mirage set Douglas up with a room where he could train for two weeks ahead of the fight. 'I rarely saw him in the gym,' said long-time casino executive Bob Halloran, who helped Wynn secure the fight. 'When he did spar, it was only for two rounds. He didn't train.'

The fight was billed as 'The Moment of Truth'. Perhaps that moment came when Douglas stepped on the scales to weigh in for the fight. He was 246 lb, 15 lb heavier than he was for Tyson and the heaviest he had weighed since 1985.

Holyfield was 24–0 with 20 knockouts, while Douglas was 30–4–1 with 20 knockouts. The pre-fight production was a bit quirky and amateurish, with Sugar Ray Leonard doing the ring introductions. Holyfield looked stoic and focused, while Douglas didn't look as confident and determined as he had when he fought Tyson. A fighter knows when he hasn't fully prepared himself for battle. Douglas must have known his time as champion was running out.

Holyfield had taunted Douglas during the promotion by calling him 'a quitter' due to his submission in his fight against Tucker. Somewhere deep inside him, Douglas must have been wondering if that were true.

He outweighed the 208-lb Holyfield by 38 lb. But it was of no advantage. 'When he moves, his body jellies,' ring announcer Ferdie Pacheco said. 'You can see the jelly in his body, particularly his breasts.'

111

Holyfield was the aggressor from the opening bell. His hand speed seemed to startle Douglas, who had enjoyed that advantage against Tyson. It was Holyfield who bounced in and out, ripping quick combinations to the ribs and head. He had Douglas backing up, struggling to find the range for his left jab.

'Keep him on the outside,' Benton told Holyfield after the first round. 'You don't have to go inside yet. I don't want that weight to be laying on you.'

Holyfield stayed on the outside in the second round, firing two and three jabs for every one delivered by the champion. Douglas tried to get aggressive in the third round, when he picked up his energy and intensity. He landed a solid right hand seconds into the round and moments later tried to land a swooping right uppercut. But Holyfield stepped back and unleashed a crisp right hand over the top that caught Douglas flush, dropping him to the canvas.

Unlike Tokyo, when he was floored by Tyson, Douglas made no attempt to get up. He flicked at his nose as if to make sure it was still attached. Then he lay prone on the canvas as referee Mills Lane counted him out. In less than nine minutes, Douglas had lost his title.

Lou Duva, Dan Duva and Shields rushed into the ring to pile on top of Holyfield. Tim Hallmark and Holyfield's Olympic teammates Meldrick Taylor and Pernell Whitaker followed close behind. As Douglas remained on the canvas getting treated by doctors, the Holyfield camp celebrated winning the undisputed heavyweight championship of the world.

'The happiest I've seen Evander was when they raised his hand as the heavyweight champion of the world,' Shields said. 'Everybody had told him he was too small. But he proved them wrong.'

Holyfield's dream of winning the heavyweight championship had come true, but not everyone was giving him credit for it. Not even after he defeated George Foreman by unanimous decision in his first title defence on 19 April 1991. Douglas was out of shape, the critics said. Foreman was a novelty act, a hamburger-eating 42 year old trying to recapture the heavyweight championship he lost to Muhammad Ali 17 years earlier. After beating Foreman by unanimous decision, Holyfield was criticised for not knocking out the old geezer.

Benton told Holyfield not to fret about the opinions of the people and the media. 'No matter what you do as a fighter, they're going to criticise you,' he told him. 'So don't take it to heart. Let it go. Just keep doing what you know how to do and that's fight. You're not going to ever satisfy everybody.'

Holyfield took his words to heart, but it didn't quench his desire to fight Tyson. He thought his chance had come when they signed an agreement to meet in Las Vegas on 8 November 1991 at Caesars Palace. Holyfield was to get $30 million, Tyson $15 million along with a hefty percentage of the pay-per-view revenue. The purses were to be the highest paid to a champion and a challenger. Industry sources estimated the fight could generate $100 million worth of income.

Tyson had re-established himself as a man to be feared by beating his former Olympic nemesis Henry Tillman and Alex Stewart by first-round knockouts and earning back-to-back wins over Donovan 'Razor' Ruddock. The loss to Douglas was now considered a fluke and largely dismissed as Tyson having an off night because he hadn't trained properly and was overconfident. Plus he was still the most marketable heavyweight in the division.

Holyfield went back into training to fight Tyson again, but again it proved to be wasted energy. The first indication the fight might not come to fruition came on 8 September 1991, when Tyson was indicted and charged with raping then 18-year-old Desiree Washington.

The indictment came after a grand jury looked into allegations that Tyson forced himself on Washington in July after she went to visit the former heavyweight champion about 1.30 a.m. at his hotel suite at the Canterbury Hotel in downtown Indianapolis. They had met while Washington was a contestant in the Black America beauty pageant being held during the Indiana Black

Expo. Washington didn't report the alleged assault until 26 hours later after consulting with her parents.

Despite the seriousness of the indictment, promoters still planned to go through with the Holyfield–Tyson fight. The indictment wasn't an indication of guilt. Plus there was $100 million at stake.

But the bout couldn't escape the dark clouds. On 19 October – Holyfield's birthday – Tyson's handlers announced he was pulling out of the fight after suffering what was described as a non-contact cartilage injury to his ribcage during training camp. Doctors estimated it would take six to eight weeks to heal. He would need additional time for training, meaning he wouldn't be ready to fight until the spring of 1992. Tyson's rape trial was set for February. The uncertainty over the outcome of the trial made it impossible to reschedule the richest bout in boxing history. Holyfield–Tyson was off again.

8

PRISON TO PAY-PER-VIEW

NO ONE KNOWS WHAT HAPPENED in Suite No. 606 at the Canterbury Hotel in Indianapolis just before 2.30 a.m. on 19 July 1991; no one except Mike Tyson and Desiree Lynn Washington.

Tyson had arrived in Indianapolis on 17 July for the Indiana Black Expo, an annual celebration of black culture that sounded like one big party to the former heavyweight champion. Don King had donated money toward the event, and Tyson was among a number of celebrities in attendance to generate publicity. Evander Holyfield was also in town.

The two boxers had ventured to the Midwest days after signing an agreement to fight for Holyfield's heavyweight championship on 8 November in Las Vegas. The start of training camp and a rib injury that would postpone the bout were still weeks away. With his divorce to Robin Givens behind him and a big payday ahead, Tyson was in good spirits.

After spending his first night in Indianapolis partying with singer Johnny Gill and other friends, Tyson woke up on 18 July and decided to lend his presence to one of the Black Expo functions. Rehearsals for the Miss Black America pageant were taking place in a ballroom at the Omni Severin Hotel in downtown Indianapolis. Tyson agreed to shoot a short rap video to promote the event. He was a kid in a candy store when he arrived as the beautiful young black girls were going through their dance steps.

Among the contestants was Miss Rhode Island, Desiree Lynn Washington. The 18 year old had just graduated from Coventry High School in Providence, where she was a cheerleader, played softball and had represented the United States during a summer tour of Russia. She was active in church and volunteered for various charities. During an interview during the pageant, she said she wanted to study politics and become the first woman and black president of the United States of America. In every respect, she was a model student with a bright future.

Courtroom testimony would reveal that during rehearsal for the promo, Tyson surveyed the group of young, attractive women and became fixated on Washington. 'You're a nice Christian girl, right?' he asked her. All of the contestants were excited to have the famous boxer in their midst, and Washington felt special to be singled out.

After giving Washington a hug, he asked her if she'd like to go out on a date later that evening. She said, 'Sure,' and gave Tyson her room number.

By the time Tyson called, it was 1.30 a.m. on 19 July. He was heading toward the Omni. By 1.50 a.m., Washington was in Tyson's limo. A few minutes later, they were walking through the lobby toward his hotel suite.

At 3.30 a.m. on 20 July, nearly 26 hours after entering the Canterbury Hotel with Tyson, Washington went to the emergency room at Methodist Hospital and reported she had been raped by Michael Gerard Tyson.

In his book, *Heavy Justice: The Trial of Mike Tyson*, special prosecutor J. Gregory Garrison offers Washington's account of what happened:

> I was really trying to get away, and the more I fought the more he became aggressive and violent. He said, 'I don't need a condom.' He says, 'We'll just have a baby.' That was one of the statements that he made. And I was just like, 'Please, I have a future ahead of me' – you know. 'I'm going to go to

college! I don't care who you are. I don't care if you're a celebrity. I just don't do this,' and I made that very, very clear to him, but it just seemed to go in one ear and out the other and he just, his words over and over again were, 'Don't fight me. Don't fight me.' And I was trying to squirm away and at that point he put his penis into my vagina and he started . . . I started crying and he said, 'Oh, you're crying, you're crying,' and he grabbed my legs and that's when he licked my vagina.

To this day, Tyson insists he didn't rape Washington and blames his conviction on what he says was 'horrible' representation by lawyer Vincent Fuller, whom he calls 'a tax attorney' hired by Don King. Fuller had represented King during a 1984 case where the promoter was found innocent of 23 counts of income-tax evasion. But he was also considered one of Indianapolis's top defence lawyers, having convinced a jury that John Hinckley Jr was insane when he shot President Ronald Reagan and three others in 1981.

It didn't help Tyson that date rape was part of the national consciousness when he was charged. William Kennedy Smith, the nephew of Senator Edward M. Kennedy, had been accused in the summer of 1991 of raping 29-year-old Patricia Bowman on a beach close to the Kennedys' vacation estate near Palm Beach, Florida. Smith would be acquitted of all charges.

Kennedy had been represented by Miami-based criminal defence attorney Roy Black. According to a source in the Tyson camp during the rape trial, Black called to offer his services. 'I can get him off,' Black said. 'There's no reason for him to spend any time in prison. I can win this case.'

The call was patched through to King, who stuck with Fuller as Tyson's attorney and launched a strategy toward generating sympathy for his client. A team of Tyson loyalists spent a month in Indianapolis talking to local townsfolk and churches, trying to rally support for Tyson. In one instance, King wanted to speak before a church congregation to cast Tyson as the true victim. But the pastor informed the promoter, 'Mr King, no one speaks from this pulpit but me.'

Noticing water stains on the roof, King suggested he make a donation to the church's building fund. 'Every church has a building fund,' said King, reaching into his pocket and pulling out a wad of bills. That Sunday, King was in the pulpit drumming up support for Tyson.

When the trial began, the defence insisted Washington was a willing participant in the sexual encounter. She had agreed to meet Tyson at 1.30 in the morning. Also, why would Tyson need to rape someone when women fawned all over him every time he stepped into the street?

'I didn't violate her in any way,' Tyson said when he took the witness stand in his own defence. 'She never told me to stop and she never said I was hurting her. She never said no, nothing.'

The defence also contended Washington cried rape after realising she was a one-night stand and Tyson didn't have the courtesy to escort her back to the limousine. The jurors didn't believe Tyson. They believed Washington.

On 10 February 1992, after thirteen days of testimony and ten hours of deliberation, an Indianapolis jury of eight men and four women found Tyson guilty of one count of rape and two counts of criminal deviate conduct.

Tyson faced six to twenty years in prison on each count. But on 25 March, Judge Patricia J. Gifford sentenced him to ten years in prison, suspending the last four years. Mike Tyson, now known as inmate No. 922335, would spend the next three years at the Indiana Youth Center before being freed with time off for good behaviour.

More than 20 years later, King remains stunned by the verdict. 'I was praying against him being found guilty,' he said. 'He was not guilty. He was naive to the fact that hell hath no fury like a woman scorned.

'Secondly, he goes to Indiana, which is a Klan state where to them we're heathens and savages. Ray Charles could see the wrong in this. But that's not what it was about. It's about being three-fifths. They don't want to give us no heroes.'

Tyson offers a similar view of why he was convicted. 'This is what it came down to,' he said. 'If you're black and you're big and you're strong, you're a rapist. If you're Jewish, you're a tax cheat. If you're Italian and you have a nice suit, you're a mobster. Those are the stereotypes that are put into our society.'

Tyson felt his sentence in a strange way was a source of vindication. 'What black man do you know that is convicted of rape in Indiana and only did three years?' he says.

Two years into his sentence, Tyson says Indiana judicial officials came to him with a compromise for his release. If he would apologise to Washington, he would be granted a release. Tyson declined the offer. 'They were trying to get me to confess,' he said. 'I couldn't confess to that shit if I didn't do it. I would have been a bigger prisoner in my mind than I ever could have been in my body. I'm not the typical black man you can do that to. Me and Cus D'Amato, we'd die for what we believe in. I'm strong enough. No one is going to make me be that kind of nigger. I'm never going to admit to that. You can kill me. You can do whatever you want to do. I didn't do that shit and that's just what it is.'

With Tyson incarcerated, Holyfield had to continue his reign as heavyweight champion against other opposition. It began once Tyson was injured in training for their scheduled fight in November 1991. Instead of Tyson, Holyfield met Bert Cooper at the Omni in his hometown of Atlanta.

Cooper was a product of Joe Frazier's gym in Philadelphia and nicknamed himself 'Smokin'. He fought in a similar style to the legendary champion. He was a puncher, compiling a record of 26–7 with 24 knockouts.

Fighting in front of his hometown crowd, Holyfield looked strong, dropping the challenger early in the first round with a left hook to the body. But the gritty Cooper stayed in the fight. He caught Holyfield with a hard right hand in the third round. The punch and follow-up combinations hurt Holyfield, causing him to stagger drunkenly face-first into the ropes. He lost his senses and his balance to the point where referee Mills Lane ruled it a knockdown.

Holyfield's title and undefeated record looked in jeopardy as Cooper closed in, landing a series of hooks to the head. Holyfield first tried to cover up. Then he tried to tie up Cooper. But his best defence began with a hard right uppercut that rocked Cooper's head backward.

The third round would end with Holyfield on the offensive. It set up a back-and-forth battle that didn't end until the seventh round, when Mills stopped the fight as Holyfield unleashed 24 unanswered punches.

In June 1992, Holyfield met Larry Holmes, the former long-time champion. After being stopped in four rounds by Tyson in 1988, Holmes had taken three years off before returning to the ring in 1991, when he had five fights, all wins against mediocre competition. A 12-round decision over the previously unbeaten Ray Mercer in February 1992 earned Holmes (54–3 with 37 KOs) another chance at the heavyweight championship he had owned for seven and a half years and successfully defended twenty times. Yet HBO's Larry Merchant wondered before the fight if Holmes, a 5–1 underdog, could 'make a fight of it'.

Using his experience and ability to spot openings in Holyfield's defence, Holmes made it an exciting fight. He conserved energy by staying on the ropes and using quick flurries to keep the champion cautious. Holyfield was forced to fight inside more than he would have liked but still landed the harder punches. In the sixth round, Holmes got some momentum when he hit Holyfield with an inadvertent elbow. It opened a nasty cut along Holyfield's right eye. But Holyfield stayed in control and earned a unanimous decision.

Critics weren't impressed. It was as if Holyfield was always fighting against two opponents. The one in the ring and the one incarcerated at the Indiana Youth Center. After all, Tyson had dropped Holmes in four rounds. Holyfield had to go the distance.

'When Tyson went to jail, they made it like it was my fault,' Holyfield said. 'They said, "You can't beat Tyson." My response was, "OK. Whatever."'

Ironically, it was in defeat that Holyfield gained true respect as a heavyweight. Riddick Bowe was 31–0 with 27 knockouts when he challenged Holyfield for the title on 13 November 1992, at the Thomas and Mack Center where the University of Nevada at Las Vegas Runnin' Rebels play basketball. Bowe was a product of the same Brownsville section of Brooklyn as Tyson.

At 6 ft 5 in., he was a mountain of man who lived up to his nickname 'Big Daddy'. He distinguished his amateur career by winning the silver medal at the 1988 Olympics in Seoul, Korea, losing gold to Lennox Lewis, who represented Canada. As a pro, he was a powerful force blessed with a good jab and hand speed.

Despite those credentials, Holyfield didn't think much of Bowe. They had sparred when Bowe was still an amateur and Holyfield was getting ready for one of his pro fights. Bowe never provided much competition. 'All I've got to do is hit him one time and put pressure on him, and he's going to quit,' Holyfield told Ronnie Shields while watching film of Bowe.

George Benton tried to change Holyfield's thinking. He knew Bowe was being trained by the great Eddie Futch and anticipated Bowe would be in top condition. This wasn't a sparring session. The heavyweight title was at stake. 'This is not the guy you sparred with,' Benton insisted. But Holyfield wasn't totally focused.

Eight months before facing Bowe, Holyfield's older brother Willie was shot and killed by his fiancée's brother. Holyfield was close to his brother, and the tragedy kept him from putting all his energy toward preparing for Bowe.

'Evander trained hard, but you could see the over-confidence in him while he was training,' Shields said. 'It's the first time I'd seen that.'

Holyfield also underestimated the impact Mackie Shilstone, a New Orleans health and fitness expert, would have on Bowe's conditioning. Bowe's work ethic was always a source of contention in his camps. 'Bowe never minded fighting in the ring or sparring,' his manager Rock Newman said. 'He just didn't want to do the other stuff.' But Shilstone, much like Tim Hallmark, used scientific and even torturous training methods to get Bowe into peak condition. He would weigh in at 235 lb, 10 lb less than his previous fight four months earlier.

Newman also played a part in rattling the Holyfield camp by asking the Nevada Athletic Commission to have more 'comprehensive' drug testing for the fight. It was a not-so-subtle allegation Holyfield was using steroids to bulk up from cruiserweight to heavyweight.

Top Rank promoter Bob Arum had raised the 's' word leading into Holyfield's fight with Foreman. At that time, Nevada tested for drugs and other foreign substances. But it didn't start testing for steroids until 2002.

Newman's suggestion angered Main Events' boss Dan Duva, who had grown tired of accusations Holyfield was using steroids. 'It gets to the point where it keeps getting written, and kids read it and they say if Evander Holyfield can succeed and get that way using steroids, maybe I should do it, too,' Duva said.

Hallmark vehemently denies ever being associated with steroids and says he has dismissed trainers and clients because he didn't want to be deemed guilty by association. He recalled the first time he and Holyfield discussed steroids.

'I can remember way back Evander calling me and saying, "I got people that want me to get on steroids." I told him, "If you do steroids, I'll never work with you again,"' Hallmark said.

He says Holyfield's response was: '"I wouldn't do steroids,

Hallmark. That's cheatin'. Man, whatever I end up doing in this sport I want to know I did it myself through God's blessing and not through something like that.'"

Holyfield never failed a steroid test during his career and has always denied using performance-enhancing drugs even after his name was linked to a 2007 investigation of an Orlando pharmacy that fraudulently prescribed steroids and HGH. In a statement issued by Main Events, Holyfield said:

> I do not use steroids. I have never used steroids. I resent that my name has been linked to known steroid users by sources who refuse to be identified in order to generate publicity for their investigation. I'm disappointed that certain members of the media fell for this ploy and chose to use my name in headlines and publish my photo alongside stories . . . about an investigation into a practice that has nothing to do with me or what I stand for.

Holyfield went into the first fight with Bowe looking to impress the critics who saw him go the distance with Foreman, hurt badly against Cooper, and fail to stop Holmes. He wanted to knock out Bowe. Instead, it turned into a classic.

The tenth round was one of the most action-packed in modern boxing history. Bowe hurt Holyfield early with a big right uppercut delivered with the force of all his size and weight. A wobbly Holyfield kept his gloves around his ears as Bowe launched a full-out attack, trying to finish the champion. He threw lumbering lefts and rights, but Holyfield wouldn't fall, forcing Bowe to punch himself to the point of exhaustion.

It's during these types of fights that a boxer's inner soul is tested. Courage, pain and resilience all combine to determine the full essence of a man. Reaching deep into his inner will, Holyfield got his second wind and began to build the reputation that would personify his career. He became a warrior, mounting an offensive attack of his own after backing

Bowe up with an uppercut. As the final seconds of the tenth round ticked off, the two fighters traded leather in the centre of the ring, almost grateful when the bell sounded. As they staggered back to their respective corners, they tapped each other in the stomach in a sign of mutual respect. The sold-out crowd at the Thomas and Mack Center roared its approval.

Bowe would win a unanimous decision to capture the heavyweight championship and hand Holyfield the first loss of his professional career. It was just the beginning of a trilogy that would captivate boxing while Tyson languished in prison.

The loss prompted Holyfield to make several changes to his team. Consistency and stability had marked his climb to the heavyweight championship. With Main Events serving as his promoters and Lou Duva, George Benton and Ronnie Shields handling his boxing training and Hallmark coordinating his conditioning, they'd proven to be an unbeatable team until facing Bowe. But Holyfield was ready for a shake-up.

He retained Hallmark, but Benton, Duva and Shields were replaced by Emanuel Steward. The changes were made in part because Holyfield wanted more independence over his career. He also knew paying one trainer was cheaper than having three.

'He wants to be a one-man show,' Lou Duva said at the time. 'I think he's making a big mistake. It reminds me of the saying, "A lawyer who represents himself takes on a fool for a client."'

The first loss to Bowe began a stretch where Holyfield was 3–3 over a period of six fights. Steward was in his corner for two wins, a twelve-round decision in a rematch with Alex Stewart and a twelve-round decision in a rematch with Bowe to recapture the undisputed heavyweight championship for a second time.

That was the infamous 'Fan Man' fight, where the action was interrupted in the seventh round when stuntman James Miller crashed his powered paraglider into the ring at Caesars Palace.

Miller landed on the top rope while his parachute was still tangled in the lights. He was pummelled to the point of unconsciousness by fans and security guards before being arrested. 'It was a heavyweight fight,' Miller said at the time, 'but I was the only guy who got knocked out.'

Forever known as the 'Fan Man,' Miller was reported missing in 22 September 2002 in the remote woods of Alaska. His decomposed body wasn't discovered until March of 2003.

After Miller crashed into the ring, it took more than 20 minutes to get the fight resumed. Holyfield was able to pull out the victory over Bowe, who had elected not to work with Shilstone and came into the ring weighing 11 lb more than he did for his first fight with Holyfield.

Having regained his title, Holyfield switched trainers again after splitting with Steward over how much the trainer should be paid for his next fight against Michael Moorer. Steward wanted $300,000. Holyfield had a lower figure in mind.

Don Turner, who had worked the corner for Holmes when he fought Holyfield, agreed to become the champion's new trainer. Turner later brought in Tommy Brooks to work the hand mitts.

'It's like found money whatever he gives me,' Turner said of his arrangement with Holyfield. 'Once they know how to fight, they can get anybody to train them. If they're a champion, they've made it on their own. The fighter enhances the trainer. I learned that long ago. It's the trainer that reminds him of what he's capable of doing in case something slips. It's just like a third-base coach. He watches the other guy and suggests what would work for his guy.'

The partnership got off to a shaky start when Holyfield tried to fight Moorer through a bad case of the flu. He also separated his shoulder during the bout and eventually lost a 12-round decision.

Media and fans began calling for Holyfield to retire. He was nearly 32 years old, had earned more than $100 million in the ring and twice won the heavyweight title. In addition to injuring his shoulder against Moorer, doctors diagnosed him with a degenerative heart condition. The condition was described by Ronald Stephens, Holyfield's physician, as a 'non-compliant left ventricle' that didn't expand and fill with blood as easily as it should have. Though he could live a normal life, he would fatigue too easily to continue his boxing career.

Holyfield (30–2 with 22 KOs) initially did retire. But he returned to the ring on 20 May 1995 to fight Ray Mercer in Atlantic City. Holyfield was confident his heart issue had either been misdiagnosed or healed during a faith-healing crusade by Benny Hinn.

Hallmark now says Holyfield never had a heart defect. He believes Holyfield was misdiagnosed the night of the Moorer fight when he went to Valley Hospital in Las Vegas to have his shoulder treated. Doctors also treated Holyfield for dehydration with a massive infusion of fluids, and Hallmark believes the heart condition resulted from a fluid build-up in his lungs.

'I walked into his room that night in the hospital and pulled the shirt off him and I thought to myself, "He looks huge,"' Hallmark said. 'Then we found out they put way too many fluids in him. His arms were enormous and his face was full. It was like he had put on 20 lb of thickness through his whole body.

'If you're way over-hydrated, it will throw off the whole cardiovascular test, including the EKG, because your whole body is an electrical system and the water has a lot to do with it. So I've always believed what they got was the result of too much water in his body and there was nothing wrong with his heart.'

Divine intervention can't be ruled out. 'If there was something wrong with his heart, I have no problem with believing that God healed him because God wanted him to continue down that road,' Hallmark said. 'Either way, I always felt like the reason why the EKG was so crazy was because he was way over-hydrated.'

Holyfield won a ten-round decision over Mercer and got another fight with Bowe in a non-title bout on 4 November 1995 at Caesars Palace. He would later reveal he was battling hepatitis at the time and had little energy. Bowe, back working with Shilstone, would score an eighth-round TKO. Amid renewed calls for his retirement, Holyfield met former middleweight champ Bobby Czyz at Madison Square Garden on 10 May 1996. Holyfield earned a fifth-round TKO but wasn't impressive in the fight.

Most thought Holyfield was past his prime. He looked like an ageing fighter on the downside of his career. He had been beaten by Moorer, battled a heart condition, suffered his first knockout loss to Bowe and was unimpressive against Czyz. Among those convinced Holyfield was washed up was Don King, who just happened to be looking for an opponent for Mike Tyson.

Tyson's release date from the Indiana Youth Center was set for 6 a.m. on Saturday, 25 March 1995. Initially, Tyson wanted to be a tough guy in prison. He clashed with prison guards, was quick-tempered with inmates and ready for conflict. But today Tyson says his prison term was a blessing in disguise. As one person close to Tyson during those days said, 'He probably would have gotten killed. He was out of control. He wasn't listening to anybody. Eventually, he was going to come across the wrong person and probably wind up dead.' Prison put a halt to Tyson's road of self-destruction.

'I was living really crazy and reckless,' Tyson said. 'I'm just glad I don't have any AIDS or got sick or got killed by somebody for sleeping with people's girlfriends or wives or sisters. I was living a crazy life before I went to prison. Everything happens for a reason. There's no way I would have lasted three years the way I was living. There's no way I would have lasted three years.'

In prison, he studied history, learned a bit of the Chinese language and read poems of Maya Angelou. He had frequent visitors. They included Spike Lee, Tupac Shakur, Whitney Houston, LL Cool J, the Rev. Al Sharpton, John Kennedy Jr and O.J. Simpson. He also became a Muslim and studied the Koran and attended classes. Though baptised by Jesse Jackson in 1988, Tyson became influenced by Muhammad Siddeeq, a 57-year-old Indianapolis high-school maths and science teacher who had spent the previous 30 years working with inmates.

Tyson was also contacted by a string of promoters looking to represent him when he was released from prison. His conviction had done little to diminish his marketability inside the ring. It may have even enhanced it. With Holyfield winning and losing, then winning and losing the heavyweight championship, the division lacked the kind of dominating champion Tyson had been in his prime.

Bob Arum wanted to match Tyson with George Foreman; Rock Newman was dreaming of a fight between Tyson and Bowe at Madison Square Garden; while Dan Duva was ready to re-visit a fight between Holyfield and Tyson. Butch Lewis, another promoter Murad Muhammad, and Shelly Finkel, who worked with Duva, also made overtures to Tyson.

But they were no match for King. He used his own four-year prison term for manslaughter during his days as a numbers runner in Cleveland to create a closer bond with Tyson. While everyone was waiting for Tyson's release, King already was moving to solidify his hold.

A court complaint filed in US District Court in 1998 when Tyson moved to sue King and Don King Productions for $100 million outlines how the promoter regained control of Tyson's career.

On 28 June 1994, or nine months before Tyson's release, King visited Tyson in prison and presented him with a seven-page contract to be his exclusive promoter. The term was for four years, with Don King Productions agreeing to promote three bouts per year. The agreement stated: 'Tyson hereby grants to DKP the sole and exclusive right to secure, arrange

Mike Tyson and Cus D'Amato in 1983. (Las Vegas Boxing Hall of Fame)

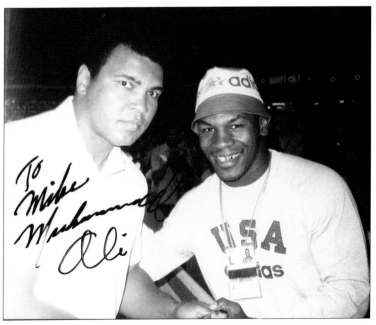

Former heavyweight champion Muhammad Ali with Mike Tyson in 1984.
(Las Vegas Boxing Hall of Fame).

Jim Jacobs, Mike Tyson and Bill Cayton pose in 1985.
(Las Vegas Boxing Hall of Fame)

Referee Mills Lane gives Mike Tyson instructions for his title bout against WBC champion Trevor Berbick in 1986 in Las Vegas. Tyson would win the fight to become the youngest heavyweight champion ever.
(Las Vegas Boxing Hall of Fame)

Boxing referee Mills Lane was called in the week of the Bite Fight to replace his good friend Mitch Halpern.
(Mills Lane Family)

Referee Mills Lane inspects the bitten ear of Evander Holyfield
(© Press Association)

An angry Mike Tyson lashes out after being disqualified for biting Evander Holyfield. (© Press Association)

An enraged Mike Tyson screams at a reporter following a rumble at a press conference for a proposed fight with Lennox Lewis. (Peter Pharaoh)

Evander Holyfield prepares for a workout before a fight with
James Toney in 2003. (Photo by Tom Casino)

Evander Holyfield prepares for a training session before his fight with James Toney. (Credit Tom Casino/Showtime)

Evander Holyfield listens to questions during a press conference before his fight with James Toney. (Tom Casino/Showtime)

Don King and Mike Tyson reunite in October 2009. Tyson worked as an announcer on one of King's fight promotions. (Don King Productions)

Mike Tyson spars playfully with pop star Michael Jackson. (Peter Pharaoh)

Mike Tyson playfully acts if he's biting the ear of Showtime announcer Jim Gray during a reunion at Barclays Center in October 2012. (Mario Costa)

Mike and Kiki Tyson. (Mario Costa)

and promote all Bouts requiring Tyson's services as a professional boxer during the term hereof.'

The agreement also stated that if Tyson won the WBC, WBA, IBF or WBO title, the agreement would be automatically extended to cover the period he held the world championship and two years following the loss of the title. Tyson signed the agreement without legal or other independent counsel.

Two months later, Tyson signed another agreement, making his two Albany friends John Horne and Rory Holloway his co-managers. 'We have been working together since 1987, John Horne as my camp coordinator and Rory Holloway as my assistant,' Tyson said in a press release issued while he was in prison. 'I am very proud of the growth and knowledge that they have shown me concerning the boxing game. I have absolutely no doubt that they will do a very admirable job on my behalf. They are also my two longest and most trusted friends who have been completely loyal to me. This starts a new chapter in my career.'

Armed with his signed exclusive promotional agreement, King set out to negotiate Tyson's financial future. King's two major objectives were signing exclusive agreements with a premium cable network (HBO or Showtime) and a casino to stage his fights. This would have been normal procedure for any promoter, but King was shrewd enough to take full advantage of his opportunity.

HBO with its deep pockets and past association with Tyson appeared to be the frontrunner. It offered King a multi-fight deal worth an estimated $80 million. Before accepting the deal, Team Tyson had a stipulation. It wanted to bar Larry Merchant from announcing any of Tyson's fights. Merchant had joined HBO in 1978 after newspaper jobs at the *Philadelphia Daily News* and the *New York Post*. He was known for his frank commentary and combative interview style.

He had been critical of attempts by King and Tyson to have Douglas's knockout win over Tyson overturned because of a long count when Douglas was knocked down in the eighth round in Tokyo. Testifying at an arbitration hearing, Merchant described it as 'guys trying to win something outside the ring that they didn't win inside the ring'.

HBO refused to adhere to the request. Whether it was an ultimate deal breaker is a matter of contention. 'I don't think it was King,' Merchant now says. 'I think it was the guys around Tyson and him trying to show that he still had control. They didn't want me to do his fights, and HBO said to him, "We're giving you an awful lot of money; you can't tell us how to do the fights." He was bringing subscriptions to HBO, and it was a very unusual thing that HBO decided to stand by an announcer over a franchise.'

According to Tyson's future lawsuit against King, five days before his release from prison King presented Tyson with a three-year agreement to fight exclusively for HBO's rival Showtime. It was just the start of a windfall that would make Tyson and King very rich men the moment Tyson walked out of prison.

On 25 March 1995, after 1,095 days of confinement, Tyson walked out of the Indiana Youth Center a free man. King, Horne, Holloway and Monica Turner, a woman he met while in prison and would eventually marry, were among those there to greet him.

Tyson wore a white skullcap and dark clothes as he slipped into a limo. He was driven a few miles to a small mosque run by Siddeeq, where he prayed alongside Muhammad Ali. From there, they boarded a Learjet to fly from Indianapolis to Ohio, where they would travel to Tyson's home on Route 534 South in Southington, Ohio.

Awaiting his arrival were several executives from Showtime, including attorney Ken Hershman and chief executive officer Matt Blank. 'He was very anxious to get rid of the team and be by himself,' Hershman said. 'After all the time of being in prison, I didn't blame him.'

Showtime had a bonus cheque of $30 million prepared for Tyson when he signed the agreement. After earning nearly

$65 million in his career, Tyson's fortune was virtually gone. Extravagant expenditures on cars, homes and clothes along with the cost of legal fees for his rape trial and lawsuits with Bill Cayton had drained his finances along with the money spent by Robin Givens during their brief marriage. Yet only one day out of prison and Tyson was about to become a very rich man again. 'Very few athletes who could pull that off, but Mike was one of them,' said Hershman.

Blank had assumed his post as president and CEO of Showtime, Viacom's premium movie and cable TV business, in February 1995. Getting the board of directors at Viacom to OK a $30 million advance to a convicted rapist coming out of prison was no slam dunk. 'We didn't know what type of fighter he'd be at that point,' Blank said. 'We didn't know if boxing fans or the broader fan base would embrace him. We had a lot of money on the line.'

Showtime was desperate to sign Tyson in order to put itself on par with HBO, which had dominated the boxing landscape since ABC and CBS began de-emphasising the sport in the late 1980s. Getting Tyson would give the network instant credibility and bolster its fledgling pay-per-view business.

What Tyson didn't know was that King had struck a separate contract with Showtime dated 17 March 1995. It called for the premium network to broadcast a series of King-promoted bouts that didn't feature Tyson, but was contingent on Tyson signing the Showtime agreement. Those fights from which King benefited financially and Tyson didn't featured King fighters such as Julio César Chávez, William Joppy, Keith Holmes and Felix Trinidad. 'We had the normal battles about maintaining the quality of the fights and keeping it at the level we wanted,' Hershman said. 'But that's a process you go through with anybody.'

King also used his role as Tyson's exclusive promoter and de facto manager to leverage a six-fight deal with the MGM Grand. Las Vegas hotels and casinos coveted big fights to attract high- rollers and gamblers at their casinos. By signing

Tyson to an exclusive deal, the MGM Grand would keep him away from the Mirage, Caesars Palace or Atlantic City.

According to legal documents, the deal also called for the MGM Grand to be the site for 11 non-Tyson fights selected by King. The contract called for King, not Tyson, to receive a $15 million advance with $10 million paid upon Tyson's release from prison. It also allowed for Don King Productions to purchase 618,557 shares of MGM Grand stock, which was guaranteed to be worth at least $30 million. King could pay for the stock out of gate receipts from his fights held at the MGM Grand.

The agreements, much like just about every other contract Tyson signed once he became the heavyweight champion, became points for litigation in future years. But at the time, Tyson was happy being a millionaire again and out of jail, and Showtime was happy to seal a deal with the former heavyweight champion.

'I'm not sure up until that point whether Showtime had made such an important announcement about its programming,' Blank said. 'They'd certainly done things in the past that were interesting. But Tyson, in spite of all his problems, was a hotly contested piece of talent. It was a big deal for us to get that talent.'

King makes no apologies for the deals he put together upon Tyson's release from prison. 'I had $77 million for him walking out of the door based upon my capability and ability to make deals,' King said in 2012. 'I had deals that were just phenomenal. They don't teach that in Yale, Harvard, Princeton and Oxford. I had the site deal, I had the TV deal and I had a stock deal. I put them all together [in] tandem and it was one of the most phenomenal deals in history; a fighter walking out of prison and walking into a $77 million deal. It was fantastic. I'm very humbled by that.'

Tyson made his long-awaited return to the ring on 19 August 1995 against Peter McNeeley at the MGM Grand. Johnny Gill, who had partied with Tyson in Indianapolis the weekend of the alleged rape, sang a long drawn-out version of the national anthem while a long list of celebrities and politicians looked on.

Tyson, now 29, hadn't fought in more than four years. His weight, 220 lb, was only four pounds heavier than his previous fight. 'Hurricane' Peter McNeeley, 36–1 with 30 knockouts, had talked a good game. A product of Medfield, Massachusetts, he had come from a boxing family. His father Tom had fought for and lost a shot at the heavyweight title when he was beaten by Floyd Patterson in 1961.

If Tyson had any ring rust, there wasn't enough time for it to show. He decked a charging McNeeley with a right hook seconds into the bout. With 1:50 left in the round, McNeeley was down again from a right uppercut from Tyson. McNeeley got up ready to fight, but as referee Mills Lane was giving him an eight-count, his corner stepped into the ring. The first fight under the new Showtime and MGM contracts ended with the crowd chanting, 'Bullshit . . . Bullshit.'

Tyson needed three rounds to defeat Buster Mathis Jr on 16 December at the Spectrum in Philadelphia. The fight fulfilled another side contract King had orchestrated with the Fox television network. But Tyson was back in the MGM on 16 March 1996, when he regained the WBC heavyweight title by stopping Frank Bruno in three rounds. Nearly six months later, his first-round destruction of Bruce Seldon on 7 September 1996, regained for him the status as the 'Baddest Man on the Planet'.

Tyson looked invincible again, which why King was confident enough to match him against the seemingly washed-up Holyfield.

Despite Holyfield's problems in the Moorer fight, Turner was confident his fighter could beat Tyson. Turner was raised in the projects in Cincinnati and had learned boxing from legends like Al Smith, Sid Bell, Jimmy Brown and Charley

Goldman. He had prepped Sugar Ray Robinson for his two fights against Paul Pender at the Boston Garden in 1960.

'Ray Robinson told me that you steal from everybody,' Turner, now in his mid-70s, said. 'Robinson used to get his workout, shower and then watch everybody train. I asked him, "Why do you watch everybody train? You're the greatest fighter that ever lived." He said, "I might pick up something. You can always learn."'

It was Turner's work with Larry Holmes that impressed Holyfield enough to give him an interview when he was looking for a trainer to replace Steward. Turner had gotten Holmes through his fight with Mercer despite Holmes suffering a detached retina. He'd also prepared Holmes well enough to go 12 gruelling rounds with Holyfield.

During their interview arranged by Shelly Finkel, Turner told Holyfield, 'You only know about one kind of distance. There's two kinds of distances: when you step inside the guy's range and when you step outside the guy's range. If you're a good fighter, you should step inside the guy's range. That means he has to readjust and you're the boss.'

Holyfield was impressed. 'Nobody has ever told me that in the years I've been fighting,' he said.

Distance would play a key factor in the first meeting between Tyson and Holyfield. Holyfield sparred 56 rounds in preparation for the mega-fight on 9 November 1996. The intention was to meet force with force. 'I knew Evander was going to beat him up,' Turner said. 'I know bullies. I was raised in the projects. I grew up around bullies. I knew Tyson was a bully. Stand your ground and he'll give.'

Few anticipated that Holyfield still had the talent, drive and power to author the performance he gave in the first fight with Tyson, not after the beatings he had taken against Bowe, the loss to Moorer and the lacklustre performance against Czyz.

'There was a legitimate view that he was no longer the dynamic fighter he had been,' Merchant said of Holyfield.

'First of all he was a small heavyweight coming into an era of big heavyweights. Then there was the issue of when he lost to Moorer and the question about his health. It seemed he was no longer the fighter he had been.'

The Nevada Athletic Commission was concerned enough about Holyfield's health to question whether it should license him for the fight. To alleviate those concerns, Holyfield submitted to an extensive examination at the Mayo Clinic, where he was given a clean bill of health. To get in peak fighting condition, Holyfield trained for 16 weeks, with Hallmark putting him through a gruelling programme that increased his cardiovascular capacity and stretched his threshold for pain.

'One of the workouts I put him through for the Mike Tyson fight was the hardest physical thing he's ever done in or out of the ring,' Hallmark said. 'Because he had the determination and focus and desire to be the best, he went through it. It would have been easy to say, "I don't need all this. I'll go back to running four or five miles in the afternoon and be done for the day." But he didn't do that.'

Holyfield did six weeks of conditioning in Houston with Hallmark before ever putting on boxing gloves. They did high-intensity weight workouts, sixteen sets to failure with a one-minute rest between. 'It was the kind of thing where you didn't know if you were going to quit halfway through it or puke everywhere,' Hallmark said.

His superior condition, his unshakeable confidence and his fierce determination to stand his ground eventually wore down Tyson in their long-awaited showdown. His 11th-round TKO was almost as stunning as Buster Douglas's upset of Tyson.

The Tyson camp, including King, had to acknowledge Holyfield's emphatic victory. He was the new heavyweight champion for a third time. 'This is a tremendous demonstration of what will and courage can do,' King told reporters after the fight. 'Holyfield rose to the occasion just as he said he would do. He did a great job. It was a great fight. The people certainly got their money's worth and then some.'

King certainly had money on his mind. He knew a rematch between Mike Tyson and Evander Holyfield would easily be the richest fight in boxing history.

9

MAN IN THE MIDDLE

MILLS LANE HAD JUST FINISHED a three-mile run across the back roads outside of Reno, Nevada, an exercise he undertook at least four times a week. It was something he dreaded when the alarm rang at 5 a.m. But it was part of his regimen, and Mills Lane was all about regimen.

After his run, he would put on boxing gloves and begin punching on a light or heavy bag, rehearsing the jabs, hooks and footwork that he learned decades ago. At age 60, Mills Bee Lane still prided himself on staying close to the 146 lb he fought at during his youth.

Most remember Lane as a referee. But he began as a boxer. He picked up the sport in the Marine Corps, where he won the All-Far East welterweight title before moving on to the University of Nevada-Reno where he won an NCAA Championship in 1960. A disciplined fighter always kept himself close to his fighting weight, and Mills Lane was all about discipline.

Boxing was always in Lane's blood. Unlike many of his contemporaries, who used the sport to escape impoverished conditions, Lane simply loved the sport even though he grew up in a world of privilege in the Deep South.

He was the grandson of his namesake Mills Bee Lane who founded Citizens & Southern Bank in 1906 in Savannah, Georgia. It grew into the largest bank in the state. His father,

Remer, however, shunned the banking business for farming and purchased an 11,000-acre plantation in rural South Carolina.

The young Mills Lane wanted to make neither banking nor farming his life's work. He wanted to be a Marine. After begging for his father's approval, he enlisted on 13 August 1956, beginning a three-year career that would instil in him the values of discipline, integrity, punctuality and loyalty that he would apply to all future aspects of his life.

It was in the Marines where Lane became the boxer he had dreamed of being when he first sat in front of a radio and listened to the second heavyweight championship fight between Joe Louis and Billy Conn. Louis' eighth-round knockout on 19 June 1946 at the Yankee Stadium got him hooked on the sport.

When the battalion boxing team asked for volunteers, he was among the first to sign up. Up to that point, he had done some informal sparring but nothing really competitive. He would soon find boxing more strenuous than he ever imagined.

Extra road work, hundreds of sit-ups, countless hours on the heavy and light bags, and endless sparring sessions were needed before he was ready for a real fight. When that time came, he made all the work worthwhile, using an in-your-face attack to capture the All-Far East welterweight title while stationed at Camp Sukiran on the island of Okinawa in the East China Sea.

After being discharged from the Marines in August of 1959, Mills decided to enrol at the University of Nevada-Reno. He had read a *Sports Illustrated* article about the school's boxing programme and figured it was a good place to go on the GI Bill, get a degree and pursue the sport he loved. He eventually enrolled for the winter semester of 1960. He chose business administration as his major but was more interested in throwing jabs, hooks and hard combinations.

Thousands of miles from his family home, Lane had to fight for everything he achieved, and the 5 ft 7 in. southpaw proved to be an excellent boxer, winning the 1960 welterweight title at the NCAA Tournament and the John S. La Rowe trophy as the tournament's outstanding boxer. This was when boxing was still an NCAA sanctioned sport.

The NCAA Championship also earned him a berth in the 1960 Olympic trials, the same trials that featured an ambitious light heavyweight from Louisville, Kentucky, named Cassius Marcellus Clay.

The trials were held at the Cow Palace in San Francisco. The Olympics were scheduled for Rome. Lane could already hear the 'Star Spangled Banner' being played while a gold medal dangled around his neck. Getting through the trials was the first step towards fulfilling that dream.

Lane's first opponent was a US Navy champion named Victor Lopez of Price, Utah. He was a nice fighter but no match for Lane's aggressive style. Lane overwhelmed and won easily, advancing to the second round against Phil Baldwin, a southpaw from Michigan.

Lane decided to box with Baldwin, thinking he could win on points. But that wasn't his style. He fought Baldwin's fight and lost the decision. Baldwin eventually joined Clay, the future Muhammad Ali, on the US team in Rome, while a disappointed Lane completed a 45–4 record as an amateur and went back to Reno to become a professional prizefighter.

Perhaps he should have known it would not be a long-term endeavour when he was promptly knocked out in 35 seconds of his pro debut on 7 April 1961. A convict named Artie Cox, who amassed a record of 7–16–1, dropped him with a right hand soon after the bell sounded to start the fight. Lane managed to stagger to his feet only to be dropped again by a dozen or so punches that separated most of the cartilage in Lane's nose.

A beating like that in a pro debut would make someone second-guess whether they belonged in the ring in the first place. But Lane was not a quitter. He would fight ten more times over the next six years, winning all ten fights before deciding he was getting hit far too often.

Going to law school seemed a better option. He embarked

on a career where he would serve as a trial prosecutor for the Washoe County District Attorney's Office in Nevada, then as a district attorney before being elected as a district court judge. His dealings with criminals who could turn vindictive were the reason he carried a snub-nosed .38 police special on him at all times. It was his version of 'protect yourself at all times'.

Lane was known as a tough prosecutor and a no-nonsense judge who was seldom prone to leniency. He had a frequent saying whether he was working his courtroom, giving an interview or at a speaking engagement. It summed up his thoughts on those who blamed their parents, their environment or other outside influences for their troubles. 'Listen, it's not because your mamma didn't breastfeed you. It's not because your daddy screamed at you. The problem is you,' Lane would say. 'And until you straighten yourself out, you're going to continue to have these difficulties.'

His hard edge yet likeable qualities landed him his own television show as 'Judge Mills Lane'. It was shot in New York, where his sons Terry and Tommy went to school.

Though the bulk of Lane's fighting was done in the courtroom, he wanted to remain involved in boxing once his pro career ended. He decided being a referee would keep him as close to the action as he could be without putting on gloves.

He soon fell in love with the profession and the responsibility of administering the rules and protecting the fighters. 'Some people get a rush out of fixing their car or jumping out of planes,' Lane wrote in his 1998 autobiography *Let's Get It On*. 'Those things don't do anything for me. I get a rush from refereeing a fight. Being an arbiter, whether it's in the courtroom or in a prizefight ring, is what I am. That's where my passion is, and I know of no other way to explain it.'

He would referee his first professional bout on 26 August 1964, a ten-round contest at the Lovelock Theater in Lovelock, Nevada. It wasn't until seven years later that he was appointed to work his first world championship fight when Betulio González defended his WBC flyweight title against Erbito

Salavarria in Maracaibo, Venezuela. And it would be seven more years before Lane worked his second world title bout. This one featured Larry Holmes and Ken Norton battling for the WBC heavyweight title on 9 June 1978. Holmes won a 15-round decision and Lane earned a spot in the regular rotation of referees for major fights.

The first time he uttered 'Let's get it on' was after giving instructions before the Holmes heavyweight championship with Gerry Cooney on 11 June 1982; it became his signature slogan.

Working a courtroom and working a boxing ring provided the perfect balance for Lane. He thrived at both.

By the time he got a phone call on the morning of 28 June 1997, he had refereed 92 world championship fights. None had been like what he was about to face. The call was from Dr Elias Ghanem's office at the Nevada Athletic Commission. Also listening by speakerphone were commissioner Dr James Nave and Marc Ratner, the executive director. Lane's help was needed. They needed him to step in for Mitch Halpern to referee.

Lane wasn't even planning to watch the pay-per-view fight that night. An avid poker player, his plan was to drive into town and spend a few hours drinking beer and playing several games of Texas hold 'em at the Club Cal Neva in downtown Reno.

But the Wednesday before the fight, the Tyson camp began objecting to the Nevada Athletic Commission's appointment of Halpern to referee the rematch. Halpern had been the third man in the ring in the first fight when he jumped between Holyfield and Tyson to stop the bout in the eleventh round when Tyson was being pummelled by Holyfield. There were no complaints from Team Tyson about the stoppage. There were also no initial objections when the commission first submitted a list of six to eight judges and three to four referees and asked each camp if there was anyone on the list it felt uncomfortable with and preferred not to be involved. That was standard procedure for every championship bout.

Team Tyson was later told the Holyfield camp had scratched referees Richard Steele and Joe Cortez from the list. But that wasn't true. Ultimately, Ratner recommended Halpern and judges Jerry Roth, Chuck Giampa and Duane Ford. The commission rubber-stamped its approval.

Halpern, 29, was considered a rising star among a highly respected list of boxing referees in Nevada. He had achieved that status through sheer hard work and a passion to be the best referee he could possibly be. Halpern came to his job in a different manner than Lane. He loved sports but did not have a boxing background.

He held the title of director of corporate direct mail at a printing shop for Station Casinos, which at various times operated eight to ten casinos in the Las Vegas area. Before that he was in advertising when he moved to Las Vegas after growing up near Huntington Beach, California.

He first met Ratner when the two worked together for Rebel Radio Sports on station KDWN. Halpern worked as the engineer for the pre- and post-game shows for Jerry Tarkanian's Running Rebels during their Final Four years. Halpern and Ratner often talked boxing and Halpern ultimately wanted to get more involved in the sport.

He initially approached Ratner about becoming one of his inspectors, whose duty it is to work the dressing-rooms and the corners to make sure boxers and trainers are abiding by the rules. But Ratner, who was a keen judge of character, knew Halpern had an aptitude for being in the ring. 'I think you're better off being a referee,' Ratner told him and introduced him to Richard Steele.

At the time, Steele was probably the top one or two referees in boxing. He was a former amateur boxer in the Marines who assembled a 12–4 record as a pro before deciding to end his career after having his ribs broken once in the ring and twice during sparring. 'I had a weak spot,' he said. Steele transitioned into refereeing and eventually set a record for most world championship fights worked.

Steele saw a lot of himself in Halpern, who was young, ambitious and eager to learn. 'He was dedicated more than anyone I've ever seen to learn this trade,' Steele said. 'Refereeing is one of the hardest things in the world to learn. You've got the physicality. You've got to know how to stay out of the fighters' way and know when to get in. He always worked hard to prepare himself to be in the best shape he possibly could.'

Steele took Halpern under his wing and brought him along slowly. Every day at lunchtime, Halpern would leave his printing job to go to different gyms and referee sparring sessions between amateurs. He would even put on gloves and spar just to get a feel for what the fighters were going through. 'For five years we went to the gyms and worked and worked,' Steele said. 'I made sure he understood the game of boxing.'

Halpern was a quick study, always focused and a sponge for soaking in information. It wasn't unusual for him to go to the gym during lunch and then return after work as well. 'He was incredibly dedicated,' said Maggie Halpern, who was married to Mitch from 1995 to 1999. 'I used to make him lunch every day so that when he came back from the gym he'd have something to eat before he went back to work.'

Halpern was on a fast track to success. He refereed his first professional fight on 13 March 1991 in Las Vegas, where Carlos Azcarate needed just 83 seconds to knock out Javier Hurtado in the first round. He would work his first world championship bout on 29 January 1994 at the newly opened MGM Grand in Las Vegas when Simon Brown settled for a majority draw with Troy Waters to retain his WBC light middleweight championship.

Two months later, he refereed his second world title bout when Julio César Vásquez stopped Armand Picar in the second round of their WBA light middleweight championship. By the time Halpern was assigned to be the referee for Tyson–Holyfield I, he had 34 championship fights on his resumé and Ratner was already predicting he would referee more world championship bouts than anyone in the history of the sport.

'He had the ability to learn from each fight,' Ratner said, 'to take constructive criticism and to get films of almost every fight that he worked. He would critique himself and call me about them.'

Among Halpern's closest confidants was Mills Lane. He was eager to learn from the ex-Marine turned district court judge. Though Halpern was half his age, Lane admired his dedication to being a referee and the extra hours he spent trying to improve. They developed a fast bond.

It grew to the point where when Lane would fly from Reno to Las Vegas to referee fights, Halpern was there to pick him up at the airport and drive him to the hotel or casino for the fight.

They would talk about their families and boxing. They talked about past fighters and current fighters, about styles of certain fighters and what to do in certain situations as a referee. 'They were very close,' Maggie Halpern said. 'Mills had a really special place in his heart for Mitch and Mitch just absolutely revered Mills. It was like a father–son relationship. Mitch just thought the world of Mills and wanted to absorb everything from Mills that he possibly could.'

Lane's sage advice was never more needed than in 1995. On 6 May that year, Mexican-born Gabriel Ruelas defended his WBC super featherweight title against 23-year-old Jimmy Garcia of Colombia at Caesars Palace in Las Vegas. It was Garcia's second attempt at winning a world title. Six months earlier he had taken a twelve-round beating when losing a unanimous decision to Genaro Hernández for the WBA super featherweight crown. Ruelas was regarded as much harder puncher than Hernández.

Halpern was assigned to referee the Ruelas–Garcia bout. It turned out to be a mismatch. Ruelas dominated the fight, landing just about every punch he threw. But Garcia was courageous, perhaps too courageous. With a record of 35–4 when he entered the ring, Garcia had never been knocked out and had been knocked down only once. His father worked his corner and searched for hope when there was none. 'One of the problems we have in boxing is having family members in the corner,' Ratner would later say. 'Sometimes they're too brave for their own good.'

Overmatched, Garcia finally went down in the tenth round and Halpern called in doctor Flip Homansky to take a look at the battered fighter. After a brief discussion, Halpern and Homansky allowed the fight to go on, while some ringside reporters shouted that it be stopped.

It wasn't until just 25 seconds remained in the 11th round that Halpern ended the one-sided assault. Moments later, Garcia collapsed in his corner. He was removed from the ring on a stretcher, and by the time he reached the ambulance he was unconscious.

The rest of the boxing card continued at the MGM Grand, including HBO's televised main event featuring Oscar De La Hoya's second-round knockout of Ruelas's younger brother Rafael. By then Garcia was undergoing surgery at the University Medical Center in Las Vegas.

Day after day, Garcia's family sat at his bedside, praying in Spanish and looking for some kind of hope as the fallen boxer who had planned to go to college lay motionless with tubes and wires keeping his heart beating. Finally, there was no hope. He was officially pronounced dead 13 days after the fight, when doctors and the family disconnected his life-support system.

Halpern was criticised in some circles for his handling of the bout. There were cries he should have stopped the fight sooner when it was clear Garcia, who won only one round of the thirty rounds scored by the three judges, had no chance. Halpern put up a brave front publicly.

'If you're asking me would I change anything, the answer is absolutely not,' he told reporters later that month. 'I don't mean to sound callous with that answer, but the man defended himself. He had his hands up and he was throwing punches. I won't change anything about the way I do my job.'

Privately, he second-guessed his actions. 'He relived it and relived it and tried to see what he would have done differently,' Maggie Halpern said. 'That was a really difficult time for him.

He got a lot of support from his peers, and the referees and judges particularly. But it was horrible how he got beat up in the press. He wasn't used to that. He was a young guy. Mitch had the biggest heart of anybody I know. He was a really, really good human being. It hit him hard that people felt he was responsible.'

Few can know the culpability someone might feel after such a tragedy, especially a referee who is charged with the responsibility of protecting fighters. Most understand it's a dark possibility each time they enter the ring. But at least one well-respected Nevada referee couldn't cope with such guilt.

Richard Green, a native of Louisiana and a Golden Gloves boxer in the 1960s, was the referee when Duk-koo Kim died as a result of injuries suffered in his fight with Ray 'Boom Boom' Mancini on 13 November 1982. Green stopped the fight in the 14th round, giving Mancini a TKO victory. But it was too late for Kim, who died four days later. Green would referee one more bout before taking his life with a handgun on 1 July 1983, at his North Las Vegas home. He was 46. As a result of Kim's death, fights were reduced from fifteen rounds to twelve, and the standing eight count was introduced.

'In my fourteen years as executive director [of the Nevada Athletic Commission], I had seven or eight people die from injuries in the ring,' said Ratner, who served in that post from 1992 to 2006. 'The last was Leavander Johnson, the IBF lightweight champion from Atlantic City who died in 2005. The guy he was fighting was Jesus Chavez. I thought he was going to survive. He lasted for five days. I did go to the hospital every day and meet with the family, and they'd say he's doing better and better. Then I went there one day and he just died. That was devastating to me. I had the best regulatory job in the world. But there's nothing worse than that.'

Lane helped Halpern in the aftermath of Garcia's death. He had gone through a similar experience while boxing as an amateur. He was competing at the 1960 NCAA Boxing Tournament at Madison, Wisconsin, when Charlie Mohr, a talented middleweight from the University of Wisconsin, suffered a fatal aneurysm after a fight. Mohr, a 22-year-old senior from Merrick, New York, seemed fine when he left the ring after being stopped at 1:49 of the second round by hard-punching Stu Bartell, a 23-year-old Navy veteran from San Jose State. Mohr walked back to his dressing-room and even signed a few autographs along the way.

When word spread that Mohr had collapsed in the locker room, Lane raced to his side. He watched as the medical team prepared to rush Mohr to the hospital, where he lapsed into a coma. Mohr died eight days later, triggering the demise of boxing as an NCAA sport.

Lane drew on that tragic experience when talking to Halpern about the Garcia fight. He theorised there could be a myriad of reasons why a fighter can die from ring injuries. Blows sustained in a previous fight, such as the beating Garcia took against Hernández, could have taken an unseen toll. There's also the health risks boxers put themselves through, gaining several pounds between fights with an undisciplined lifestyle then rapidly losing it to make weight before a bout. The potential for dehydration makes boxers vulnerable to injury. It's a practice that disgusted Lane. It's why he still ran three miles four times a week at 5 a.m. and hit the light and heavy bag at 5.30.

'It's not your fault,' he told Halpern during one of those car rides from the airport to the hotel. 'All you can do is referee to the best of your ability and as long as you do that, you can look yourself in the mirror and say you did the right thing.'

Halpern seemed to have dealt with the tragedy and moved on. He was excited about the Tyson–Holyfield assignment but knew Ratner was taking a risk giving him the job. He was young and there were other referees seemingly more qualified. It would be Halpern's first heavyweight championship fight. 'I have to do the absolute best I've ever done because this is huge,' he told his wife, Maggie, who remembers her husband being excited yet confident he could do the job.

Others weren't so sure. At 5 ft 9 in. and a lean 160 lb, Halpern's size, or lack of it, was questioned going into the match and became a factor as soon as the bell rang. He had to physically separate the fighters nine times in the first round and step between them when they exchanged punches after the bell. It set the tone for a physical fight where Halpern repeatedly had to use his hands to get between the fighters and pull them apart from their frequent clinches. But he was authoritative with his instructions: 'Step back! . . . No punches! . . . Let go! . . . Work out of it!' he shouted over and over again.

Ferdie Pacheco, commentating from ringside for Showtime, wasn't initially impressed. 'He's too young and too little for these big, big guys,' Pacheco said during the second round. But the dark-haired, moustachioed Halpern was firm throughout the fight. When Tyson and Holyfield clashed heads in the sixth round and a cut opened over Tyson's left eye, Halpern immediately stopped the action and appropriately ruled the cut was caused by an accidental head butt. He spent the rest of the round warning both fighters to watch their heads until Holyfield dropped Tyson later in the round with a left hook to the body.

In the seventh, when Holyfield and Tyson locked arms and were reluctant to separate, Halpern called time and pointed his finger at Holyfield, warning him, 'When I say break, you step back.'

Twice in the seventh, Tyson complained to Halpern about Holyfield using his head as a weapon. But Halpern would warn Tyson about holding Holyfield's arms. Later in the seventh, after a particularly vicious clash of heads instigated by a charging Tyson, Halpern had to stop the action and summon Homansky to look at Tyson's cut. He then walked over to Holyfield and said, 'I'm not going to warn you again, watch the head. Let's keep this clean.'

With Holyfield keeping his head low and Tyson holding in the clinches, Halpern had his hands full. But he stayed in control.

At the end of the tenth round, Holyfield rocked Tyson with

a thunderous right hook and looked to finish him. But with less than ten seconds remaining, Halpern stayed close. When the bell sounded, he grabbed Holyfield to pull him from his assault.

A referee's duty is to know when to stop a fight and when to let it continue. It involves instinct, timing and quick decision making. If Halpern waited too long in the Garcia fight, he wasn't going to make that mistake again.

When Holyfield continued the barrage in the 11th, Halpern promptly stopped the fight 37 seconds into the round by stepping between the fighters as he waved his right hand in the air before wrapping his arms around a slumping Tyson. There were no complaints from Tyson's corner.

Tyson even defused complaints about Holyfield head butts, telling Showtime's Jim Gray, 'He head butted me, but I probably head butted him, too.'

Halpern would referee ten more fights before his name was called to wear his bowtie for Holyfield–Tyson II. It's rare when the same ref works a rematch, and though initially surprised Halpern was excited about the opportunity, partly because he planned to put his $10,000 fee in a college trust fund for his two-year-old daughter, Maris.

That plan began to change the week of the fight, when Tyson's promoter Don King and co-manager John Horne complained about Halpern being selected as the referee for the rematch. 'There ain't no way in hell Mike is gonna fight with this guy in the ring,' Horne bellowed. 'Absolutely not. It's not fair. We didn't have confidence in him the first fight and we don't have confidence in him that he can handle these two big guys again.'

The Nevada Athletic Commission called an emergency meeting to discuss Tyson's objection and announced on Thursday it had voted 4–1 to deny the protest. Halpern would referee the fight. But Horne wouldn't relent. 'This has nothing to do with Mitch Halpern,' Horne said. 'It has to do with having the same referee in back-to-back fights. He just seen Mike Tyson get pummelled in the 11th round. That is not a good sign for either of these fighters. There's no way we can perform 100 per cent under these conditions.'

Late that Friday night, after doing some soul-searching while on a treadmill, Halpern called Ratner and told him he was removing himself from the fight. 'I don't want to be the centre of controversy,' Halpern told Ratner. 'If somebody doesn't want me to be in there that bad, I'm not going to do it. I appreciate you guys choosing me. But I'm going to respectfully not take the assignment.'

On Saturday morning, Ratner called Lane to confirm he would take the fight. There would be no hold 'em poker. Instead, Lane quickly packed and caught a plane from Reno to Las Vegas. Little did Lane know he was about to be in the centre of the most infamous fight in boxing history.

Halpern watched the fight on television and was relieved he'd been spared from being part of the chaos. He continued with his life and his career, refereeing 87 world championship fights, including Felix Trinidad's victory over Oscar De La Hoya and Lennox Lewis's triumph over Holyfield in their rematch.

When Halpern bounced around a ring, he seemed unfazed by the adversity he sometimes encountered. Through Garcia's death, having to give up the Holyfield–Tyson rematch and the end of his marriage in 1999, Halpern was regarded as one of the best referees in the world. But his destiny changed on the morning of 21 August 2000.

Las Vegas police were called to his home in South Las Vegas, where they found him dead from what police called 'an obvious self-inflicted gunshot wound'. He was 33. To this day, his friends and colleagues struggle to find reasons why Halpern took his life at the height of his career.

'I was stunned and broken hearted,' Steele said. 'He was a nice kid. He was a great referee. He was just coming out of a divorce, but he seemed really good. I'd just talked to him. He was driving back from California with his daughter. I told him to "drive safely and I'll see you when you get here". When they told me what happened, it definitely broke my heart. It's one of the worst things that's ever happened to me in my life.'

Royce Feour, the long-time boxing writer at the *Las Vegas Review-Journal*, covered many of the fights Halpern worked. 'I don't know what kind of personal problems he had, but he must have had some demons somewhere, which I never recognised. He became a world-class referee so young. I don't think there was ever as young a referee as good as he was.'

Maggie Halpern doesn't believe her ex-husband intentionally took his life. 'It was not premeditated or intended,' she says. 'It was definitely something that was spur of the moment. That was not his nature at all. Mitch did not know how to use guns and here he was with a weapon that if you pulled the trigger once, it had a safety on it that no bullet would come out. I'll go to my grave believing he did not think it was loaded.'

Halpern's daughter Maris has grown up with pictures in her bedroom of her father in his bow tie refereeing the first Holyfield–Tyson fight. But her favourite picture is one of him sitting on the beach with her in his lap. 'He was a great man,' Maggie says.

College beckons for Maris and if she gets her wish she'll attend a prominent university. What few knew is that after 'The Bite Fight' Lane handed Halpern an envelope. It was for half of the $10,000 fee he earned on 28 June 1997, so Halpern could start his daughter's college fund.

10

WHEN RAGE TAKES OVER

GOSPEL MUSIC FILLED THE LOCKER room at the MGM Grand as Evander Holyfield sang along in his loudest voice. This was part of his normal pre-fight ritual. Facing Mike Tyson for a second time, Holyfield was filled with a sense of peace the scriptures say passes all understanding.

Focusing on his faith, on the word of God and its music was how Holyfield tackled the fear that can overwhelm any fighter moments before a major bout. As strong and as confident as Holyfield appeared in the ring, he had been dealing with fear since he was an amateur and didn't want to face Ricky Womack, the talented amateur from Detroit. Even though he had beaten Tyson once, Holyfield knew he would be facing a more determined and desperate opponent in the rematch. Holyfield had fear. All boxers do.

'The object of fear is to make you forget what you're supposed to do or make you not do what you're supposed to do,' Holyfield said. 'It's not like you say I want to be that way. But your nerves just kick up. If you're not thinking about anything, the fear will come back. So my whole thing was to read the word to calm my nerves down because as soon as the mind gets blank the fear would start coming back.'

Holyfield had turned the first fight with Tyson into a referendum on religion. Tyson gave praise to Allah before every press conference, while Holyfield proclaimed Jesus Christ as the only true God. There are many who point to Holyfield's religious beliefs as the foundation for his ring success.

Hallmark, also a devout Christian, would pray with Holyfield before each workout and quote scriptures during fights or encourage Holyfield to pray in what Christians call 'tongues'.

'I know his confidence was in God, not me, not Lou [Duva], not anybody,' Hallmark said. 'He just had confidence in God that this was what he was supposed to do in his own strength and leave the rest in God's hands, and that's essentially what we did.'

Riddick Bowe's manager Rock Newman thought Holyfield was getting divine assistance during his battles with his fighter. 'I admired his sense of belief in faith and I genuinely believe that helped propel him also,' Newman said. 'Whether what he believed is rooted in reality or hocus pocus, he believed it and I think his belief strengthened him. It gave him a foundation and it was a reservoir that he went to and called on that made him the warrior that he was.'

Don Turner, who would work with Holyfield from 1994 to 2004, offers a different opinion. He felt the fighter's religious convictions kept him from being all he could be in the ring. 'If Holyfield wasn't religious, he would have been a much better fighter,' Turner said. 'He always had to pray first. That way when he was winning, he contributed his winning [to the fact that] God was listening. Religion is good in a church. But in a fight it's not going to help you. Is God going to be on one guy's side and against the other guy? If that worked, you wouldn't have to train.'

Little did anyone know holy hell was about to break loose on 28 June 1997. The rematch had been postponed from its original date of 10 May after Tyson suffered a cut over his eye while training. Dr Ira Trocki, the plastic surgeon from Atlantic City, made sure the cut would not be a factor. 'None of his old cuts that I fixed ever reopened,' Trocki insisted. 'His cuts were all new ones.'

Trocki was back in Tyson's corner for the rematch, as was

Stacey McKinley, the assistant trainer who worked with many of King's fighters. But Jay Bright had been replaced by the verbose Richie Giachetti, who looks like a cross between wrestling manager Captain Lou Albano and Jackie Gleason. Giachetti trained Tyson for his four victories after the loss to Buster Douglas.

When Tyson emerged from prison, Giachetti and King were at odds, embroiled in a lawsuit over Giachetti's work with another King fighter, Oliver McCall. As Giachetti put it, 'They wanted to save a dollar and lose millions.'

When his dispute with King was resolved, Giachetti was brought in to add experience and structure to Tyson's camp. He had been around boxing for 25 years at the time, having helped King promote his first show, a Muhammad Ali exhibition in Cleveland. He also worked with Larry Holmes and Earnie Shavers. More importantly, Tyson respected him. Giachetti helped him rebound after losing his title to Douglas to score victories over Henry Tillman, Alex Stewart and twice over Razor Ruddock. But it had been six years since they last worked together.

Giachetti's primary objective was to work on Tyson's balance and footwork in preparation for the rematch. He also wanted him to use his jab more. 'The jab is everything with boxing, especially when you get a guy to jab and throw the hook off it or an uppercut,' Giachetti said. 'You gotta be first, though. You've got to get there first and keep the pressure on. That's been my philosophy and I've won from it.'

Getting Tyson to focus and train wasn't always easy. After his release from prison, he basically trained when he wanted without anyone to tell him otherwise. But Giachetti was old-school. The power struggle was never-ending.

'We were sparring one day and he didn't feel good and the guys were getting to him,' Giachetti said. 'I told him, "You're not throwing punches. You just want knockouts." I told him to keep sparring and work through it. He jumped out of the ring and hit me in the privates. I finally put duct tape around his gloves so he couldn't take the gloves off.'

Giachetti didn't mind the mini-battles and knew conflict was part of training any boxer, including Tyson. 'The biggest thing is we communicated,' Giachetti said. 'I wasn't afraid of him. He got mad a lot, but so what? You can get mad. If I'm not getting fired ten times a day I'm not doing my job.'

By the time fight week arrived, Giachetti was confident his fighter was ready to regain the heavyweight title. When Tyson arrived in Las Vegas, he wasn't the over-confident braggart he'd been in the first fight. At times he was subdued and reflective. He may have offered an insight to his fragile mental state days before the fight during a sit-down with reporters at Don King's home in Las Vegas. 'Basically, I've been taken advantage of all my life,' Tyson said. 'I've been abused. I've been dehumanised, humiliated and I've been betrayed. That's basically been my life. I'm kind of bitter. I'm kind of angry at certain people. But it keeps you sharp and witty by being revengeful and bitter.'

Before the first fight with Holyfield, the legendary trainer Emanuel Steward had warned King it would 'be a big mistake putting Mike in there with Evander'. When Steward worked with Holyfield for his second fight with Bowe, Holyfield often talked about Tyson, who was in prison at the time. 'I wish Mike wasn't locked up,' Holyfield told Steward. 'Mike is just a little bully. When you stand up to Mike, Mike falls apart. He can't hold up to somebody challenging him.'

King wasn't impressed. 'Man, we can hardly get the guy licensed,' he told Steward, heading into the first fight. 'We're just worried about Mike killing him.'

King and Tyson weren't as confident heading into the rematch. They were concerned enough to secretly ask the Nevada Athletic Commission that Holyfield take a steroid test prior to the bout. Holyfield was not obliged to consent to such a test but agreed with the stipulation the results wouldn't be revealed until after the fight.

With that psychological edge, Holyfield entered the ring to a thunderous roar. He wore a purple and white robe with his warrior emblem on the back. He bounced around on his toes, looking fit and confident. He'd gone through another gruelling training camp under Tim Hallmark, and he was ready to prove his first victory over Tyson was no fluke. His entire team was confident, from his trainer to his attorney Jim Thomas, who had predicted victory during the pre-fight press conference.

'Mike Tyson is a truly great fighter,' Thomas said days before the fight. 'I've admired his skills since the first time I saw him. But he got soundly beaten by Evander last time, and Evander is now stronger, faster and more confident. I don't know how the outcome would be different.'

Thomas's remarks temporarily quieted Steve 'Crocodile' Fitch, Tyson's hired cheerleader, who often wore camouflage fatigues and dark shades. He was a professional trash talker and was constantly screaming about how Tyson was about to destroy Holyfield, who ignored him. 'If you feel that words hurt you, that's when you get out of character,' Holyfield said.

A crowd of 18,000 packed the MGM Grand to see if the outcome might be different. Whitney Houston, Michael J. Fox, Magic Johnson, James Caan and Michael Jackson were among the celebrities in attendance.

Showtime CEO Matt Blank was settling in at ringside with a group of influential guests from politics, entertainment and sport. This was to be the biggest night in the young history of Showtime Event Television. It would validate risking all that money and the favours to Don King to sign Tyson to an exclusive contract. The rematch was tracking to exceed 1.8 million pay-per-view buys, more than the 1.6 million for Tyson–Holyfield I. That would generate at least $90 million from pay-per-view and $40 million at the gate.

'We all thought the rematch was going to be the most memorable fight in heavyweight history,' Blank said. 'It was, but not for the reason that we expected.'

Despite the loss in November, Tyson was a 2–1 betting favourite, though the assembled boxing media had more faith in Holyfield. Prior to the first fight, only Ron Borges of the *Boston Globe* had had the foresight to pick Holyfield, who had told him how Tyson backed off after their stare-down over the pool table at practice for the Olympics. For the second fight, a poll by the *Las Vegas Review-Journal* had the media favouring Holyfield 39–23–2.

As the challenger, Tyson, two days short of his 31st birthday, entered the ring first. Gone was the snarl he entered with for his first fight with Holyfield. While Crocodile spewed nonsense in his corner, Tyson paced around the ring with a white poncho draped over his shoulders awaiting Holyfield's arrival. He looked nervous and uncertain, as did King.

It was Jimmy Lennon Jr's job to be the ringmaster of the festivities. As a youngster, Lennon wasn't sure if he wanted to follow in the footsteps of his father, the famous ring announcer who had introduced some of the greatest fighters in boxing history. Jimmy Lennon Jr went to UCLA and graduated in psychology and education. He would become a school principal in West Los Angeles, a job he would keep for a decade beyond Holyfield–Tyson II.

But the call of the ring always tugged at Lennon. He would interview fighters with his dad and announce some of the undercard bouts. He did amateur events on the side to make a few extra bucks and eventually worked his way up to the point where when his father's health failed Jimmy Lennon Jr was ready to continue the family legacy.

As lead announcer for Showtime, Lennon had worked hundreds of championship fights. But a heavyweight championship fight was always special, especially one involving Tyson. 'There's nothing like a Mike Tyson ring walk and the energy of that,' Lennon Jr said. 'When he comes in and starts pacing in the corner, there's a tremendous build-up. I've done Super Bowls, World Series and all that stuff. But that's nothing compared to a Mike Tyson fight. My all-time favourite introduction is to introduce Tyson because of that feeling. It's the most exciting atmosphere in the ring.'

Ding, ding, ding.

The build-up begins with the familiar sound of the bell. It

alerts everyone that the introductions are about to take place and the bout is set to begin. Lennon's words roll out with rhythm. 'The city of entertainment, the MGM Grand in Las Vegas, Nevada, it's time for our main event of the evening . . .' Lennon said into the microphone while standing in the centre of a crowded ring.

Dressed in his customary black tuxedo, Lennon acknowledged the network sponsors, ringside judges and other officials. Mills Lane, fresh from Reno, stood in a neutral corner ready to referee his 96th world title fight.

'OK, fight fans, here we go, the time has come,' Lennon bellowed in his familiar build-up. 'And now, ladies and gentlemen in attendance and boxing fans joining us around the world, it is Showtime.'

Ding, ding, ding.

There is no more electric moment in sports than when prizefighters are introduced. Weeks and months of anticipation have built to this crescendo, where in moments two gladiators charge into the centre of a ring and do battle. 'Your hair stands up on your arms,' Ken Hershman said. 'It's like nothing you can describe.'

Hershman settled into his seat in the tenth row. Surrounded by co-workers and friends, he put $20 into a pot and made the prediction the fight would end in the third round. Fifteen years later, he would say, 'Sure enough it ended in the third round, but not in any way that anyone had ever predicted. I won the bet and proceeded to have the worst night of my professional career.'

As Lennon introduced the fighters, first Tyson and then Holyfield, the roars were decisively louder for Holyfield, who smiled as Tommy Brooks pulled off his robe when Lennon called for the champion. 'Please welcome only the second man in history to capture the heavyweight crown three times, the former undisputed cruiserweight world champion, the former undisputed heavyweight world champion; ladies and gentlemen, here is boxing's warrior spirit, the current WBA heavyweight champion of the world, introducing Evander "The Ree-al Dee-al" Ho-ly-field!'

Ding, ding, ding . . .

'What struck me more than anything else was the supreme calm and confidence Evander projected,' Hershman said. 'For so long we saw the people who were afraid and visibly afraid of Mike: the Frank Brunos of the world who were crossing themselves at every step. You just saw they were somewhat defeated before they got through those ropes. Looking at Evander, I was struck by how different he was.'

Back in New York, Teddy Atlas was at the home of *New York Post* columnist and boxing historian Jack Newfield, who often invited a mix of politicians, actors, sports figures and simple boxing fans to his home for big fights. Someone asked Atlas what his prediction was for the bout. 'Holyfield will win by disqualification,' Atlas said. He had said the same thing to a couple of reporters who called earlier in the week for his thoughts after the Tyson camp complained about Halpern being the referee.

'This is his way out,' Atlas told them. '[Tyson] couldn't fight this fight because he already knows this guy is everything he can't handle. This guy is a man. [Tyson] can't overrun him physically and he can't intimidate him, so he can't fight him. He knows he's going to get exposed. He had to get out of there. He was setting the stage for his great escape.'

Mills Lane brought the two fighters to the centre of the ring. The crowd stood, hoping to witness a fight that would be talked about for years to come. As Lane went over his instructions, Holyfield stared straight at Tyson, who stared back. But Tyson broke the gaze, lowering his head while Holyfield never moved his eyes. When Lane finished with his familiar 'Let's get it on,' they tapped gloves and went back to their corners. Within moments, it was just Holyfield, Tyson and Lane in the ring.

Ding.

The two boxers stepped to each other as Tyson launched the

first combination, a left–right that missed. Holyfield countered with a left hook that drew only air. But as Tyson tried another combination, Holyfield darted inside, his head colliding with the left side of Tyson's face. Someone yelled from Tyson's corner, 'Watch the head butts.' Lane broke the clinch but said nothing to either fighter.

Moments later they clinched again, and this time Tyson wrapped his left arm over Holyfield's right arm and wouldn't let it go even when Lane tried to intervene. 'Let's stop the rough stuff,' Lane told the two fighters.

As the round entered its second half, Giachetti screamed from the corner, 'Jab first! Jab first!' Wearing his traditional black trunks and black shoes, Tyson looked fit and quick, almost like he did in his prime. But he was headhunting with hooks and combinations, trying for the quick knockout that once came so easily. 'Jab first . . . Jab first,' Giachetti yelled.

Holyfield spent the rest of the first round trying to stay inside and forcing Tyson to fight backing up. In the days before the fight, he made no secret of his game plan. 'He knows he can't fight going backwards,' Holyfield said. 'He has to press forward. That will make it easier for me to get him out of there. It's the guy who has more weapons, and I have more weapons. He's going to come out shooting all he can shoot. I have to weather the storm. Once I do that, that will play on his mind and I know he don't want to go 11 or 12 rounds.'

Once inside, Holyfield lowered his head to keep from getting caught with one of Tyson's hooks. He also wanted leverage to push Tyson backwards when they were in the clinches. Just before the bell rang to end the first round, Holyfield landed a hard right hook to Tyson's crouching head, followed by a left and another right. It was enough to win the round. When the bell sounded, they were locked arm in arm. But they broke cleanly. There was no hitting after the bell as they'd done after the first round of the first fight.

'Stay with the jab. Stay with the jab,' Giachetti told Tyson in the corner. 'I want you to now jab for the throat. You're moving good. Keep off the centre. You've gotta keep punching. Don't wait.'

The second round began with a quick clinch, forcing Lane to step in and pull the boxers apart. Once separated, they feinted with their gloves up, waiting for the other to punch. Tyson flinched and Holyfield stepped back. Finally, Tyson lunged in with a left hand. But when he tried to follow with a right, Holyfield ducked under the punch and came up. His head clashed with the right side of Tyson's face.

As they clinched again, Tyson looked at Lane, saying, 'He head butted me.' Lane pushed Holyfield back and called time as blood began to trickle from just underneath Tyson's right eyebrow. Lane sent the two boxers to their corners and signalled to the judges. 'That's a butt. That's a butt,' he told each of them. He did not deduct a point.

Among those not surprised by the early clash of heads was Bobby Czyz, who was at ringside announcing the bout for Showtime. He had been in the ring with Holyfield as a fighter and was familiar with his roughhouse tactics.

'After every fight, Evander Holyfield evokes Jesus Christ's name, God's name and the Lord and all that, but during the fight he'll elbow you, he'll thumb you, he'll forearm you, he'll hit you low, he doesn't care,' Czyz said. 'He'll do all the subtle little things that aren't such a nice-guy type of thing.'

With the fight resumed, Holyfield went right back to his plan of staying close and not leaving Tyson any room to punch. To prevent Tyson hitting him with a vicious uppercut, he kept his chin on Tyson's shoulder before pushing him off.

It was quickly turning into an ugly bout. Late in the second round, Holyfield charged in again, throwing a left hook to Tyson's body. Tyson dropped his head as Holyfield charged, causing another clash of heads. As Holyfield pushed him back into the corner with his head on Tyson's cheek, Tyson looked again at Lane. The referee hardly acknowledged Tyson, breaking the fighters from the corner and getting them back into the centre of the ring.

Holyfield picked up the pace, swinging hard with a left and then a right hook that Tyson ducked. Near the end of the second, they clinched again, this time with Tyson's right arm around Holyfield's left elbow. As Holyfield backed him into the corner, Tyson leaned down on his right arm, pushing in Holyfield's left elbow in a deliberate move that could have snapped the bone. It went unnoticed by Lane but not by Holyfield, who growled as he pushed Tyson back.

Lane sensed the mounting anger and tried to regain control by stopping the bout and lecturing both fighters about their antics. 'You both know better than that,' he said. His plea was barely acknowledged.

As the second round ended, Trocki went to work on the cut. When he squeezed the slit brow together, Tyson yelled, 'Ouch!' Trocki says he intentionally drew the reaction. 'Mike was bleeding all over the place and he was cut real bad,' Trocki said. 'He was not really thinking about the fight. He was just angry. So I squeezed the cut real hard to stop the bleeding and wake Mike up and get him back in focus.'

Trocki was confident the cut wouldn't become an issue. He was a plastic surgeon, not a cut man and prided himself on that. He had fixed Tyson's cuts after the first fight with Holyfield and the cut he suffered during training camp to postpone the rematch. 'Most cut men have no clue what they're doing,' he said. 'They're not physicians and they're not plastic surgeons dealing with life-and-death emergencies and dealing with cuts and bleeding. I've seen cut men use some strange concoctions to stop bleeding. Technically there's only certain things you're allowed to use and most of those can only be prescribed by a physician.'

In the opposite corner, Hallmark reminded Holyfield, 'Don't be anxious. Let your spirit go forth. It's not what you feel; it's what you know. However you feel he feels worse.'

Turner liked what he saw in the first two rounds. Tyson was getting frustrated and desperate. Since the first fight, Turner had done all he could to rattle the Tyson camp. 'Psychological warfare,' he called it.

Prior to the first bout, he walked fearlessly into their dressing-room, reached into a bucket and pulled out a bottle of water to drink. When reprimanded by one of Tyson's entourage, Turner said, calmly, 'I was thirsty. I saw some water and I drank it. If you don't like it, as soon as Holyfield becomes champ and Tyson's ex-champ, I'm going to put my foot in your ass.'

Earlier, the old sage had told Tyson, 'I'm from the same place you're from, the ghetto. But the difference between me and you is I didn't snatch no purses.'

Now he was seeing Tyson look to Lane for help. He knew the bully was getting bullied. 'Short punches inside,' Turner told Holyfield as he headed out for the third round.

Tommy Brooks offered his own encouragement: 'Look, this guy is ready to quit. You've got to make him want to quit.'

As the bell sounded for round three, Tyson got off his stool and headed to the centre of the ring. But Giachetti was still on the ring apron yelling for Tyson's attention. 'Mike . . . Mike,' he screamed.

In Giachetti's hand was Tyson's mouthpiece, which hadn't been replaced before Tyson left the stool. Holyfield had noticed, pointing to his own mouth with his glove to get Lane's attention.

In the aftermath of the Bite Fight, there were many who believed Tyson never had his mouthpiece in during the round. But replays clearly show that wasn't true. Lane even called time and watched as Tyson went back to the corner to get the mouthpiece reinserted.

'I think he knew what he was going to do,' Thomas said. 'I don't see a veteran like him accidentally coming out with no mouthpiece. That just would never happen.'

As the third round began, Tyson was the aggressor. He landed a hard straight right and two left hooks that backed up Holyfield. Another straight right followed by a left sent Holyfield with his back to the ropes. The crowd began to chant, 'Tyson . . . Tyson . . . Tyson . . . Tyson.'

Chuck Giampa, a veteran boxing judge from Las Vegas, was scoring the fight along with fellow Las Vegas judges Jerry Roth and Duane Ford. They were among the best in the business and had judged a number of Tyson and Holyfield fights in the past. Only Roth had worked the first fight. Giampa, sitting near the Holyfield corner, had given the first two rounds to Holyfield but liked the work Tyson was doing in round three.

'When you do a Tyson fight, or any of the big heavyweights, you can always count their punches,' Giampa said. 'Those types of fights are easier to score than a flyweight or a bantamweight where there's a lot of punches and you really have to separate the aggressor versus who is more effective. In a heavyweight fight, it's very easy. You don't have the volume of punches, but you have the effectiveness of punches that makes it easier to choose from. I just thought Tyson, in my estimation, was a little more effective with his punches.'

Yet just when it looked like the bout was going to be competitive and fulfil all of the high expectations, it turned bizarre. With 36 seconds left in the round, Tyson threw a wild left hook that Holyfield ducked. The momentum of the punch sent Tyson over Holyfield's right shoulder. Holyfield buried his face on Tyson's right shoulder to avoid the uppercut. It put his right ear next to Tyson's face. It was then Tyson turned, opened his mouth and looked like someone biting on a tough piece of jerky.

Suddenly, 18,000 people in the arena and millions watching on television weren't sure what was happening. Holyfield broke free from Tyson's grip and began hopping high in the air, like a cat on hot coals. With blood dripping down his neck, he spun around and stomped the canvas. He pointed to his ear with his glove.

'What happened here?' Steve Albert asked a worldwide audience while announcing the fight for Showtime.

'I think he got bit on the ear,' said analyst Ferdie Pacheco.

'Holyfield got bit by a dirty Mike Tyson,' Albert said.

Lane called time to pick up Tyson's mouthpiece, which had fallen to the canvas after his teeth released their grip from Holyfield's ear. The referee was still unsure exactly what had happened. As Holyfield turned his back, Tyson pushed him with his gloves into the ropes as if they were tussling in a P.E. class. Holyfield bounced off the ropes and began pointing to his ear again as Lane signalled for time. 'What I felt was incredible pain,' Holyfield would say later. 'It was a shocking thing.'

The blood pouring from Holyfield's right ear made it clear he had been bitten. It was up to Lane to sort out what to do next.

In his 27 years as a referee, this was a first for Lane. There was no standard rulebook for how to handle the situation. He first admonished Tyson and told him was going to take a point away. Then he went to Holyfield's corner and as he inspected the injury, Turner said repeatedly, 'He bit his ear . . . He bit his ear.'

Lane then signalled Marc Ratner, the executive director of the Nevada Athletic Commission, to the ring apron as ringside doctor Flip Homansky went to assist Holyfield. At that point, Ratner wasn't sure what had happened. 'I thought he got hit in the balls and somehow it pinched him with the cup,' Ratner said. 'That's why I thought he was jumping around like that.'

Giampa wasn't sure what had happened either. Tyson had his back to him when he chomped on Holyfield's ear. 'I thought maybe it was a head butt,' Giampa said. 'But when Ratner was on the apron discussing it with Mills Lane, I looked at the ring and saw a piece of flesh on the canvas. That's when I realised something happened.'

Jim Gray was working as Showtime's behind-the-scenes and in-the-ring interviewer. He was seated at ringside next to Lennon, just as shocked as everyone else in the building. Gray had known Tyson since he was a 16-year-old amateur. He'd never known him to be violent, much less out of control. It's why Gray couldn't believe he was seeing flesh come out of Tyson's mouth. 'Nobody could believe it,' Gray said.

As a snarling Tyson paced in his corner, Lane informed Ratner about the bite. 'He bit his ear. He's disqualified,' Lane said initially. 'He's out. He's disqualified. He bit his ear. I can see the bite marks.'

'You really want to disqualify him?' Ratner asked calmly.

It was a natural response in an unnatural situation for Ratner, who, with his greying hair, spectacles and bushy moustache offered a calm demeanour in the growing confusion. In addition to working for the commission, he was a football official for the Mountain West Conference and the commissioner of the Southern Nevada Officials Association.

'One of the first things when an official says to you they want to throw somebody out, you say, "Are you sure you want to throw them out?"' Ratner explained years after the Bite Fight. 'It's just to make the guy really think about it and take a step back. Here it is, the biggest fight of my career, the biggest fight of all time. So I said that to him.'

Lane did take a step back. He next went to Homansky. 'Can he go on?' he asked Homansky.

'Yes,' Homansky said.

Lane then marched over to Holyfield's corner to inform them it would be 'a two-point deduction. The fight will go on.'

Lane then marched over to Tyson's corner. He took Tyson by the arm and told Giachetti, 'He bit him in the ear.'

Tyson tried to lie. 'It was a punch,' he said.

'Bullshit,' Lane snapped. 'It's going to cost him two points.' One for the push and one for the bite.'

As Lane informed the judges of his decision, Hallmark kept telling Holyfield to pray in the spirit. 'He was bleeding pretty bad,' Hallmark said. 'And Evander like a lot of people if they see their own body bleeding it can be alarming. I just kept telling him to stay focused on what he was doing.'

The first thing Holyfield thought was, instead of an eye for eye, how about a bite for a bite? 'I was angry,' he said. 'I said to myself don't do it halfway. You do it all the way. If I bite him, I'm going to bite his whole ear off. That's what crossed my mind.'

Getting bitten or biting wasn't unfamiliar to Holyfield. He used to bite for survival as a kid. 'When my brothers and I would be wrestling and I'd say "I give" and they keep pressing me, I'd bite them,' Holyfield said. 'When you bite people, the reaction is they're going to jump because they don't expect it.'

Holyfield calmed down enough to realise his first instinct to bite back wasn't a good idea. 'All of a sudden I realised if I would have reached out and bit him back they would have every right to get rid of the whole game because you've got the two best boxers gorging each other,' he said.

Brooks yelled at Lane, Tyson 'should be disqualified for that.' Turner later said he was surprised Lane allowed the fight to continue. The bite was clear grounds for disqualification. As Holyfield's trainer, he could have demanded more justice. But he didn't. 'I believe in letting the referee do his job because I'm going to do mine,' Turner said.

Brooks, however, was angry. 'You're a fucking coward,' he yelled across the ring. Then he yelled at Lane to stop the fight. 'But I guess it was a shock to Mills, too,' Brooks said.

In the span of two minutes and twenty seconds that seemed like an eternity, Lane had made several rapid-fire decisions under extreme pressure. First he was going to disqualify Tyson, then he talked to Ratner, then he called for the ring doctor, then he decided to deduct two points and allow the fight to continue. The judge who sent criminals to jail was giving Tyson a second chance.

While all this was happening in the ring, security around the building was being put on a high alert. As soon as Tyson bit Holyfield, the security on the second level of the Grand Garden Arena was instructed to move into position around the ring in case it needed to be sealed off. At this point it was just a precaution. But the crowd Tyson attracted to his fights had always put the hotel security on edge.

The third round resumed with 34 seconds remaining. The rage was still evident on Tyson's face. He was no longer there to play by the rules. Lane had warned Tyson if he did anything like that again he would be disqualified. Having left Jack Newfield's party, Teddy Atlas was at home watching the fight on television. When he heard Lane's warning of a disqualification for a second incident, he knew things would get uglier. 'He's going to have to bite him again,' Atlas told his wife, Elaine. 'He wants to get disqualified.'

It took just fourteen seconds before the two fighters clinched and Tyson wasted no time biting Holyfield on his left ear. Lane again didn't see the second bite and allowed the two boxers to wage what had turned into a street fight.

The bell sounded to end the third round, and Holyfield and Tyson headed to their respective corners almost as if nothing unordinary had taken place. Giampa and the other judges submitted their scoring for the round. With the two-point deduction for Tyson, Holyfield had won the round 9–8, putting him ahead 29–26 on all three cards. Even the ring-card girl was oblivious as the shapely brunette stepped through the ropes and paraded around with a white card with the number four over her head.

But when Turner saw the second bite, he went straight to Lane to show him the damage. After seeing the second bite, Lane walked over to Tyson's corner and told him, 'You're disqualified.' Giachetti tried to argue for another round. 'I'll get him under control,' he said. Tyson at first feigned a look of innocence. Then he looked over at Holyfield and all hell broke loose.

By now the ring was filled with Las Vegas Metro police officers, hotel security, promoters, commission officials and the entourages of both fighters. Tyson tried to get through all of them to get to Holyfield. Initially, assistant trainer Stacey McKinley tried to hold Tyson back but thought better of it when the enraged boxer turned and cocked his fist toward him. Then Tyson turned and began swinging at two uniformed officers who avoided the blows. 'Mike Tyson has apparently lost his reason. His rationale,' Albert told the Showtime audience. 'He seems possessed right now.'

Ratner stood just outside the ring watching in disbelief. 'I had never seen anything like this from any fighter or from him. It was shocking,' he said. 'It was very chaotic and very frightening. There was so many people in there and the police were in there and you could see the fury in Tyson.'

As Hallmark stood in front of Holyfield to shield him, Turner stood next to Holyfield and pulled a five-inch switchblade out of his pocket and clicked the knife open. Brooks spotted the potential weapon and said, 'You're going to get locked up with that thing.'

Turner had always carried the knife into the ring with him just in case something happened. A riot at Madison Square Garden during the Riddick Bowe–Andrew Golota fight nearly two years earlier had made those closest to the ring aware of their vulnerability in a mob atmosphere. Several people were injured during the melee at the Garden, including trainer Lou Duva, who had to be carried off on a stretcher. Turner was taking no chances. 'I pulled out my knife, but I knew Tyson wasn't going to come near me with that nonsense,' Turner said. 'He was just shadowboxing.'

Hallmark also flashed back to the Bowe–Golota riot and positioned himself in front of Holyfield to protect the boxer and himself. 'I remember thinking, "I'm not going to take a cheap shot,"' Hallmark said. 'I wasn't going to get hit without seeing it. I was at least going to give myself a chance. I've been cheap shotted before and got my nose broken, so I was just trying to prepare myself. I was very, very mad and angry at the whole atmosphere and where it was going. I just wanted to be ready if it got over to where I was that I wasn't going to get hurt without putting up a fight or protecting myself or grabbing somebody or whatever.'

As the police moved in to contain Tyson, Giachetti wrapped his heavy arms and big belly around the boxer and pushed him back into the corner.

'Everybody was scared to hold him and I just grabbed him,' Giachetti said. 'He didn't fight me. That was the respect. It was just crazy. Everybody jumped in the ring and they all came after us. It was like the whole world was against us at the time. It was the most shocking thing. I really thought we'd win the fight. But when rage takes over, it's unbelievable.'

Tyson made one last plunge for Holyfield but didn't get far. He was pinned like a caged animal. 'When you're a professional boxer, you're not supposed let your anger get in the way of being a professional,' Trocki said. 'But in a street fight, you do whatever you have to do to win. It's a life-and-death struggle. You're fighting for survival. I think that's what Mike felt.'

Amid the bedlam, Holyfield and his team were told they needed to immediately leave the ring. Security formed a human alley as they hustled Holyfield from the ring to his dressing-room. Tyson soon followed, but his departure came under a blanket of cups, soda, popcorn and beer thrown his way as he pushed through a barricade of bodies blocking his path. At one point, Tyson tried to get to a heckler. But security and his entourage pushed him forward.

Later, during a brief interview with Showtime's Jim Gray, Holyfield said Tyson's actions were out of fear and that he was looking for a way to get out of the fight. 'An easy way to get out of the fight is to foul because you know you're going to get disqualified instead of fighting through it,' Holyfield said as blood trickled from his ear. 'That doesn't show any courage whatsoever. Everybody knows how to get out of a fight. All you have to do is foul. And then you can say, "Well, he didn't beat me."

'If you feel you can whip me, why you can't whop me with the gloves on? This is a boxing match. This is not a rumble when the fight is over, you really get brave and you want to fight. You had a chance to fight. Why do you have to bite me on my ear?'

Team Tyson moved quickly into damage control and tried to paint their fighter as being justified for his actions because of Holyfield's head butts. That's the case they presented to Jim Gray, who was waiting outside Tyson's lockerroom for interviews. First, he spoke to John Horne, who claimed Holyfield had turned it into 'a street fight'. Then King emerged and under persistent questioning by Gray conceded Tyson had gone too far. 'The proper reaction is not to bite,' King told Gray. 'But I guess when a guy feels he's pleading with the referee to give him some consideration and he doesn't get the consideration then he just goes beyond reason.'

Gray convinced King to bring out Tyson for a brief interview by appealing to the promoter's ego. 'No matter what anybody thinks of Don, Don doesn't want to shortchange the people and he doesn't want to be viewed as someone who can't deliver,' Gray said.

When Tyson finally emerged from his locker room to speak with Gray, he was still fuming. He painted himself as the victim. 'He butted me in the first round, then he butted me again in the second round,' Tyson said, with a three-inch gash over his right eye clearly visible. 'As soon as he butted me, I watched him and he looked right at me and I saw that he kept going for my eye, and he butted me again. He kept going under and coming up and charging into me. No one warned him and no one took any points from him. What am I to do? This is my career. I can't continue getting butted like that. I got children to raise. This guy keeps butting me and trying to get me stopped on cuts. I got to retaliate.'

Gray tried to bring reason into Tyson's thinking, but the anger was still too raw. 'Holyfield's not the tough warrior everyone says he is,' Tyson said. 'He got little nicks on his ear and I've got one eye. He's not impaired. He's got ears. Look at me, look at me. I've got to go home and my kids are going to be scared of me.'

Gray would win an Emmy for his work that night. 'Jim is a controversial figure,' Showtime's Matt Blank said. 'But that night at personal peril he took on Mike Tyson pretty hard and pretty strong.'

Back inside the arena, Jimmy Lennon Jr stood in the centre of the ring looking like he was giving the last call at an emptying bar. The fighters had gone to their locker rooms and there still had been no announcement of what actually happened. Those watching the fight on pay-per-view knew. But those in the arena only saw mass chaos after the third round had ended. Finally Lennon took the microphone: 'The winner by way of disqualification and still the WBA heavyweight champion of the world, Evander "The Real Deal" Holyfield.'

There was no joy in Lennon's voice. 'The end was so disappointing,' he said. 'Boxing is a sport I really believe in and I love. I want other people to appreciate it for what it is and what it stands for. And it stands for things I stand for: good sportsmanship, win or lose. It's one on one. I was really disappointed this happened in such a big fight.'

Czyz was equally disappointed. 'As a fan, I was pissed. As a broadcaster, I was pissed. As a former fighter, I was pissed,' he said. 'You had what could have been one of the greatest rematches in history unfold in spectacular fashion. It was spectacular. But not in a good way.'

Gray thought boxing would be viewed around the world as a sport gone mad. 'I thought boxing would be severely damaged,' he said. 'I thought this was something that would live forever. The passage of time wasn't going to make this better. But it just became part of the ring. It just became one of the things that happened that everybody remembers. It was all part of being the youngest champion ever, the train wreck and the allure that captivated everybody.'

'It was a once in a ten lifetimes type thing,' Czyz added. 'Through all the decades that fighting has been around, I don't think anyone has ever seen that. I have seen people that have been bit in the shoulder. I got bit once and I head-butted him. It's not a nice guys' sport. It's not polite like golf. It's a whole lot different. The mindset is different from any other sport. Second place is last place.'

Because Tyson got off the stool without his mouthpiece, many think he planned to bite Holyfield in the third round. But HBO analyst Larry Merchant isn't among them. 'I don't think it was a calculated plan,' he said. 'I think it can be fairly claimed that some combination of frustration and rage led to that moment, that Tyson sensed very early that the second fight wasn't going to be any different from the first one and that he resorted to his street worst, that he was going to get some kind of victory out of defeat and that was to take a piece out of the guy.'

Perhaps Atlas knew better than anyone why Tyson snapped. Despite his fame, riches and indestructible image, Tyson wasn't far removed emotionally from the insecure 12 year old he first met in Cus D'Amato's gym in the Catskills. 'He became a 230-lb monster who could punch like a bastard and was taught how to put punches together and throw all of them with power,' Atlas said. 'Even though he could do all those things he was never far removed from the guy that didn't stand up for himself, that hid behind walls, that got picked on, that got called stinky because he had body odour and the guy that did things like mugging old women.

'I thought it was always a struggle for him to be a chameleon and really believe he was a warrior like Jack Dempsey and the guys he talked about and romanticised about and copied. The hard part was when he couldn't hit [his opponent] in the liver and make them quiver and make them disappear. When that wasn't enough to dismiss somebody, he was in a lot of fucking trouble.'

Watching on television from his home was Mitch Halpern, the referee who stepped aside because Team Tyson didn't want him in the ring. In the end, he was glad he wasn't there to become a scapegoat. 'After the fight, Mitch was relieved because it was such a joke with the whole ear-biting incident,' his then wife Maggie said.

That night Halpern summed it up for just about every disappointed boxing fan. 'The real losers are the fans,' he said. 'Think about all the people all over the world who paid to see the fight. They geared up to see a fight like the first one, and they didn't get it.'

11

LET THE CHIPS FALL

THE ANNOUNCEMENT BY JIMMY LENNON Jr did little to soothe an already agitated crowd. Few in the sold-out MGM Grand Garden Arena knew what had sparked the mob scene in the ring. From their view, the third round had resumed and ended without incident. Then suddenly the fight had been stopped with no explanation given.

The bedlam that erupted with Tyson going berserk and swinging at random added to the confusion. 'There was such pandemonium and such delay before the decision was announced,' Lennon recalled. 'People at ringside were begging me for a decision because they didn't know what happened. "Please, what is it? What is it?" they said. There were many, many minutes before anyone knew.'

When Lennon told the crowd Tyson had been disqualified, it caused an angry reaction. Many in attendance became irate. They were angry the fight was stopped before a decisive verdict, angry their money and emotions had been wasted, and angry bets had been lost. They came to see something special, certainly more than three rounds.

Some in the stands began to seek retribution. Watching tennis matches makes people want to play tennis. Watching boxing can make some people want to fight. The rage Tyson displayed in the ring moments earlier infected the crowd. When Tyson left the arena, it was just the beginning of the unruliness.

Fights soon broke out in the stands as Holyfield fans and Tyson fans argued over which fighter was to blame for the unsatisfying finish. Las Vegas Metro police and hotel security rushed in and were wrestling with fans that had got out of control. 'The sense was this could escalate into something unmanageable pretty quickly,' said Ron Borges, who was at ringside covering the fight for the *Boston Globe*.

Thousands began to flee the arena to escape danger. Others sought to create chaos. A mob mentality began to fill the building, creating an emotionally charged environment.

This was the MGM's worst fear. Hotel security had been on high alert during every Tyson fight since he defeated Bruce Seldon on 7 September 1996. That's the night Tupac Shakur was gunned down on the Las Vegas strip. Tyson and Tupac were close friends. They partied together, chased women together. Tupac had visited Tyson when he was in prison and Tyson had once advised Tupac to calm down after the rapper became embroiled in several incidents of raucous behaviour. It was Tyson who also warned Tupac to watch whom he associated with. He told him not everyone who claimed to be his friend always had his best interests at heart. It was real talk.

To this day, Tyson says fans around the world ask him more about his relationship with Tupac than his boxing career. 'People always ask me about Tupac,' Tyson says. 'All the Caucasian kids, all the Middle Eastern kids, from Kazakhstan, Laos and the Congo, they always ask me what Tupac was like. Tupac is bigger than me. When the freedom fighters go into battle, they play Tupac's music. Tupac has no idea of his influence. I have so much respect for what he accomplished at a young age.'

When asked about Tupac, Tyson tells of a friend who 'had a lot of fury and a lot of fire. But he was the kindest man in the world. He would give you the shirt off his back,' Tyson said. 'He was very generous. But he had a lot of fire and he was fearless.'

Tupac became a fixture during Tyson's comeback fights after prison. He was among the first to congratulate him with a hug after Tyson defeated English heavyweight Frank Bruno on 16 March 1996, to recapture the WBC heavyweight title. And he was there to cheer his friend against Seldon.

It was a comfortable union of bad-boy images. Tyson, a champion boxer and nonconformist, was a hero in the hip-hop subculture that craved Tupac's music. His prison sentence had only added to his street cred. Tyson's fights were now attracting a clientele that made Las Vegas nervous. There were still plenty of people dressed to impress, as is the norm for a heavyweight fight in Vegas. But this younger so-called street element with baggy pants, gold chains and gang connections had hotel security on edge.

'There was always a palpable undercurrent of tension and danger in a Tyson fight,' Ken Hershman said. 'It was the Super Bowl of boxing every time he fought. But it also had this undercurrent of danger to it.'

Such was the case the night Seldon and Tyson entered the ring for a fight that lasted less than two minutes. Born in Atlantic City, Seldon had won the vacant WBA title by beating Tony Tucker. He was making his second defence against Tyson, who owned the WBC belt.

Seldon made sure he didn't get beat up. At 1:46 of the first round he went down from a Tyson right hand to the head. Seldon, who had been competitive to that point, scrambled back to his feet. But Tyson floored him again seconds later with a darting left hook. Seldon was again on his stomach. As referee Richard Steele counted, he got to his feet. But his eyes were glassy and his legs were wobbly. He staggered into Steele's arms, prompting the referee to stop the fight.

'The second punch is the one that really got me,' Seldon would later say. 'That's the one when I dropped my hands.'

On his way back to his locker room, Tyson was greeted by an elated Tupac. It seemed the rapper was even more excited than the fighter about the victory. 'We hugged and we talked,' Tyson said. 'I just had my daughter and I said, "I'm going to spend some time with my daughter and I'll come out and see you."' It was the last time Tyson would see Tupac alive.

Later that evening, Tupac and his entourage were caught on surveillance tape brawling with a known gang member of the Southside Crips, prompting hotel security and Las Vegas law enforcement to clear the lobby before trouble escalated. Tupac hustled out before police arrived, leaving with record producer Marion 'Suge' Knight, who was driving in his BMW 750.

At 11.15 p.m., they stopped at a light at Flamingo Road near Koval Lane. A four-door white Cadillac pulled up to the passenger side where Tupac was riding. As the window of the Cadillac slowly rolled down, a gun appeared, releasing a hail of bullets. Tupac was hit in the chest, pelvis and the thigh. Knight was grazed by fragments. Six days later, Tupac Shakur died of internal bleeding. He was 25.

The assassination was a shocking event even by Las Vegas standards and though the shooting was committed on the Strip, it was somehow linked to the element of danger that followed Tyson.

'He drew an unbelievable clientele,' said a casino supervisor at the MGM Grand, who has worked at the hotel since its opening. 'It's all kind of different people that come out from underneath the rocks to watch and be part of the activities any time there was a Tyson fight at the hotel. A lot of those people didn't even have tickets or come to gamble. They came to just be part of the scene, and a lot of them were very scary.'

Tupac's murder was still fresh on the minds of hotel security and Las Vegas visitors when Tyson and Holyfield fought for the first time two months after Tupac's death and again when their rematch came nine months after the shooting.

Holyfield's methodical beat-down of Tyson in the first fight subdued a crowd expecting to celebrate a Tyson victory. But the chaos in the aftermath of the rematch ignited a near-riot that spilled into the halls of the MGM and its casinos.

There are two main exits out of the MGM Grand Garden Arena. The lower-level exit is used primarily by employees, ring officials and VIPs arriving and leaving in private limos. The upper-level exit feeds into a large corridor that snakes past restaurants and shops towards the casino. It's barely the width of a two-lane road.

The fights and unruliness that erupted in the arena had caused a mass rush for the exits. With hundreds if not thousands of scared and angry people pushing and shoving out of the arena, it was packed pandemonium. 'A lot of people were fearing for their lives,' said one casino employee. 'Things were total chaos.'

As the fans pushed out of the Grand Garden Arena, a fight broke out in the front lobby between two huge men. Three others jumped in. Seconds later someone yelled, 'A gun. He's got a gun.' Police ran to the scene, drew their guns and told bystanders to hit the floor. The spooked crowd ran from the lobby into the casino to escape danger. That's when gunshots were heard. At least it sounded like gunshots.

The MGM was quickly engulfed in bedlam. The crowd escaping the fights in the arena collided with the crowd fleeing the sound of gunshots in the lobby. It was a collision of panicked people. Young, old, rich, poor, VIPs and nobodies, they all feared for their lives. 'It was a tidal wave of people running into the casino,' said a dealer who was on duty that night. 'It was scary.'

Gaming tables were overturned, drinks were spilled, poker chips were knocked off the tables and bodies were trampled. Even the dealers took cover, not knowing how dangerous the situation might get.

Fearing a full-scale riot, the unprecedented decision was made to temporarily close the casino for the first time in its history. Restaurants had already closed their doors to keep the unruly crowd out. Bars stopped serving drinks. Shops locked their doors. Remembering the Tupac shooting, Las Vegas Metro shut down a two-block portion of the strip from Tropicana Avenue to Koval Lane. The MGM was on lockdown.

'It was one of the craziest damn things I've ever seen,' Brian Rogers said. Rogers had come to the Holyfield–Tyson rematch to work as a ringside paramedic for Mercy Ambulance. He thought his evening would follow the pattern of the previous fights he had worked, assisting the ringside doctor and transporting injured fighters to the hospital if needed. But on this night, he found himself in the midst of a mini-riot.

'At first I didn't know what I was getting myself into,' he said. 'People were fainting. People were fighting. It was a scary time.'

There were a number of people who sustained injuries in the melee, and the uncertainty of whether gunshots had been fired kept everyone on alert. The paramedics, the fire department and Metro police set up a command post in the valet area and shuttled those injured from the hotel down the driveway and into an ambulance. 'We were trying not to put anyone else in harm's way,' Rogers said. 'There were some sounds that sounded like rapid gunfire out in the parking area. I heard it myself. We all took no chances and assumed for a while that it was shots fired.'

Inside the casino, looters were taking advantage of the disarray. As much as $200,000 worth of chips and casino markers were stolen from tables and floors. Among those stuffing their pockets with chips was a future NBA Hall of Famer who will go nameless since no charges were filed. 'It's funny,' said someone who was an executive at MGM Grand at the time. 'The veteran player was the one doing what he did, while the rookie who probably didn't have any money stood back and watched him.'

The MGM quickly spread the word along the strip for other casinos not to cash in their stolen chips. Most of the money was eventually recovered after surveillance video was examined and the culprits were tracked. What the NBA player and other thieves didn't know is that the poker chips were coded. The $25,000 chips, called 'pumpkins', have a code embedded in them so they can be traced. Chips worth $5,000 known as 'browns' and $1,000 chips known as 'yellows' are tracked by the casino supervisors. 'Our job depends on knowing where each one of them is on the table and how they were acquired,' said a casino supervisor. 'That money has to be verified before cashing.'

It took nearly an hour for the casino to be cleared and order to be restored. Rogers estimated that nearly 50 people were injured during the stampede. Of those, 16 were transported to local hospitals with broken bones and other assorted injuries. One female suffered chest pains. When calm was restored, police officers and security personnel began investigating what had happened.

Bill Doak was also looking for answers. Doak was the public relations director for the MGM Grand that night. His pre-fight responsibilities were enormous and ranged from making sure high-rollers and VIPs staying at the 5,000-room hotel were happy, to assisting the worldwide media in attendance. He helped promote private and public events, press conferences and weigh-ins leading up to Holyfield–Tyson II. Only when the fight was ready to begin did Doak get a chance to exhale.

As was his custom, he stayed in the press room to watch the fight on a television monitor. He had other members of his PR team at ringside. 'Everything had gone smoothly during the week and according to plan,' Doak said. 'The fight was about to come off and I was happy knowing we were about to deliver a great event.'

It wasn't long before Doak went from relaxed to stunned disbelief after watching Tyson bite Holyfield's ears. 'I remember just staring at the screen on the monitor saying, "I can't believe this is happening."'

Initially, Doak thought his primary responsibility would be to coordinate a post-fight press conference. He knew the media would want to talk to all parties involved. But soon he found himself embroiled in trying to sort out what was happening in the casino. 'It was a mess,' he said.

An estimated 40 per cent of the gaming revenue generated during a big fight weekend is taken in during the hours just before and after the fight, and the Las Vegas economy was hoping the Holyfield–Tyson rematch would offset a slow summer. But the closing of the casino, including the high-roller pit, couldn't have come at a more critical time. Some areas of the casino were closed for nearly an hour. Some were closed up to three hours.

'It was a pretty big disaster,' Doak said. 'That's when the casino makes back all its money in time and effort when it comes to hosting these big fights. That casino drop severely impacted the night. For all intents and purposes it was a disaster for us at the MGM.'

Doak, who now owns his own Las Vegas public relations firm, says there was never any evidence that gunshots were fired. No one reported being struck by a bullet, no hospitals reported anyone being treated for a gunshot wound at the MGM, no bullet holes were found, and no spent cartridges were located. Doak said the noise mistaken for gunshots came from either champagne bottles opening or brass standards bouncing on the marble floors.

'To this day, nobody knows the real story,' Showtime CEO Matt Blank says. 'It's everything from shots were actually fired to blanks were fired to it was a robbery attempt in the casino and it was a diversion. I don't think anybody really knows what happened. But for those on site, it was shots fired. People were hiding in the bathrooms. There was a good deal of pandemonium.'

There are those who worked at the MGM that night who insist they heard gunshots. 'Undoubtedly,' said one casino operator. 'Officially, they never came out and said that. But from the people I've talked to and worked with and were there that evening there undoubtedly were gunshots.'

Even 15 years later, Doak concedes, 'There were some issues

that still today I'm probably still under a confidentiality agreement not to discuss.'

As part of their investigation, police wanted to confiscate tapes of the Holyfield–Tyson fight from the Showtime truck where the director and producers monitor the event. The tapes would show exactly what happened in the ring and whether Tyson had struck any of the police officers, making him open to assault charges. If Tyson were charged with assault, his probation could be revoked and he could be sent back to prison.

Ken Hershman's immediate task was to keep that from happening. Showtime had long planned to replay the fight the following week and wanted to maintain possession of the tapes to ensure that happened.

His cell phone began ringing as soon as the fight ended. As the lawyer for the fight he had possession of the contracts that covered the liability issues that Showtime might face as a result of what happened.

But Hershman had left the contracts in his hotel room at the MGM, never anticipating the scenario he was facing. 'I got caught in that mass exodus of the MGM,' he said. 'I remember it being really terrifying. Gunshots went off and tables were overturned. I was in the middle of that trying to battle my way to get to the room. I finally got out of the crowd and into my room and then had to go back down to the arena. That's when I met up with police who were guarding all the entrances back in.'

The police weren't letting anybody back in the arena. In fact, no one was being let in anywhere without the proper credentials. Hershman was initially told by the police he needed a yellow VIP sticker to get back in the arena. Those were normally given to the camps of the fighters and other officials who needed floor access. Hershman didn't think he needed one because he planned to view the fight from the stands.

'I'm the lawyer and I've got the contract,' Hershman told the police. 'I've got to deal with the fall-out.'

After offering his work identification, Hershman got back

into the arena and worked his way to the truck in time to grab the tapes of the bout. Within an hour, Hershman, Gray, Blank and the rest of the Showtime team gathered at Emeril's Restaurant inside the MGM for an emergency meeting to try to make sense of what had just happened.

They needed to address the potential damage and other repercussions the network might be facing and plan some sort of action even though the situation was unprecedented. Economically, the fight was a huge success, becoming the highest-grossing boxing match in history. Pay-per-view buys totalled more than 1.99 million, generating nearly $100 million. The gate was $17,277,000. Closed-circuit sales at more than 1,600 locations generated another $6 million. The fight was seen in 97 foreign countries where sales totalled $21 million.

How much of that income was in jeopardy? Would pay-per-view money need to be refunded? Was Showtime vulnerable to lawsuits? Who would handle the cable companies? What would they tell the press? And how could they salvage Tyson's career and earn back their huge investment?

'We didn't know what the Athletic Commission was going to do,' Hershman said. 'We didn't know if there were going to be any police charges because there were rumours he swung at a cop in the ring. We didn't know if there were going to be assault charges. We had no idea what was going down. We were really in more of a fact-finding mode. Let's get the facts and make no rash decisions.'

There were no immediate answers. To Blank, the night remains surreal. 'It's one of those evenings that was so over the top that you can't exaggerate it,' he said. 'You can't add colour to it because there's so much colour. There you are sitting with Muhammad Ali and Jack Nicholson and our biggest customers and hundreds and hundreds of guests all seated at ringside. Then all of a sudden they find themselves in the middle of a major worldwide news story. It was a pretty amazing [*sic*].

'We were all devastated at Showtime because it was potentially a huge economic blow to us,' he added. 'We had made significant advances to Tyson and didn't know if he would ever fight again.'

While commotion raged in the casino of the MGM, the quietest place now was the Grand Garden Arena. Among those cleaning up the mess was 28-year-old Mitch Libonati.

He wasn't just a maintenance worker. He was a boxing fan. Libonati always wanted to make his mark in the sport. He just wasn't sure how he would do it. Born in Thousand Oaks, California, he had moved to Las Vegas in 1992 in pursuit of that dream. He even opened a boxing gym and managed a few pro fighters. But that was small-time stuff. Libonati wanted a taste of the big time.

He heard through the grapevine the MGM Grand was looking for a house corner man to work its boxing events. The job called for someone to make sure the ring and the corners were orderly when the fighters entered. He made sure the turnbuckles were straight and even assisted trainers when they needed towels or gauze or help cutting off gloves.

While the job was hardly glamorous, it got Libonati the best seat in the arena to watch some of boxing's greatest fighters: Julio César Chávez, Felix Trinidad, Oscar De La Hoya, George Foreman, Evander Holyfield and Mike Tyson.

'I took pride in that arena on fight night,' Libonati said. 'My dream at the time was to someday get myself in that ring with somebody I represented and make a name for myself.'

He worked the night Tyson made his return from prison by beating Peter McNeeley, and the nights he beat Bruno and Seldon. 'To see him do his thing and see that electricity and that environment, that was hot,' Libonati said. 'As a young cat who saw the celebrities that he brought and that crowd and that environment, it was lights out every time. My heart was excited.'

He also worked the night Evander Holyfield and Tyson met for the first time and was captivated by their raw energy. 'To see the Warrior and Mike go at it, that was a fight,' he said.

He was just as excited to be working the rematch. Like everyone else, he came to the arena that night expecting to witness boxing history, another memorable battle, instead he wound up trying to keep people from rushing the ring.

He was on the apron when Tyson went wild after being disqualified for biting Holyfield on the ear. Libonati had seen the bite. He even saw Tyson spit something out. 'Whatever it was, I knew it was down there somewhere,' he said.

With the arena empty, Libonati went on a search, figuring he had little chance of finding whatever it was he saw flying from Tyson's lips just after Holyfield went hopping mad around the ring with blood streaming from his ear.

Libonati stood in the middle of the ring and started looking closely at the canvas where mayhem had erupted earlier. Just as he was about to give up his search and go back to his regular duties, he spotted something. It was brown, bloodied and shrivelled. 'It was right there in the centre of the ring,' Libonati said. 'It was the chewed-off piece of Holyfield's ear.'

Libonati picked up the piece of ear and wrapped it up in a latex glove. His first thought was to get it to Holyfield as quick as possible. He alerted a policeman and headed to the locker room where Holyfield was getting some initial treatment before being transported to the hospital.

Libonati knocked on the door. Michael Grant, a 6 ft 7 in. heavyweight contender from Chicago who had helped Holyfield train and was part of his small entourage, answered the door. 'Here I am, this little white dude with a piece of something, and I'm telling him I've got something important for Evander,' Libonati said. 'I said, "He needs this. I've got the piece of his ear right here."'

Grant eyed the little man up and down and then grabbed the latex glove and closed the door. Grant handed the glove to Holyfield's physician Dr Robert Voy. It was then placed in a red bio-hazard bag carried by paramedics in case fragile material needs to be preserved and transported.

Before Libonati could turn around, he was swarmed by media

waiting for Holyfield. He told them his story and a few days later he was on David Letterman's couch telling the story again of how he found Holyfield's ear.

Libonati had always wanted to be known for something he did in boxing. But somehow his 15 minutes of fame proved overwhelming. 'My phone was ringing like crazy and for what? Finding an ear,' he says 15 years later. 'All I know is I did what I had to do. I let it go from there.'

At least he tried to let it go. Libonati had wanted to be known for managing a top fighter, not as someone who found a piece of shrivelled-up ear. Others might have basked in the limelight. But for Libonati it was not the notoriety he had envisioned. 'I became insecure and didn't show up for work any more,' he said. 'I haven't had my face around the fight game since bite night.'

After nearly two hours of discussion during the meeting of Showtime officials, Blank made the unprecedented call to release clips of the bite with the Showtime logo burned into it. Normally, after a pay-per-view event the clips released wouldn't show knockdowns or other key moments during a fight. They would show just enough to get people interested in watching the delayed broadcast the following week.

'We made a decision this would be the most important news story in America if not the world the next day,' Blank said. 'We decided to put that clip out and burn our name in it thinking we would probably get hundreds of millions of pieces of coverage.'

When Blank got back to his room as the sun was rising over Las Vegas, he clicked on his television. The network news opened with an eight-minute report on the Bite Fight. There was the clip of Mike Tyson biting Evander Holyfield's ear with the Showtime logo in the corner. 'We took advantage of the moment,' Blank says 15 years later. 'This was a major news story and we were part of that news story.'

Also part of the story was the reaction of the Nevada Athletic

Commission. The media covering the fight had assembled for what traditionally would be a post-fight press conference with the respective fighters, trainers, managers and promoters to discuss the bout.

But with Holyfield headed to the hospital to get his ear treated and Tyson heading home to avoid further discussion about what had transpired, the commission had the starring role as the world waited to hear what sanctions Tyson would face.

Marc Ratner announced the commission was suspending Tyson and withholding his $30 million purse. An emergency meeting would be held within a week to determine further penalties.

'We knew we had to hold the purse that night,' Ratner said. 'We wanted to let the press know that Tyson wasn't going to get paid and that there would be a hearing in the future.'

A weary Ratner began his journey home, knowing the ramifications of the Bite Fight were just beginning. 'It was something I never dreamt I would see,' he said. 'I knew that night it certainly wasn't going to be over. I was getting calls from different media people until I finally turned my phone off. I was dreading Monday because I knew the kind of calls I would get.'

When Ratner went to exit the MGM Grand, he saw the panicked crowd reacting to what it thought was gunshots. With the help of a security guard, he exited out a back door and hurried through the pool area to get to his car. 'I saw the panic in the people,' he said. 'I saw people rushing in the casinos. That's the only time I was a little bit frightened because I could see the panic and people screaming. It was wild.'

Doak didn't leave the MGM Grand until 5 a.m. More than 15 years later he still can't believe what transpired that night. 'Even when I think back to it what I think about most is that so many things can go wrong for the host of an event like that,' he said. 'The coordination that goes on within the VIP services of our property for the biggest gate ever sold, you have to execute so many things well just to host an event like that. To know everything went fairly well except for Mike ended up biting Evander Holyfield's ear off is just unbelievable. I remember just staring at the monitor and saying, "I can't believe this is happening.'"

12

EAR PIECE

JULIO GARCIA SAT COMFORTABLY AT a pool party in south-east Las Vegas, enjoying a relaxing evening with family and friends. His plan was to eat a few hamburgers, smoke a few cigars and watch the Evander Holyfield–Mike Tyson rematch on pay-per-view.

A prominent plastic surgeon, Garcia was close to the boxing game in Las Vegas, having treated the cuts and injuries of numerous fighters. He was also a lifelong fan of the sport. His dad was an orthopaedic surgeon in their native Cuba and often took care of members of the Cuban boxing team before the family moved from Cuba to Chicago when Julio was five. After moving to Las Vegas to establish his practice, Garcia treated Tyson for small cuts he received during training and some of his early prizefights.

It was rare for Garcia not to at least be on call for a fight as big as the Holyfield–Tyson rematch. But he looked forward to not having to worry about being on duty.

'I was in a T-shirt, shorts and sandals, smoking a cigar and getting ready to watch the fight with some friends,' Garcia said. 'I was looking forward to a good fight like everyone else.'

About the time Garcia struck a match to light up another cigar, he watched in disbelief as Tyson bit Holyfield on both ears during the third round of their heavyweight championship bout. It was at that moment Garcia thought to himself, 'Some poor guy is going to get called in and have to sew him up.'

Five minutes later, Garcia's beeper began to buzz. It was the emergency room at Valley Hospital calling to say they would prefer that he come down and treat Holyfield instead of the doctor that was on duty.

'I can be there in about 20 minutes,' Garcia said on the telephone. 'I just have to stop home and change my clothes.'

There was no time for that. 'You have to get here right now,' the voice on the other end insisted. 'Mr Holyfield is on his way.'

It seemed like a normal request considering the circumstances, but Garcia faced a dilemma. He was a successful plastic surgeon in Las Vegas with a thriving practice and respected enough to be personally requested to treat the heavyweight champion of the world. But he knew the media was likely to be at the hospital following Holyfield and showing up in a T-shirt and shorts might be detrimental to Garcia's health.

'My fear was my mother was going to see me dressed like that and she'd kill me after seeing me on TV,' Garcia says nearly 15 years after that night. 'If you knew my mother, you'd never want to make her mad. That's why I was terrified.'

Wearing his T-shirt and shorts, Dr Julio Garcia headed to Valley Hospital, thinking about how he might get past reporters without his 62-year-old mother seeing him on news reports in Chicago.

Meanwhile, Holyfield was being transported from the MGM to Valley Hospital by Mercy Ambulance. Brian Rogers, the paramedic contracted to be on duty for the fight, was in the ambulance with the wounded warrior. Next to Rogers was the red bio-hazard bag that contained the skin from Holyfield's bitten ear discovered by Mitch Libonati.

Rogers had been with Holyfield since minutes after the fight abruptly ended. It was standard procedure for the paramedic on duty to accompany the ringside doctor to each boxer's dressing-room after the bout ended to monitor post-fight drug tests and check on their condition.

They first entered Tyson's locker room. It was filled with his corner men, his entourage and security people. Also in the room were King, Giachetti, his co-managers John Horne and Rory Holloway, Trocki, Stacey McKinley and Steve Finch aka Crocodile, whose mouth had run non-stop before the fight but now had little to say. There were also members of the Nation of Islam offering support. Tyson was still raging. Still wearing his boxing gloves, he was fuming with anger and wanted to strike something.

'He was screaming and punching the walls,' Rogers said. 'He was hitting things so hard, things were shaking. The guy was in a fit of rage like I've never seen before. He had that look in his eye. His people were all trying to talk to him and calm him down from a distance. But there weren't too many challenging him.'

Rogers decided to let Tyson cool off and headed to Holyfield's locker room. Initially, the scene there was just as chaotic as Tyson's. There were shouts of anger and disbelief, but then Holyfield asked Jim Thomas, his adviser and attorney, to quiet the room so he could lead everyone in a prayer of forgiveness for Tyson.

'When Evander first got in the locker room and saw his ear, he was angry,' Tim Hallmark said. 'But Evander knows a lot about what the word of God says and one of its basic fundamental truths is forgiveness. That isn't always easy to follow through with. That night, he said, "I need to forgive Mike." When he said that, I thought this guy is a lot deeper spiritually than I may have given him credit for.'

Holyfield admits he was 'mad' and 'ticked off' when he looked in the mirror and saw the extent of his injuries. A piece of his ear was gone, a sport he loved had been disgraced, and a chance to validate his victory over Tyson had been stolen. 'I was praying, "Lord, you should have let me knock him out." Then God said, "It's not about that. It's about forgiving." That's when I said I have to forgive him. After saying it a second time, it became more comfortable to forgive him.'

It was decided Thomas would remain at the MGM and attend

the post-fight press conference to counter any claims that Holyfield had intentionally head-butted Tyson. Holyfield, meanwhile, was set to be transported to the hospital to have his ear repaired. Rogers suggested Holyfield exit the dressing-room on a stretcher so he could be manoeuvred more easily through the crowd of reporters and onlookers.

Holyfield initially objected to that idea. But the champion eventually relented. It was also decided to cover his face with a towel so photographers couldn't get a picture of his injured ear.

Before Rogers left the locker room, Flip Homansky, the ringside doctor, handed him the red bio-hazard bag. Rogers recalls Homansky telling him, 'The ear is in here.'

Rogers says he placed the red hazard bag into another plastic bag and put ice around it and wrapped it tight before transporting Holyfield to the ambulance. 'I never looked inside the actual bio-hazard bag,' Rogers said. 'I just put it in the baggie.'

Inside the ambulance, Holyfield remained in good spirits, testing Rogers' knowledge of various Bible verses. It is a six-mile drive up I-15 North from the MGM to the Valley Hospital Medical Center, a frequent destination for boxers injured in the ring. Rogers was still trying to reconcile the crazy events of a night that would get even crazier. 'It was one of those things where we all knew Evander got bit. But it was more like "What just happened?"' Rogers said.

When they arrived at the hospital, Holyfield was taken straight to a pre-op holding area instead of the emergency room. After dropping off Holyfield and the red bio-hazard bag, Rogers thought his night was done. Then he got a call in the ambulance: 'Get back to the MGM. All hell is breaking loose.'

Dr Julio Garcia, still wearing his T-shirt and shorts, arrived at Valley Hospital a few minutes after Holyfield and ahead of the national media. The plastic surgeon had treated a number of wounds caused by bites in his career, mostly the result of late-night bar fights. His immediate concern with Holyfield was the risk of infection.

'Traditionally, human bites are the most prone to infection,' Garcia said. 'They're worse than a dog bite. We have more bacteria in our mouth than a dog has. You get into a bar fight and you punch somebody in the mouth, if your knuckles get caught, we've got to take you to the operating room and irrigate that out because the bacteria can get in your joint and destroy the joint. Human saliva is really bad. So he needed to get it cleaned out without a doubt.'

The doctor was handed the red bio-hazard bag and told it contained a piece of Holyfield's ear. He opened it and looked inside. 'They had the piece of skin but not the cartilage,' Garcia said.

The doctor then turned to Holyfield. A quick examination showed he had a piece the size of a thumbnail missing from his right ear. There were also abrasions on the left ear. 'You could actually see the tooth marks on the remaining cartilage of both ears,' Garcia said.

As he prepared to change and scrub to work on Holyfield's ear, Garcia left the red bio-hazard bag at the nurses' station. But by the time he returned, the red bag with the skin from Holyfield's ear was missing.

It remains one of the unsolved mysteries of Tyson–Holyfield II. Despite an extensive search, the red bag and the skin from Holyfield's ear was never seen again.

Garcia suspects it might have been accidentally thrown away. Or someone could have intentionally taken it. 'It's not a locked facility,' he said. 'Any person could have come into that area and taken it.'

Rogers, speeding back to the MGM to help with the chaos there, got a call asking if he knew where the missing piece of ear was. 'All I can tell you is I didn't take it,' Rogers said. 'You really think I'd take somebody's ear?'

The loss of the skin meant Garcia would have to perform a more complicated procedure to repair Holyfield's ear. On the right ear, he applied a local anaesthesia. Then he made a little flap and raised the skin from the back of the ear and pulled it forward to cover the gap left from the missing cartilage. He then closed up the hole in the back of the ear with stitches. The second bite on the left ear didn't do as much damage. The cartilage was intact.

Holyfield was a model patient throughout the 45-minute procedure. Afterwards, he joked that perhaps he looked mean now that his ears covered in bandages resembled those of a Doberman pinscher.

After Holyfield put on his sweats and signed autographs for the staff and nurses, Garcia asked him for a favour. He knew there was a horde of media outside that would not only want to talk to Holyfield but also the surgeon that repaired his ears. Out of his scrubs, Garcia was again in a T-shirt and shorts, and fearful his mother might see him on television.

'I asked Holyfield if I could go out with his entourage that were all dressed casually so no one would know it was me,' Garcia said.

As Holyfield and his team exited the hospital, Garcia held on to the back of the fighter's shoulder and kept a low profile. When the media descended on Holyfield, Garcia slipped off to the side unnoticed.

He had successfully ducked the media and avoided his mother's wrath. After doing several dozen interviews over the telephone once he got home, Garcia thought he was done for the night until he received another telephone call. Someone had found the cartilage of Holyfield's ear while cleaning up at the MGM.

Replacing the cartilage would have been crucial to restoring Holyfield's damaged ear to its original appearance. But it was 1.30 a.m., too much time had passed. For starters, Holyfield was already asleep in his hotel suite. Second, the cartilage was unusable because it had been trampled and contaminated. 'It wouldn't have been a good idea to try to use it,' Garcia said.

What happened to the cartilage remains another unsolved mystery of Holyfield–Tyson II. One story is someone from Holyfield's camp wound up with the cartilage and sold it for auction in New York, where it was purchased for $25,000 by a stockbroker.

Some have been led to believe the cartilage lies in a trophy case displayed in the memorabilia section at the Montgomery Inn Boathouse Restaurant in Cincinnati. The display includes a sign that reads: 'Evander Holyfield, 28 June 1997'.

'It's actually a joke,' said Alexis Gregory, the granddaughter of the founder of the restaurant. 'We had a piece of chicken that we put in the case about five years ago. People always ask if it's real. We have all kinds of memorabilia, but that's the one everyone wants to see. We have people call from all over the country to ask about it. It's kind of funny how far it's gotten.'

Sitting in a hotel suite at the MGM 15 years after their rematch, Holyfield is convinced Tyson bit him out of fear. 'People don't bite because they're mean. People bite because they're scared,' he said. 'They want to get out of there. Tyson wanted to get out of there and I realised he wanted to get out of there. There was no doubt in my mind he wanted to get out of there.'

Holyfield knew this because he sometimes bit his brothers when they wrestled as kids. He also bit an opponent when he was boxing as an amateur. In 1980, Holyfield met Telum 'Jakey' Winters in a semi-final bout in the Georgia Gloves Tournament in Atlanta. Winters was a natural athlete who had come from a tough background in Macon, Georgia.

His father, Melvin Winters, was a promising middleweight in the 1960s. He trained under Angelo Dundee and compiled a 27-3-1 record with 19 knockouts. Just when his career was taking root, Melvin Winters was shot and killed on 12 June 1970 by a girlfriend during a heated domestic dispute. At eight years old, Jakey became the man of the house, forced to protect his younger brother and sister and their mother while still in grammar school. 'He grew up at an early age,' said Burt Gordon, who was Jakey's best friend when they were kids. 'He was always a parent, I guess.'

Though he excelled at all sports, boxing was his passion. He was nicknamed 'Jakey' after Jake LaMotta, whom his father had befriended when he trained in Miami. Jakey didn't know much about his dad, who wasn't home much when he was alive. But the youngster coveted a *Ring* magazine article written about middleweight contender Mel 'Stormy' Winters. 'I knew all about my father and how popular he was through my scrapbook,' Jakey once said.

At age 11, his mother Joanne took him to a local gym in Macon and asked Jack Cantrell, who would train amateur boxers for 35 years, to teach her son to be a fighter. Over the next seven years, Jakey Winters would compile an amateur record of 102 wins in a 112 bouts, mostly as a welterweight. He was Georgia's open-division 147-lb Golden Gloves champion from 1974 to 1983.

'Jakey would throw a 100 rapid-fire punches and put boxers on the defence,' Cantrell said. 'You either had to cover up or quit. He was in such better condition than most amateurs. I never had a boxer train like he did. The harder he trained, the harder he wanted to train. He often told me, "I can't lose." He wanted to be as good as his father.'

A young Holyfield was outmatched the night he met Jakey Winters, who had beaten him when both were nine year olds. Strong, fast and fearless, Winters smothered Holyfield with his punches and dropped him with a left hook to the body and right to the head in the second round. A frustrated Holyfield got up, and when the two fell into a clinch Winters banged Holyfield's head with his shoulder. An angry Holyfield retaliated by spitting out his mouthpiece and biting Winters on the shoulder. Holyfield had a point taken away and the fight went the three-round distance with Winters earning a unanimous decision.

Holyfield's bite barely broke the skin, and the incident was largely forgotten until Tyson bit Holyfield 17 years later. 'Jakey never had any animosity about it,' Gordon said. 'It was the highlight of his life that he and Evander had actually fought when they were kids.'

Jakey's dreams of becoming a successful professional fighter were derailed before they could begin. In 1980, his mother was shot and killed when a gun went off while she and her boyfriend fought after a night of drinking. Just 18, Jakey was now the head of his family. 'He had to take the parental role and put everything else on the back burner,' Gordon said. 'He had to go to work and take care of his brother, sister and grandparents and provide for them.'

Three different times he tried to jump-start a pro career, but retired after compiling a 4–3–1 record with three knockouts over a nine-year span. He left Georgia and settled in Florida where he married and became a financial adviser. With his life on the upswing, he was diagnosed with colon cancer. He died on 28 October 2011. He was 49. 'If I had to go back and pick one of them to be a world champion I would have said it was going to be Jakey before I ever said Evander,' Gordon said. 'But that's just the way things turned out.'

That night against Jakey Winters gave Holyfield more of an understanding about Tyson's actions than anyone knew. He had felt that frustration, that sense of anger born from hopelessness.

'When Tyson bit me, it was, "I want out of this,"' Holyfield said. 'When Mills Lane gave him another chance and he thought I was going to be scared and I came on him, then he bit me again. He was saying, "I just want out of this." Then he got disqualified and he was walking around. All that was a thing of acting like "I'm mean". People don't bite people because they're mean. That's the most beautiful cover-up in the world. He just wanted out.'

That's the consensus of the Holyfield camp. 'After the first fight, I had the utmost respect for him,' Brooks said. 'He talked all that trash and took his ass-whipping like a man and then comes back and does some garbage like that. I had lost all respect for him. He just wanted to get out of there. He knew he was probably going to get knocked out because he came so close to getting knocked out the last time.'

Later, Holyfield would tell Brooks, 'When you trap a rat in

a corner, he's going to do anything he can to do get out of that corner. Mike was in that same situation.'

Holyfield could have had reconstructive surgery on the ear when he returned to Atlanta but elected not to. To this day, he insists it's not a badge of honour. 'It's something that happened that represents forgiveness,' he says. It also represents the most meaningful victory of his career.

Mike Tyson had planned a post-fight party at his Las Vegas home. His 31st birthday would be two days after his rematch with Holyfield, and the hope was to start with a victory party and turn it into an early birthday celebration. But by the time Tyson got home he was in no mood to celebrate.

Many of the invited guests didn't bother to show up, knowing it would be an uncomfortable atmosphere after what had gone on at the MGM. Only close family and friends showed up. And most of them stayed only briefly.

Among those stopping by was Trocki, who had patched up Tyson's cuts at the MGM and wanted to check on any further damage. 'Mike was upstairs in his room,' Trocki said. 'I just went to see how he was feeling. He was pretty hurt and I wanted to make sure there were no other injuries like head trauma.'

King stopped by to check on Tyson but also made a quick exit. The promoter would spend the rest of the night trying to figure out how to salvage Tyson's boxing career. The contracts with Showtime and the MGM Grand had yet to be fulfilled, and the last thing King wanted was for those deals to be voided. If he lost $100 million while Tyson was in prison, he could lose just as much if Tyson was suspended indefinitely.

'He was really depressed,' King recalled of Tyson's mental state that night. 'He couldn't cope with what had happened. He was frustrated. He said Holyfield was butting him and nobody was calling the butts. It was trying to make some rationalisation out of an irrational situation.'

A distraught Tyson sat in his upstairs room. He had been overheard in his locker room at Grand Garden Arena, saying,

'It's over. I know it's over. My career is over.' In the quiet of his home, he was starting to understand the potential consequences of his actions.

A suspension was certain; a lifetime ban was a possibility, and there was also a chance he could go back to prison for violation of his parole if videotapes confirmed he had punched one of the police officers in the ring. He was about to become a father again, with his wife Monica ready to give birth to their second child that August. Now his career seemed in ruins and his freedom was threatened.

He also was being vilified in the media. Ferdie Pacheco broadcasting for Showtime didn't hold back his disgust. 'I don't think anybody can make any justification or rationalisation for something as bizarre as not one but two bites,' he told the pay-per-view audience. 'Something clicked inside of Mike's brain. I've been saying Mike Tyson is an unpredictable and confused young man. I don't think you can see any evidence of mental confusion and unpredictability more than we just saw there with one fighter biting another fighter in the same round two times and taking a chunk out of his ear. End of the story, this guy is one confused individual.'

Fellow broadcaster Steve Albert was equally incensed: 'I thought this was an inexcusable, despicable, illegal exhibition by Mike Tyson.'

The front page of the *New York Post* the day after the fight ran the headline 'Dracula'. Tyson was being called 'a street thug' . . . 'pathetic' . . . 'a coward'. Famed sports columnist Jim Murray of the *Los Angeles Times* wrote that Tyson should never be given a licence to box again. Even the President of the United States Bill Clinton weighed in saying he was 'horrified' by what Tyson had done.

Czyz said Tyson's actions were premeditated. 'Mike didn't just bite the ear,' he said. 'He bit through and then he made sure he ripped it off. That's a conscious effort of frustration and wanting to cause some damage.'

Ten years earlier, Tyson had been the darling of boxing. He

had destroyed Michael Spinks in 91 seconds and was adored worldwide. He seemed invincible and the only words he heard or read were those of admiration and praise. There was talk of breaking Rocky Marciano's record for consecutive wins without a loss. And Tyson was being mentioned alongside the legends he worshipped. Now he was being called a disgrace to boxing, the worst kind of fighter: a biter, a cheater, a quitter.

Steve Lott, who was in Tyson's corner until after the Spinks fight, says Tyson's meltdown had less to do with Holyfield and more to do with how his life was unravelling. 'He remembered being a hero,' Lott said. 'He remembered Cus and how disappointed Cus would be in him. He remembered how disappointed everybody who used to be around him like Jim [Jacobs] and Bill [Cayton] and me would be in him. Everyone around him was a jerk-off and every newspaper was reporting him being a jerk-off. There was the rape conviction and spending three years in jail for something Mike may or may not have done. All the money he could have made was gone. Everything that could possibly go wrong was going wrong. He goes to the arena and hears boos. His emotional strength is gone. It's just a shell. There was nothing left, and he decides he doesn't want to be there.'

Fifteen years after Holyfield–Tyson II, there is no short answer for why Tyson did what he did. 'He was head-butting me and I really lost it,' Tyson says. 'I was mad. I was getting dizzier and I felt like I was blacking out like I did in the first fight. Then I really panicked. He had just kicked my ass six months before I didn't want that to happen, so I just went for the gusto. I lost my discipline as a fighter and just went for broke.'

In the days and weeks following what is now known as the Bite Fight, every action and decision was analysed, especially those of referee Mills Lane. This would be the signature fight of his 34-year career. He would referee for one more year before retiring after Thomas Hearns stopped Jay Snyder in the first round at the Joe Louis Arena in Detroit on 6 November 1998.

Many second-guessed why he didn't disqualify Tyson after the first bite, which was his initial reaction. Lane offered insight to his thinking in his book *Let's Get It On*, saying:

> In a fight of this magnitude, the referee is carrying a lot of unasked-for baggage. I'm referring to the responsibility of overseeing something like $65 million in purses for this one fight, plus hundreds of millions of dollars in future earnings for the winner. In addition, you've also got the vested interest of all fight fans – those who in good faith paid a grand for ringside seats or $100 for a ticket or laid down $50 to see the fight on pay-per-view television. Professional boxing would die were it not for the loyalty of its fans worldwide.'

Lane didn't shy away from the controversy, and his notoriety skyrocketed after the fight as he made appearances on *Larry King*, ABC television and the *Jay Leno Show*. His folksy nature and no-nonsense approach led to his own television reality series *Judge Mills Lane* that ran from August 1998 to September 2001.

In the midst of developing another television programme, tragedy struck boxing's best-known referee in March 2002 when he suffered a debilitating stroke. Lane was stricken while he was in Reno and his family was in New York, where his sons Tommy and Terry were attending school. It was hours before one of Lane's partners discovered him. The lack of immediate treatment caused Lane to lose his speech and some of his mobility. He is now seldom seen publicly.

'It came out of nowhere,' said Terry Lane, who, along with his brother Tommy, carries on the mantle of their father's legacy through Let's Get It On Promotions. 'He ate right, worked out and ran like a beast. My dad was the picture of health. It was one of those things you can't make sense of. Even now I can't make sense of it. It's a tragic thing. But he's still around to see what we're doing. It could have been worse.'

13

DAMAGE CONTROL

THE MORNING AFTER HOLYFIELD—TYSON II, Don King placed a call to Sig Rogich, a Las Vegas-based expert at managing a media crisis. If there ever was a media crisis, Mike Tyson was in the middle of it after getting disqualified for biting Evander Holyfield on the ear.

Within 24 hours, the story of what happened at the MGM Grand had gone worldwide, with Tyson being portrayed as a madman in boxing gloves. The one-time superstar was being vilified across the globe. The sport itself was also under scrutiny.

King's immediate concern was the hearing the Nevada Athletic Commission had scheduled for Wednesday, four days after the fight. The five commissioners would determine what punishment Tyson would suffer for his actions. There were already calls from national and international media for Tyson to be banned from boxing for life. Such a penalty was a possibility that could cost King and Tyson untold millions. 'It was damage control to try to get him not suspended for life,' King said.

Rogich might have been the only man to keep Tyson from being banished from boxing, if not returned to prison for his barbaric actions in the ring. He owned Rogich Communications, a crisis management and political consulting firm based in Las Vegas. He had also served as the media adviser to presidents Bush and Reagan. Rogich was also familiar with the inner workings of the Nevada Athletic Commission, having served a term as one of its commissioners.

His first priority was to make Tyson human again. When last seen, he was remorseless, justifying his actions by blaming Holyfield for intentionally head-butting him. To temper that perception, Rogich helped craft an apology Tyson would deliver two days after the fight.

Tyson appeared at the MGM Grand's Hollywood Theater, showing up 47 minutes late for a press conference he had called. He dressed in a tan sports jacket and sported a bandage covering a stitched cut over his right eye. Over the next four minutes and sixteen seconds he read the following statement in an unemotional tone:

Thank you for this opportunity.

Saturday night was the worst night of my professional career as a boxer and I am here today to apologise, to ask the people who expected more from Mike Tyson to forgive me for snapping in that ring and doing something that I have never done before and will never do again.

I apologise to the world, to my family and to the Nevada State Athletic Commission that has always treated me fairly, to Judge Patricia Gifford who knows that I am proud to be living up to the terms of my probation. I apologise to the MGM, to Showtime, to Don King, my promoter, to my team and to this wonderful city of Las Vegas that has hosted so many famous boxing events.

I cannot tell you why, exactly, I acted like I did other than to say that when the butting occurred and I thought I might lose because of the severity of the cut above my eye, I just snapped and I reacted and did what many athletes have done and have paid the price for. You have seen it in basketball with fist fights on the floor and in baseball with riots on the field and even spitting in the face of an official.

For an athlete in the heat of battle to suddenly lose it is not new, but it's not right and for me it doesn't change anything. I was wrong.

And I expect to pay the price like a man. I expect the Nevada State Athletic Commission to hand down a severe penalty and I am here today to say I will not fight it. I only ask that I not be penalised for life for this mistake. I will instruct my managers and promoters to waive any time restrictions so the penalties can begin immediately so that I can show the boxing fans of the world that I am willing to accept what I have coming to me.

I have also told everyone associated with me that I will not stand for any more of the nasty and insulting comments made to Evander Holyfield and his boxing team.

Evander, I am sorry. You are a champion and I respect that. I am only saddened that this fight did not go further so that the boxing fans of the world might see for themselves who would come out on top. When you butted in that first round, accidentally or not, I snapped in reaction and the rest is history.

To those of you who say that I should never fight again, I can only say that I am just 31 years old, in the prime of my career, and I have made it this far because I had no other way. I grew up in the streets. I fought my way out and I will not go back again. I learned the hard way from the past because I didn't have the luxury of schools, or people, to help me at a time when I needed it the most.

And I will learn from this horrible mistake, too. I have reached out since Saturday to ask my God to help me and to renew my faith as a true believer. I have also reached out since Saturday to the medical professionals for help, to tell me why I did what I did and I will have that help.

Now I will continue to train not just my body but my mind too, so that if it's possible I can put this behind me and so that I will know that it can never happen again. I only ask that you forgive me as you have forgiven others of us in professional sports so that I can be given a chance to redeem myself when my family, my friends, my doctors and most of all my God tell me I am ready to do so.

Thank you.

Tyson left the stage without taking questions. 'All in all I thought Tyson came across sincere,' said Mike Marley, who was Don King's public relations man at the time. 'But I can say the response to the apology was underwhelming. People were still in shock even though there was a gap between the cannibalism and the apology.'

Tyson was not in attendance when the Nevada Athletic Commission convened on 9 July 1997 at the Las Vegas City Council Chambers to determine what sanctions he would face. The room, which held 300 people, was packed. Another 100 or so people mingled outside.

Tyson was not required to attend the hearing and Rogich had advised him to stay away, citing the potential of a melee if he had appeared. There were also concerns Tyson might get angry if questioned about his actions. 'No one wanted him there,' said a person close to the Tyson camp. 'He would have been too much of a reminder of what happened.'

Representing Tyson's interests was Oscar Goodman, a well-known defence lawyer in Las Vegas whose past clients included several organised-crime figures. In future years, he would serve as the mayor of Las Vegas from 1999 to 2011.

Goodman made it clear that Tyson meant no disrespect by not attending the hearing, pointing to his earlier apology. 'All he was going to say was, "I'm sorry," and he's done that already,' Goodman told the commission. 'How many times does a man have to say, "I'm sorry. I'm sorry. I'm sorry?"'

Unimpressed, it took commissioners Luther Mack, a restaurateur from Reno, Nat Carasali, a casino owner from Las Vegas, Jim Nave, a veterinarian from Las Vegas, Lorenzo Fertitta, who owns an investment company, and chairman Dr Elias Ghanem, little time to vote unanimously to revoke Tyson's boxing licence for at least one year and fine him $3 million. The rest of the 48-minute hearing became a sideshow of 20 speakers offering public testimony, including noted Los Angeles attorney Gloria Allred, who encouraged the commission to adopt a policy to prevent sex offenders from fighting for world titles.

Tyson's spiritual adviser Muhammad Siddeeq also spoke, professing his belief that Tyson could live 'a responsible and honourable life'.

It would take years before Tyson would get to that point. While the hearing was underway, Tyson left Las Vegas and headed to New York to find some seclusion. His favourite spot was atop an abandoned building on 118th Street in Harlem where he kept a pigeon coop. He would go there with his confidant and friend Mario Costa, a bar and restaurant owner from Jersey City he first met in the Catskills. Costa had dabbled in boxing, providing support to fighters like Nino Gonzalez, Matthew Hilton, Frans Botha and Arturo Gatti. To this day, he is one of Tyson's closest friends.

Costa and Tyson sat atop the building in Harlem discussing what happened in the Holyfield fight and why he had so much rage.

'Mike got cut in the first fight, so the second time when Mills Lane comes to the dressing-room and talks about the rules and regulations, he asked if there were any questions. Mike told him to watch the head because Holyfield was very bad with the butts. So please warn him or something,' Costa said. 'Mills Lane never really liked Mike. He was an ex-prosecutor and an ex-judge, and he thought Holyfield was a nice guy and a gentleman, and Mike Tyson was a hoodlum that was no good. That's the way Mike felt.

'When he gets cuts in the second fight, you can see Mike trying to tell Mills Lane to ask Evander to watch his head or take a point. But Mills didn't do anything. Mike thought the ref was on Holyfield's side. That's why he lost it.'

Costa said Tyson was also envious of Holyfield and angry at the portrayal that their fights were cast as good versus evil. 'Mike always thought that everybody thought Holyfield was the nice guy and Mr Proper,' Costa said. 'He didn't like that. When you look deep into Holyfield, maybe he's not that good of a guy. Mike would say, "I'm the bad guy because everybody knows everything I do. But he's the car salesman, quiet." It's the quiet guys you have to watch out for.'

Tyson says what some people viewed as being a bad guy was simply part of his act of intimidation. It sold tickets and weakened his opponents. 'They all tried to make me out to be a bully,' he said. 'They just didn't like my shtick when I was boxing. It stepped on people's manhood and made them feel wimpy. That was my whole MO. I had those guys feeling less than a man. I intimidated them without even talking to them. My appearance made them uncomfortable, like most strong-looking black men do. Strong, black-looking men make people uncomfortable. They even make black people uncomfortable.'

Tyson was also getting beaten down by the business of boxing and having his life played out in the tabloids. 'I think his love for the game was mostly when Cus was alive and making him believe he was going to be this great fighter,' Costa said. 'At first, he didn't know what this old guy was talking about. He was just a kid from Brooklyn. Then he really got into going to the gym because you had white kids, you had Spanish kids and you had black kids all up in the Catskills. It got to the point where he wanted to prove to Cus that he was going to be the best of all of them. And he did that. But then came all the partying and all the money. If you're not prepared and you don't have the right people around you, you get completely lost.

'He felt people were around him just for the money,' Costa went on. 'There was Don King, there was the entourage. He would say a lot of times, "You're not here for me. You're here for the pay cheque. You're here for the money that you get at the end of the week." He always had this big entourage, and it was just too chaotic and too crazy,' Costa said.

After having his licence revoked, Tyson began to listen to those questioning his association with Don King. Tyson eventually lost trust in King when questions over his finances arose and Tyson also learned the IRS was demanding he pay $12 million in back taxes.

Tyson confronted King at the exclusive Bel Air Hotel in Los Angeles where he was staying. An eyewitness to the event said

Tyson then 'bitch slapped' King, pummelling the promoter with his open hand. When Tyson tried to leave in a limo, King followed Tyson, but Tyson kept him out by kicking King in the chest with his feet.

The next day, Tyson contacted Jeff Wald, a Los Angeles-based entertainment executive who had promoted a couple of fights for George Foreman and later would be part of the Contender television series featuring relatively unknown professional boxers trying to seek fame. Tyson wanted Wald to help him take control of his financial situation.

Wald had known Tyson since he was 20 and had visited him when he was in prison. Wald never wavered in his faith in Tyson, not during the rape conviction – 'he didn't rape the girl,' Wald said – and not after the rematch with Holyfield. 'I was at that fight and when Holyfield head-butted him I could hear Mike yelling at Mills Lane about the head butt and Mills Lane looked through him like he was glass,' Wald said. 'He looked right through him. My take is that it was Mike's final straw. Nobody heard him during the rape trial either. He was railroaded by Don, and he was railroaded by his lawyer, who had never tried a criminal case before.

'Nihilism comes from no hope and nobody caring,' Wald went on. 'That's why kids kill each other in the ghetto. I saw Mike's face when he looked at Mills Lane, and he didn't know anything else to do. When you get to the point where people don't listen to you and you think they don't care about you, you do a stupid thing and that was a stupid thing. But he did it out of that feeling and out of anger.'

In one of his first public statements since his apology, Tyson announced in February 1998 he had dismissed Holloway and Horne as his managers and was forming Mike Tyson Enterprises. 'I'm in the process of moving forward with my life,' he said in the statement released by Wald's offices.

A month after announcing his independence, Tyson filed a $100 million lawsuit against King in the US District Court in Manhattan accusing the promoter of financial fraud and bilking the former heavyweight champion of millions of dollars. The suit accused King of 'fundamental breaches of trust and fraudulent acts' including duping Tyson into signing an exclusive promotional contract while he was still in prison.

On paper, Tyson had earned $127 million in purses since leaving prison. But the lawsuit accused King of diverting millions of Tyson's monies by way of secret reductions in Tyson's profit participation, accounting manipulations and improper deductions. At the centre of the lawsuit were the contracts with Showtime, MGM and Fox that King put together upon Tyson's release from prison. The suit accused King of receiving 'in excess of $100 million' from those deals 'while leaving Tyson with only a disproportionately small fraction of that amount'.

The lawsuit, which demanded a jury trial, also alleged King billed Tyson for bogus consulting fees paid to his wife, son-in-law, his two sons Carl and Eric and his daughter Debbie for being president of the Mike Tyson Fan Club. Renovations at Don King Productions corporate headquarters in New York and a house owned by King in Las Vegas were also allegedly charged to Tyson's account.

The lawsuit also alleged that King installed Horne and Holloway as 'puppet' managers who took $4.3 million out of the Showtime deal and along with King took as much as 50 per cent of Tyson's purses before he stepped into the ring.

King says Tyson was manipulated by outside influences that took advantage of his frustration of having his boxing licence revoked. 'Idle time is the Devil's workshop,' King said. 'There was a lot of people whispering in his ear to get him to do things that eventually he would be sorry for. Nevertheless, that was Tyson.

'The end result is Tyson did himself more damage than anyone else, running through his money because he certainly had it. He had hundreds of millions, not just millions. And I gave him a sense of pride and dignity and stature and esteem.'

King even defended the role of Horne, a failed stand-up comic, and Holloway, a teenage friend of Tyson from Albany.

(Tyson would also sue them for arranging the deal that made King his exclusive promoter and gave the co-managers 20 per cent of his purses and 30 per cent to King.)

'I'm that if a man is hungry and you give him a fish, he's going to be hungry again. But if you teach him how to fish, he can eat fish until he can establish and expand on his menu,' King said. 'To these two kids John Horne and Rory Holloway, it was like a classroom. It was on-the-job training and they did remarkably well with Mike and all the opponents of liberty and freedom and feeding poison to Tyson. They did a pretty credible job. It was a growing process for all of them. It was a rewarding experience.'

The lawsuit was central to Tyson paying up the $38 million in debt he had compiled. But that would take years to work its way through the court system. His immediate task was regaining his boxing licence. Instead of applying for reinstatement in Nevada, Tyson went before the State Control Board in New Jersey on 29 July 2008 to apply for a licence in the Garden State.

With Shelly Finkel serving as his new adviser, and accompanied by Larry Holmes, Tyson offered remorse for biting Holyfield's ear, saying he became 'desperate, irate and I just snapped.

'I'm sorry for what I did,' he added. 'It will haunt me for the rest of my life.'

But any chance to gain some empathy was lost when, after 40 minutes of questioning about his rape conviction and biting Holyfield, Tyson got angry, using an expletive.

Tyson ultimately withdrew his application in New Jersey and went back to the Nevada Athletic Commission to have his licence reinstated. Before it would consider that, the NAC requested Tyson undergo a series of psychological evaluations at Massachusetts General Hospital to determine whether he was fit enough to return to the ring.

Six different psychologists and psychiatrists conducted a battery of neurological and psychological tests over a five-day period in September 1998. The report submitted to the NAC said Tyson suffered from depression, anger, low self-esteem and irritability and lacked impulse control. While there was no way to predict whether he would lose his temper in a future boxing match, the report concluded that he was mentally fit to return to the ring.

Tyson appeared at a hearing of the NAC on 19 October 1998. Nearly 16 months after the Bite Fight, the NAC voted 4–1 to restore his licence.

Tyson was free to fight again, but the purpose had gone from the love of the sport to paying off the debt he owed. With King no longer running Tyson, a new support group was assembled. Wald served in an unofficial role as adviser, Finkel, who once managed Holyfield, began to operate as Tyson's manager. Dan Goossen, who owned a promotion company called America Presents, served as the promoter, while Tommy Brooks, Holyfield's assistant trainer, was asked to be Tyson's new trainer. Tyson's return was set for 16 January 1999 at the MGM Grand against Francois Botha.

Brooks hadn't looked to leave Holyfield, but teaming with Tyson gave him a chance to be the head trainer and make head trainer money. But the partnership didn't get off to a smooth start.

'I went to Phoenix and didn't see Mike for a whole week,' Brooks said. 'I was getting upset with Shelly, asking him, "Do you guys want a trainer or don't you?" Shelly would say, "It's more complicated than you think."'

When Tyson did show, he was driving a 600 Mercedes Benz. Brooks got in the back seat and was amazed how it moved. Tyson turned in astonishment: 'You've never been in a Benz before? That cheap-ass Holyfield should have bought you one for what you guys did to me.'

It would be the last time they mentioned the Holyfield fight. The two worked together for six weeks before the Botha fight. 'I wanted him to get back to moving his head and putting his punches together,' Brooks said. 'He was extremely fast.'

The night of the Bite Fight, Brooks had called Tyson a coward for his actions. But he would develop a different opinion after working with him. 'He was a real sweet guy,' Brooks said. 'When he trained, he trained hard.'

Nearly 19 months after the Bite Fight, Tyson returned to the same arena where chaos had reigned the last time he stepped into the ring. McKinley was still serving as Tyson's assistant trainer and Trocki was handling the cuts, with Crocodile still adding the vocal support. Showtime did the broadcast.

The MGM wasn't thrilled to have Tyson back but had two more fights coming on his contract. There was an air of apprehension in the building as Tyson entered the ring. Botha, a 30-year-old burly South African with a record of 39–1 with 24 KOs, was a former IBF heavyweight champion. Known as the 'White Buffalo', Botha had stood up at the press conference before the fight and declared, 'I'm the real nigger here. I was born in Africa. Ain't nobody here born in Africa. I'm the real nigger here.' Tyson wasn't amused.

Now 32, Tyson entered the ring with a 45–3 record, 39 KOs and plenty of ring rust. The crowd offered a mixture of boos and applause when he was introduced.

The fight began with Tyson trying to land wild hooks that caught mostly air. Botha countered with sharp jabs and combinations that landed consistently and opened a cut over Tyson's right eye. It didn't take Tyson long to get frustrated, and the MGM began to fear a repeat of what had happened in the Holyfield fight.

With only seconds remaining in the first round, Tyson grabbed Botha's arm during a clinch and tried to break it. As Botha groaned, referee Richard Steele tried to separate the fighters, but Tyson wouldn't release his grip. In an instant, the ring was filled with corner men and security as the pay-per-view announcer shouted, 'It's bedlam in the ring.'

Brooks couldn't believe what he was seeing. 'I thought, "Jesus, here we go again, another Holyfield situation."' He raced across the ring, grabbed Tyson and dragged him back into his corner as Las Vegas Metro police stood on the ring apron. When order was restored, Steele checked with Ratner. Steele then warned both boxers, telling Tyson, 'You can't win with a foul. You've been here once before, Mike.'

He told the same to Botha. 'You can't win with a foul.'

In the second round, Steele took a point away as Tyson continued to bend Botha's arm in the clinches. 'You can't win with a foul,' he repeated.

The fight remained rugged but without further controversy. Botha won rounds by staying outside and using his boxing ability. But in the sixth round, Tyson landed a hard right hand that dropped Botha to the canvas. He didn't get up. 'If I got up, I think he would have killed me,' Botha said after the fight. 'I've never been hit that hard in my life.'

Tyson was hit hard a month later when he was jailed in Maryland for assaulting two motorists after a fender-bender. He was released after serving three and a half months.

Tyson's second fight back wasn't without controversy either. Matched against Orlin Norris at the MGM in a non-pay-per-view bout, Tyson hit Norris with a short left hook after the bell sounded to end the first round. Norris, a former cruiserweight champion, dropped to the canvas, falling awkwardly with his right leg under him. Steele, again the referee, took away two points from Tyson and gave him a stern warning. But when the bell rang to begin round two, Norris remained on his stool. He claimed he had injured his right knee when it buckled under him as he fell to the canvas.

Las Vegas Metro police and hotel security again flooded the ring as Ratner, Steele and ring doctor Flip Homansky tried to sort out the situation. Eventually, the fight was ruled a no-contest. The crowd of 12,000 booed its displeasure.

The outcome didn't sit well with Showtime either. The company had reinvested in Tyson, shelling out $13 million to help pay off the tax liens on his homes, so he could sell them and help pay off his debt.

It also didn't sit well with the Nevada Athletic Commission.

Tyson's $8.7 million purse was withheld for nearly a week. In releasing the purse, the NAC told Tyson essentially he was no longer welcome in Nevada. 'We're not prepared to have any hoodlums fight in the state of Nevada,' said Dr Elias Ghanem, chairman of the NAC.

Tyson would fight his next four fights in Manchester, England; Glasgow, Scotland; The Palace at Auburn Hills outside Detroit; and Copenhagen, Denmark. He would go 3–0 with one no-contest after testing positive for marijuana in his TKO victory over Andrew Golota at Auburn Hills. His next fight would be a blockbuster against Lennox Lewis for the undisputed heavyweight championship. But it wasn't an easy journey to get the two of them in the ring.

On 19 January 2002, Monica Turner filed for divorce to end her five-year marriage to Mike Tyson on grounds of adultery. Three days later, Tyson was in the Millennium Hotel's Hudson Theater in New York for a press conference to announce a 6 April bout with Lewis at the MGM Grand.

Ross Greenburg, the president of HBO Sports, said the deal was 'probably the most difficult negotiation of my life'. It was complex primarily because Lewis was under contract to HBO, while Tyson still had a debt to pay to Showtime. 'I had to strike a deal with Showtime and come up with a way HBO would be protected,' Greenburg said.

It was eventually worked out that HBO and Showtime would each use their own announcers for the fight. If Lewis won, HBO would have to pay Showtime $3 million for the rights to the delay, and vice versa if Tyson won.

With all the details worked out, Greenburg had planned to make a special presentation during the press conference. He had kept the videotape of a young Mike Tyson Jimmy Jacobs had given him years ago to create interest in the young boxer from the Catskills. 'As part of my speech, I was going to talk about that tape and the beginnings of finding out about Mike Tyson,' Greenburg said. 'I thought Mike would get a kick out of it.'

Greenburg never got the chance to make his presentation. He was behind a curtain on stage, sitting at a table alongside WBC president José Sulaimán and other dignitaries. In front of the curtain, Tyson was introduced first. When Lewis, then the heavyweight champion, appeared, Tyson walked towards him. Lewis's bodyguard pushed Tyson, who threw a left hook. Lewis answered with an overhand right. In an instant, bodies began rolling all over the stage. Large men fighting like children crashed into the curtain and the table where Greenburg and Sulaimán were sitting. Sulaimán was knocked unconscious and had to be treated at a hospital. Greenburg lost his tape. 'It flew out of my hands and I ran out of there,' Greenburg said. 'I have no idea where that tape is today.'

Tyson suffered a small cut to the top of his head and reportedly bit Lewis in the leg. Before leaving the stage, Tyson directed a vulgar tirade at a reporter, who yelled, 'You should be in a straitjacket.'

As they were leaving the Theatre, a calmer Tyson asked Finkel, 'The fight was big, but this is going to make it bigger. Isn't it?'

It certainly made it later. A week after the rumble, the Nevada Athletic Commission denied him a licence, forcing promoters to search for another venue in another state. Attempts to place the fight in California, Georgia, Texas and Washington D.C., all failed before the unlikely location of Memphis, Tennessee, agreed to accept the bout and pay a $12.5 million site fee. It would be held on at the 20,000-seat Pyramid on the banks of the Mississippi River on 8 June 2002.

Tyson's first task was to find a new trainer. Brooks was let go over money. 'Shelly called me and asked me how much I wanted for the fight and I think I said a million dollars,' Brooks said. 'He said, "It's not there."' Brooks would work his way down to $750,000 before being told by Finkel 'It's not there,' despite Tyson making $20 million on the fight.

Eventually, Brooks was told Tyson would be trained by someone else. It turned out to be Ronnie Shields.

Brooks had no hard feelings. 'I made a lot of money working with Mike,' he said. Brooks also sensed Tyson was losing interest in the sport. 'I just thought he lost all hope of being a champion again,' Brooks said. 'He was just going through the motions. When I heard that he was fighting Lewis and I found out he was training in Maui, I thought how in the hell are you going to train in Maui. With all those beautiful women down there, it's not the right frame of mind to be in. For a fight like that you've got to go to desolation. Not Maui.'

Despite the tropical surroundings, Tyson was in a crude mood with reporters leading up to the Lewis fight. But he was not much of a challenge to Lewis, who knocked him out in the eighth round. Tyson was cut over both eyes. He looked like a fighter ready for retirement. 'I was pretty much finished,' Tyson said. 'I was getting high and fooling around with a bunch of chicks. I didn't have fighting in my heart no more.'

Nonetheless, eight months later, he was back in Memphis with a tattoo on his face. It was enough to intimidate Clifford Etienne, who was knocked out in the first round by a right hand. It would be the final victory of Tyson's career.

Ideally, Tyson should have retired then. But he needed money. He agreed to face Danny Williams of England on 30 July 2004, in Louisville, Kentucky. It went without fanfare until two weeks before the fight when Tyson settled his lawsuit with King for $14 million. Eight million was paid immediately with the other six million spread over the following two years.

It was fraction of the $100 million he was seeking. All of the money eventually went to the IRS, various creditors and his now ex-wife Monica. On paper, Tyson seemed to have a strong case. But a verdict could have been strung out for years and there was no guarantee he would win.

Brooks was no lawyer, but he found it hard to totally fault King. 'If somebody sticks a blank contract in front of you and you sign it, who are you going to blame? You can't blame Don King,' Brooks said. 'It's business. That's why you have to have lawyers watching lawyers.'

There are those who felt Tyson was talked into settling the lawsuit to keep him fighting. If he had won the lawsuit, he would have retired with plenty of money. Settling for the $14 million ensured he had to continue fighting to pay his remaining debts.

'I carry the weight of the fool alone,' Tyson said, 'but other people contributed to it. I didn't know any better. I was just going along for the ride. I didn't have any money and I thought it was the best thing to do. I didn't really know much about all that stuff. I was just desperate back then.'

An uninterested Tyson would be stopped by Williams in the fourth round on 30 July 2004, and eleven months later he went six rounds before basically quitting on his stool against Kevin McBride in Washington D.C.

After the fight, Tyson retired. 'I can't do this any more,' Tyson said. 'I don't have the heart for it. I'm not interested in fighting any more. I'm not going to disgrace the sport. This is my ending.'

14

THE LOVE OF THE GAME

EVANDER HOLYFIELD WAS AWAKE IN his hotel suite when Jim Thomas came through the door the morning after the rematch with Tyson. Thomas had returned from a nearby pharmacy where he collected a prescription for pain medicine to quiet the throbbing ache in Holyfield's wounded right ear.

'How you feeling?' Thomas asked.

Holyfield smiled: 'I just got paid $34 million for three rounds. I'm ready to do it again.'

Holyfield left that night for South Africa to meet with Nelson Mandela, a trip arranged through his sponsorship deal with Coca-Cola. When he returned, his first priority was to plot a path to become the undisputed heavyweight champion of the world again. To do that, he had to win the other two major belts. The IBF championship belonged to Michael Moorer, while the WBC championship was owned by Lennox Lewis.

Holyfield would gain the IBF portion on 8 November 1997, when he dropped Moorer five times before Dr Flip Homansky stopped the fight after eight rounds at the Thomas & Mack Centre. After a successful defence against Vaughn Bean at the Georgia Dome, a fight with Lewis was arranged for the undisputed heavyweight championship on 13 March 1999 at Madison Square Garden.

It was billed as the biggest heavyweight fight at the Garden since Ali–Frazier I on 8 March 1971. An undisputed champion was becoming a rarity in boxing with the evolution of multiple sanctioning bodies all insisting champions fight their mandatory challengers or be stripped of their belt.

There had not been a unified heavyweight champion since Riddick Bowe defeated Holyfield in their first fight in 1992. Bowe subsequently vacated the WBC belt, dropping it in a garbage can to avoid fighting Lewis, who was the WBC's mandatory challenger at the time and had beaten Bowe for the gold medal at the 1988 Olympic Games. Lewis, who was born in England but fought for Canada at the Games, went on to win the vacant WBC belt by beating Tony Tucker in 1993. Overshadowed by Holyfield and Tyson, Lewis didn't get the recognition or respect normally accorded the WBC champion.

His reputation as a fighter and worthy champion took a huge hit when in his third title defence he was knocked out with one punch by unheralded Oliver McCall in the second round of their bout in 1994. Lewis would regain the title in a bizarre rematch in 1997 when McCall had an emotional tear-filled breakdown in the fifth round at the Hilton Hotel in Las Vegas.

Still searching for a signature win that would validate his championship, Lewis wanted to fight Holyfield, and Holyfield wanted to fight Lewis in order to become the undisputed champion. But attempts to match the pair were complicated by financial and network issues.

Lewis was under contract to HBO, while Holyfield felt loyal to Showtime, which had televised his fights after his career looked finished prior to beating Tyson. Eventually, a compromise was reached, with HBO designated to handle the pay-per-view broadcast.

Holyfield was happy to get the fight and the $20 million purse. But his mood changed during a telephone conference call with the media where Lewis labelled him a 'hypocrite' for calling himself a Christian and fathering children out of wedlock.

After the Bean fight, the *Atlanta-Journal Constitution* published a story where Holyfield admitted he had fathered two children out of wedlock in the same year his wife Janice gave birth to their first child. It gave him nine children altogether: one with Janice, three with his first wife Paulette, whom he divorced in 1991, and five born out of wedlock to four different women.

An angry Holyfield responded by predicting he would knock Lewis out in the third round. It was out of character for Holyfield to make predictions before a fight and it stunned Thomas when he heard the news while travelling in Europe. 'How did he let himself get baited into doing that?' Thomas said. 'Evander is usually such a level-headed guy and he got furious at that.'

Reflecting on that fight, Holyfield admits he made a mistake getting emotional and guaranteeing a third-round knockout on such a huge stage. 'Why in the world would I say something like that about somebody as big as that and just as good as me?' Holyfield said. 'But I said it out of anger because he told me I was a hypocrite because I had these kids out of wedlock and that really hurt my feelings and allowed me to say that stupid stuff. I wanted to knock him out because he offended me.'

Throughout his career, Holyfield guarded against getting emotional about his opponents or during fights. As mad as he was when Tyson first bit his ear, Holyfield eventually regained his composure knowing there was a chance for the fight to continue. Tim Hallmark remembers Holyfield saying an angry fighter is easier to defeat. 'I remember when he told me way back in the day, a guy can't do his best when he's real mad. You can be intense, but you can't be mad. You'll throw a punch and get knocked out.'

But Lewis calling him a hypocrite touched a nerve. It was one thing to question Holyfield's boxing skills. It was another to question his religious beliefs. He had admitted to making mistakes in his life, including impregnating two other women while his wife Janice was pregnant. He had never claimed to be perfect. 'I accept that I've made mistakes in my life,' Holyfield said at the time. 'But if you are a Christian, you are human. What matters is what you do to make amends for those errors.'

Making the guarantee to knock out Lewis was another error. It became the talk of the pre-fight build-up. By the night of the fight, Holyfield had convinced himself his prediction would come true.

The Garden, also known as the Mecca of Boxing, was packed for the tenth heavyweight championship fight in its history. Holyfield entered the ring upbeat, singing a gospel song as he bounced into the ring. Lewis arrived more focused and serene.

The first two rounds were uneventful, with Holyfield landing a total of just eight punches, while Lewis was a bit more active, landing forty-two.

While sitting on his stool before the third round, Holyfield told his corner men, 'This is the round he go out, y'all.'

Don Turner warned him, 'Don't get careless.'

Halfway through the round, Holyfield backed the 6 ft 5 in. Lewis into a corner and landed a solid combination. The crowd of 19,000 rose in anticipation of the knockout Holyfield had guaranteed. But Lewis fought behind his long jab and pushed off enough when necessary. The bell sounded with Holyfield looking discouraged as he headed back to corner. He had won the round but failed to deliver his promise of a knockout.

Tim Hallmark knew Lewis had won the psychological battle by surviving the round. 'I've said for years a lot of these fights can be lost or won the week of the fight depending on what you let get under your skin or what you might say to an opponent,' Hallmark said. 'I think Lewis Lennox used that to get Evander angry.'

What those in the Garden didn't know was Holyfield entered the ring suffering from severe cramps in his legs. He couldn't squat to properly deliver his punches or move the way he would have liked.

'He was cramping up badly in the locker room before the fight,' Thomas said. 'But you can't call off a fight that big because you don't feel good. You never feel perfect. He went out there not feeling really well, but he believed his prophecy would come through. When Lennox weathered that storm,

Evander started slumping and really feeling the cramping. Lennox was confident after that.'

Holyfield admitted he thought about quitting on his stool as the fight progressed. Lewis was boxing smartly, setting up his punches with his long jab and wearing down Holyfield with his size and weight.

'When I didn't knock him out in that third round, all the air was gone,' Holyfield said when recalling the fight. 'The boy bust my eardrum in the next round. The only reason why I stayed in there to go through all that was because of what I said to Buster Douglas. I told Buster Douglas when he was talking all that noise, I told him, "I watched you fight Tony Tucker and you quit; once a quitter always a quitter."'

Holyfield also looked into the crowd between rounds and saw his 14-year-old son Evander Jr, sitting at ringside. 'I was getting ready to quit,' Holyfield said. 'But my son was right there, and he was looking pitiful because I had told everybody that I was going to knock this boy out in the third round.

'I realised I built my whole career up to this point doing all these wonderful things and now my eardrum is bust and I'm sick and all this, and if I get out of this ring, they're going to tell my kid, "That pressure hit your daddy and he quit,"' Holyfield said. That's what kept him fighting against Lewis.

'I went through all that to keep people from judging my kid by me,' Holyfield said. 'Even though I've accomplished all that I've accomplished, the one thing they'll tell my son is, "You're just like your daddy." I never want my kid to have to hear that. So I knew I needed to stay in that ring, sick and cramping. The boy busted my eardrum. I was messed up. He could have got me out. When they called that a draw I was like, "Lord, thank you."'

When the bell sounded to end the 12th round, Lewis raised his right fist in triumph. He along with just about everyone else in the building on 33rd Street in Manhattan thought he had won the undisputed championship.

The punch stats overwhelmingly favoured the Brit. He was

credited with 348 landed to Holyfield's 130. Of Lewis's punches landed, 187 were jabs to 52 for Holyfield.

HBO's unofficial judge Harold Lederman scored the bout 117–113 for Lewis. 'No question. No doubt about it,' Lederman said.

But the scoring of the official judges stunned the crowd. Eugenia Williams from Atlantic City scored the fight 115–113 for Holyfield. Stanley Christodoulou of Johannesburg, South Africa, saw Lewis winning 116–113, while Larry O'Connell of London called it a draw, 115–115. Each fighter retained his respective belts. 'That's a travesty, an outrage,' HBO's Jim Lampley told the pay-per-view audience.

Holyfield blames Lewis for making the fight as close as it was. 'That was a very passive fight he fought,' Holyfield said. 'This boy could have killed me and he didn't do nothing. He didn't want to take the chance. That's the reason the fight ended up a draw because he was so dog-gone passive.'

The controversy over the decision didn't end that night. A New York state Senate hearing was held to investigate the scoring. Williams said her vision was obscured at times by photographers and after watching a tape of the bout she would have scored it a draw instead of giving Holyfield the edge.

Williams, who had been a judge for ten years, had her personal life dissected to the point it was reported she had filed for bankruptcy, supposedly making her vulnerable to having her judgment influenced for financial benefit. The Manhattan District Attorney and the New York State Athletic Commission also conducted their own investigations, while others pointed a finger at Don King, now Holyfield's promoter, for having influenced the judging.

'They blame me for everything,' King says in retrospect. 'Everything that goes wrong, the Johnstown Flood, the Lindbergh kidnapping, whatever comes up, I was to blame because I was in the forefront contradicting the notion of white superiority. I was doing phenomenal things, but they're always going to dehumanise it.'

Nothing unethical or illegal was uncovered in the investigations, forcing a rematch eight months later on 13 November 1999 in Las Vegas. Jim Thomas knew Holyfield was in for an uphill battle when he heard the crowd respond as King entered the ring before the fighters.

'I thought that fight got decided when Don King came into the ring and there was one of the worst choruses of boos I've ever heard at a sporting event,' Thomas said. 'There were about 7,000 Brits there who thought he stole the first fight. Whether it was conscious or unconscious, I don't think the judges in that fight wanted it to look like they were Don King pawns. I think they had some psychological incentives to see it Lennox's way.'

Nearly 13 years later, Holyfield insists he won the rematch with Lewis, a 12-round battle where he felt better and performed with more aggression. But with Mitch Halpern working as the referee, all three judges gave Lewis a unanimous decision. Chuck Giampa had it 116–112, Jerry Roth 115–113 and Bill Graham scored it 117–111.

Thomas believes Lennox got the decision in the rematch as retribution for what happened in the first fight. He says it would have been better if Holyfield had lost in New York. 'Then he would have been the underdog in the second fight and there would have been no resentment and he would have gotten the decision,' Thomas said. 'But I think everybody thought it was so unfair to Lennox the first time around that we've got to fix this.'

Giampa, who judged 132 world championship fights over a 25-year career, said he wasn't influenced by the crowd at Holyfield–Lewis II or the controversy of the previous fight at Madison Square Garden. 'That never entered my mind,' he said. 'During a fight, the previous round doesn't enter my mind. I never even thought about the previous fight and what went on. I know it was a hot topic when it happened. But it never crossed my mind. That's the way I was trained. You have to judge three minutes at a time.'

But there was one big difference surrounding the judges that night. Normally, judges arrive at the arena early in the afternoon and mingle wherever they please. But Marc Ratner, the executive director of the Nevada Athletic Commission, had guaranteed there would be no controversy surrounding the scoring of the rematch. To avoid any hint of impropriety, he ordered the judges not to arrive at the Thomas and Mack Center until 6 p.m., or approximately two hours before the fight. They were also instructed not to discuss anything about the fight with anybody, not to sit with the other ring officials or speak to the media or each other.

'It wasn't a difficult fight to score,' Giampa said, 'but there was a lot of pre-fight pressure due to the fact Marc guaranteed there would not be any controversy. That probably was one of more stressful fights I've done because you don't know what the other scores are.'

Holyfield has no doubts he should have been given the decision over Lewis. 'I beat him that second fight,' he said. 'Regardless of what the judges said, I beat him that second fight. But he fought me back. That's when he won my respect. Even though I didn't feel like he won, I realised he could fight, too. I hit him with everything. He would have gone down with everybody else. But the sucker didn't go down with me. He fought back and showed me he had ability. When the fight was over and they gave it to him, it didn't bother me. Man gets decision. God gets victory.'

Yet, without the belts, Holyfield was unfulfilled. It was his intention to defeat Lewis and retire as the undisputed heavyweight champion. That was his plan. Though he may have felt he won the fight, he was not ready to end his career until his goal was achieved.

Those who knew Holyfield understood that when he set his mind to do something he would not waver regardless of what others felt. That focus and determination drove him to make the 1984 Olympic team after he was told he'd never amount to anything. It also drove him to become the heavyweight champion when many said he was too small to fight as a heavyweight. 'Evander would never doubt himself,' Main Events promoter Kathy Duva said. 'It's his greatest strength and also his greatest liability.'

His name recognition and reputation kept him a marketable fighter, and it wasn't long before he got another title shot. On 12 August 2000, the 37-year-old Holyfield met John Ruiz for the WBA heavyweight championship Lewis vacated to fight Michael Grant instead of Ruiz.

An awkward boxer of Puerto Rican heritage from Chelsea, Massachusetts, Ruiz entered with 11 straight wins to regain his place among heavyweight contenders after being viciously knocked out in 19 seconds by David Tua in 1996. Ruiz was unknown and lightly regarded, which is why Lewis had little interest in fighting him. But to Holyfield this was more than just another title shot.

A win would make him the first four-time heavyweight champion. Beating Muhammad Ali's record of a three-time champion was never a goal, Holyfield insists. It was simply a result of not getting the decision in his second fight against Lewis.

'For whatever reason, they made a decision to give that fight to Lennox Lewis,' Holyfield said. 'That's the reason Ali's record is broken. My goal was to be the undisputed heavyweight champion of the world. If I'm the undisputed heavyweight champion of the world, I would have retired. I didn't have any incentive to break a person's record. I got in it for the love of the game and to be the very best I could be.'

Holyfield earned a unanimous decision over Ruiz to capture the WBA title, but Ruiz's management complained of low blows and head butts to the point where a rematch was ordered. Holyfield and Ruiz would wind up fighting three times over the span of sixteen months, with Ruiz winning the second fight by decision and the third ending in a draw.

While Holyfield's trilogy with Riddick Bowe was a classic, his trilogy with Ruiz was 36 rounds best forgotten. Ruiz's style was more of a barroom brawler than boxer. 'I've never fought a guy that was so green that he hit me on the knee with his head,' Holyfield said. 'The guy would just grab and hold. I fight the man three times. I win one, they gave one to him and they called the other one a draw. In the draw, I beat the daylights out of him. In the one they say he won, I hit him to the stomach and he rolls over and lays on his stomach. He grabs his crotch and Don King says Evander hit the guy low. He was knocked out already. Nobody protested or nobody went back to look at the count.'

Determined to regain the undisputed heavyweight championship, a beltless Holyfield took on Hasim Rahman on 1 June 2002. It's a fight best remembered for the huge haematoma that grew on Rahman's forehead, causing the fight to be stopped in the eighth round in Atlantic City. Rahman said the grotesque swelling was caused by a head butt, a familiar theme in just about every Holyfield fight since the Bite Fight. While some accused him of being a dirty fighter, Holyfield's stance was that he was simply being smart. 'Every fighter knows to keep your head down or you get your head knocked off,' he said.

Holyfield would later say he fought Rahman with severe pain in his shoulders from injuries that included a torn rotator cuff. He underwent arthroscopic surgery, but instead of contemplating retirement he remained focused on his goal of regaining the undisputed heavyweight championship.

A year away from boxing to recover from the surgery would have been the norm, but when a chance arose to fight Chris Byrd for the vacant IBF belt, Holyfield accepted the fight.

They met on 14 December 2002 in Atlantic City. It was six months after the Rahman fight and the shoulder surgery. Byrd, an elusive southpaw from Flint, Michigan, dominated the 40-year-old Holyfield, peppering him with jabs all night. Holyfield looked slow and indecisive. Two of the judges scored nine of the twelve rounds for Byrd.

Holyfield blamed the poor showing on not giving his shoulders enough time to heal. But it was the first of three consecutive losses that raised concern Holyfield would wind up being a fighter who stayed too long in boxing and suffered the consequences for the rest of his life.

Boxing is not a sport to compete in until you're 60. It's not golf. There are far too many cases of fighters suffering dementia or displaying what's commonly known as 'punch-drunk' syndrome in their later years. Repeated blows to the head eventually cause damage and every boxing follower knew Holyfield had been in his share of wars during his career.

Many in the boxing media urged Holyfield to retire as far back as the Bowe trilogy and again after his second fight with Lewis. But it would be a disappointing performance against James Toney on 4 October 2003 in Las Vegas followed by another loss to Larry Donald a year later at Madison Square Garden that had people within his own camp telling Holyfield it was time to quit.

Toney was a brash-talking former middleweight champ from Grand Rapids, Michigan, who had never fought in the heavyweight division. Holyfield initially wanted to fight another former middleweight champion, Roy Jones Jr, who had just won the WBA heavyweight title from Ruiz, but negotiations fell through. Holyfield figured he'd make a quick $5 million by beating Toney and then wait for his next title shot.

But Holyfield looked like a washed-up fighter that night. Toney pounded the former four-time heavyweight champion repeatedly with right hands, much to the chagrin of Don Turner, Holyfield's trainer. After the eighth round, Turner warned Holyfield that if he kept getting hit with the right hand he was going to stop the fight. In the ninth round, Toney dropped a stumbling Holyfield with a series of combinations to the head and body. Holyfield got up and was standing while taking the mandatory eight-count from referee Jay Nady, but Turner threw in the towel to stop the fight. The trainer raced to Holyfield and embraced him as if protecting a son from danger.

Turner now says he saw deterioration in Holyfield's skills long before the Toney fight. 'After the second Lennox Lewis fight, he couldn't see the right coming any more,' Turner said. 'His reflexes were dulling. He started complaining in the gym. He really didn't want to do it any more, but he was getting so much money he was going to keep doing it. He thought he was good enough to skate through. He started turning down sparring partners. When they start complaining, you know it's time.'

Thomas, who had gone from Holyfield's litigator to adviser, friend and staunch defender, thought it was time, too. The night after the Toney fight, they sat alone when Holyfield admitted, 'I could see the openings, but they were gone by the time I punched. I could see his hands coming and I couldn't stop them.'

'What do you think that means?' Thomas asked.

'Well, maybe it means it's time,' Holyfield said.

Thomas felt relief, thinking Holyfield had decided to retire. 'I'm so proud of you that you're not going to hang on,' he told Holyfield. 'I've got a lot of things we can talk about that you can do.' Holyfield seemed receptive.

'I just thought that would have been the perfect time,' Thomas said. 'I thought he was done.'

The next morning, Holyfield called Thomas and told him to fire Don Turner.

'Fire Don? Why would I fire Don?' Thomas asked.

'Because he threw in the towel,' Holyfield said.

'He threw in the towel because I was screaming in his ear to throw it in,' Thomas said.

Their conversation ended with Holyfield telling Thomas that he was going to be the undisputed heavyweight champion of the world again and if Thomas didn't believe it he couldn't be his adviser any longer. It effectively ended their business and personal relationship. After travelling the world together since Holyfield first became champion by beating Buster Douglas, they hardly spoke for the next eight years.

Despite their split, Thomas didn't second-guess the decision. 'My view is you don't really lose your skills in a straight line, you just have more bad days,' he said. 'His reflexes were declining as everybody's do eventually. I just thought it was time to go.'

Though Turner was never officially fired, he never heard from Holyfield again after the Toney fight. 'As long as I think I did the right thing, that's all that matters,' Turner said. 'And the way his career went, I know I did the right thing. I love him. If I had stayed, it would have been blood money from then on.'

When Holyfield took on Donald on 13 November 2004 at the Garden, Ronnie Shields, one of his first trainers at Main Events, was in his corner. But they had worked together for just three weeks. The 42-year-old Holyfield performed so poorly in losing a 12-round decision that Ron Scott Stevens, the chairman of the New York State Athletic Commission, suspended his boxing licence citing diminished skills.

Holyfield felt robbed of his livelihood and vowed to fight again. But now Hallmark was wondering if faith was turning into foolishness. Age, attrition and injuries were taking their toll. 'I saw what happened when the plan came together for a number of years and saw when you couldn't even get the plan up and going and it was fight time,' Hallmark said. 'I think deep down in his heart he was walking into that ring not as prepared as he had been in the past and not as prepared as he could be.'

Having worked with other Olympic and professional athletes, Hallmark knows their mentality and battles with injury and Father Time.

'That's part of every athlete's life you've ever talked to, whether it's a quarterback or basketball player or soccer player where they went into games where they weren't as prepared or didn't have a good training camp or were a little bit injured,' Hallmark said. 'But that's part of the game. It's just kind of different in boxing. Football, basketball and baseball, it's a team sport. They got somebody else to stick in or help them. In boxing, you set that date and it's not a tag-team. You can't say, "I don't feel good. Will you go in?"

'He's the guy that climbs in the ring. When we had really good camps, you felt like you climbed into the ring with him ready to go and you paid your dues. Unfortunately, on the fights where you knew he wasn't prepared, you climbed into the ring knowing he wasn't prepared.'

Holyfield would come to view the suspension as a blessing in disguise. He underwent extensive shoulder surgery after the Donald fight and was sidelined for 21 months before getting medical clearance to fight again.

His return wasn't universally celebrated. But after four straight wins against non-descript opponents, Holyfield got back-to-back titles shots, losing to WBO champion Sultan Ibragimov and WBA champion Nikolay Valuev. Shields had seen enough after the loss to Ibragimov. 'I don't think you need to fight any more,' he told Holyfield after they returned from the bout in Russia. 'You should have beaten a guy like that. He's not even in your class and you couldn't pull the trigger.'

Holyfield said he might have eaten something that adversely affected his performance that night. Shields wasn't buying it. 'Evander, c'mon, man. The worst thing in the world is to make excuses,' Shields said. 'You can't make excuses in this sport. You've either got it or you don't have it, and, Evander, I think you've lost it. I think right now is the time for you to say, "I've had my run. I think it's over."'

At age 45, Holyfield wasn't ready to retire. 'I respect you so much and we're going to always be friends,' he told Shields. 'But I'm not quitting until I'm the undisputed heavyweight champion of the world. If you don't want to do it any more, I'll have to do it without you.'

Hallmark would stay with Holyfield for one more fight after the loss to Valuev, the 7-ft Russian giant of minimal skill. Even though Holyfield earned an eight-round TKO over Frans Botha in Las Vegas on 10 April 2010, Hallmark didn't like what he had seen during the training camp leading up to the fight.

'I just saw a couple of things in the last camp I worked with him on that concerned me about his ability to react to certain types of punches,' Hallmark said. 'I love Evander too much just to go along to get along. So I explained I felt like it would be wiser for him to do something else maybe outside of the ring. It got to a point where he didn't respond as well as he needed to. I felt like if he fought somebody with really good hand speed, he may not be able to do as well as he had in the past. I always said if I saw something physical that would keep him from being his best that I would step off of it.

'That's the decision I made and I never once regretted it,' Hallmark said. 'It's unfortunate that we didn't agree on that decision. But Evander's a fighter. It's real simple. He makes the decision and you decide whether you want to be part of it or not.'

Now Thomas, Turner, Shields and Hallmark had advised Holyfield to retire from boxing. He ignored their opinions and pressed on, continuing to say he wanted to win the undisputed heavyweight championship again before leaving the ring.

It is rare when a superstar athlete doesn't struggle with retirement. The money, the fame, the adulation and their innate thirst for competition all conspire to keep most of them active long past their prime. What fuelled their excellence, their self-belief and desire to defy their critics can also blind them to their own deficiencies and misjudgements.

'The thing that made him great was ignoring what people told him his limitations were,' Thomas said of Holyfield. 'He just stopped listening to that. It made it harder for him to let go than probably some other people.'

When he was a young child, Holyfield's mother told him not to quit until he accomplished his goal. It's something that sticks with him today. His belief in attaining whatever he believes he can achieve is also cemented in scripture often sewn into his boxing trunks and robe: Philippians 4:13, 'I can do all things through Christ who strengthens me.'

That in essence is why Holyfield, having turned 50, hasn't officially retired. 'When it comes down to it,' he said, 'the Bible tells you that everything works for those who believe in God.'

Holyfield believes in God, and Holyfield believes in Holyfield.

15

LIFE ON LIFE'S TERMS

THE LINE OF PEOPLE WAITING to get into the Longacre Theater on West 48th Street in New York City stretches from 7th Avenue to 8th Avenue. The entrance is somewhere in the middle. It's Times Square, the Theater District. The last place you might expect Mike Tyson.

Men, women and young adults dressed from suits to jeans stand in the summer light waiting to see the former heavyweight champion perform on Broadway. They are there for the premiere of *Undisputed Truth*, the one-man show where Tyson, now aged 46, appears on centre stage to talk about his life and career.

The two-hour autobiography was conceived by Tyson and his wife Kiki Tyson. It made an initial run in Las Vegas from 13 to 18 April 2012, where it received mostly positive reviews. Spike Lee, the renowned Brooklyn-born director of *Do The Right Thing* and *Jungle Fever* liked the show enough to make it his directorial debut on Broadway.

Fifteen years after biting Evander Holyfield's ears, Tyson will sell out the 1,009-seat theatre to an eclectic crowd mixed with tourists, boxing fans and locals willing to pay up to $300 to hear what he says.

'I know what you are probably thinking,' Tyson tells the crowd when the curtain rises. 'What the hell is Mike Tyson doing on Broadway? To be honest, I wonder, too.'

It has been an incomparable journey to say the least. After retiring from boxing in 2005, Tyson sank into an abyss of alcohol, drug abuse, weight gain and addiction. He was in and out of rehab three different times and looked headed for the kind of disastrous ending many people feared.

Kiki was there for much of that. Married in 2009, they initially met during his fight with Buster Mathis in Philadelphia in 1995. King and Kiki's father, Shamsud-din Ali, a Muslim cleric from Philadelphia with strong political ties, had done business together and Ali would often bring his daughter to their meetings. She always wanted to talk to Tyson. 'Stay away from her,' King told Tyson more than once. 'Don't go talking to that girl. Leave these people alone. These are not the people to mess with.'

'It was like a moth to a flame,' Kiki said.

They would reconnect in 2003–04 and began living together while she was in New York City. 'That was a disaster,' Kiki said. 'He was cheating and being a pig.'

Tyson admits he wasn't ready for a commitment. 'At that particular time I was an idiot, and I believed that it was normal protocol that everyone should want to be with me,' he said. 'That's what I was taught in life. I didn't know people could really care about you because you're really not that bad of a schmuck. I never thought we'd be in this kind of relationship, never in a hundred years.'

Tyson's philandering ways became a secondary concern when Kiki was charged with federal theft after an investigation into her father's business practices. She was sentenced to six months in prison on April Fool's Day 2007. A week before reporting to prison, she learned she was pregnant with Tyson's child.

'Then she went to prison when I'm in addiction and I'm just running rampant in the streets,' Tyson said. 'I wasn't really thinking about taking care of no woman or having a commitment even though it's really what I wanted to do: have a commitment, raise a family and try to be courageous regardless of my past discrepancies. I wanted to be courageous and try to be a man and raise a family and respect a woman and never cheat. I'd never done that.'

They spoke only once during the six months Kiki was in jail. 'I called once and heard partying in the background,' she said. 'I couldn't stress myself out like that.'

She was released on Mischief Night and would have their daughter, Milan, on Christmas Day, the same birth date as Tyson's mother.

Yet the first time Tyson would see their child was at the Los Angeles premiere of the *Tyson*, the 2008 documentary directed by James Toback. Kiki had moved to Las Vegas initially planning to live with Tyson, but because they were both convicted felons Arizona laws forbade them to live together. 'It was ridiculous,' she says. 'We have a child together but can't live together.'

She would move into a townhouse, not sure if she was fully committed to Tyson or living in Las Vegas. 'I was really humiliated because I had no place to go and I had my baby. I told myself I'm going to give myself six months because I know he's not going to be committed, he's going to screw up, it's not going to work. That's fine. I'm going to come out here for six months to get on my feet and then come back to New York and figure out what my plan is.'

Tyson attended the premiere of his documentary while in the middle of a rehab stay in Los Angeles. He was sent there after failing a urine test stemming from a 2007 guilty plea for cocaine possession and driving under the influence. It was either rehab or a return to prison.

While at the premiere, Tyson met his three-week old baby, but their visit wasn't long. A chaperone connected with the rehab centre had escorted Tyson to the event. As soon as the festivities concluded, he escorted Tyson back to rehab in Los Angeles.

'I'm thinking this is not going to work,' Kiki said. 'We were broke and didn't have money at all. I was thinking about getting into the welfare line.'

By the time Milan was two months old, a flood at Tyson's

home prompted him to defy the law and move in with Kiki. The entourages were long gone and so was the money. Having to depend on each other for survival, it was the first time Tyson began to see himself as someone with a chance at real family.

But he couldn't escape his addiction. 'He would relapse and I would always have this uncomfortable feeling waiting for the other shoe to drop,' Kiki said. 'He would go on binges for two days. We were always trying to find him so he didn't kill himself.'

The worst was a night when Tyson was missing and Kiki found an Internet report saying Mike Tyson had died of an overdose. 'We'd look on line to make sure he hadn't got arrested and then it said, "Mike Tyson dies at age 44 while out partying for his birthday,"' Kiki said. 'His birthday had just passed the week before.'

Calls were made to the coroner's office before Tyson finally surfaced, ending a two-day search. 'I was shaking,' Kiki said. 'I just knew he was dead.'

It took tragedy to convince Tyson of the value of life. On 26 May 2009, Tyson's four-year-old daughter Exodus died after her neck got caught in a treadmill cord at her home in Phoenix. Exodus was found by her seven-year-old brother Miguel. Both children lived with their mother Sol Xochitl, a former girlfriend of Tyson, who was living in Las Vegas at the time.

The tragedy was devastating to Tyson, who went through all the emotions a father would when losing a child. Why wasn't he there? Was there something he could have done? Why hadn't they spent more time together?

Through the tears, Tyson vowed to become a better father to his children and a better husband to Kiki, whom he married shortly afterwards. It began the transformation of Mike Tyson from a boxer who was disdained after disgracing his sport to a man being re-embraced by those who remain fascinated by his life, personality and ring triumphs.

'Look at me now,' Tyson says in the summer of 2012. 'I'm just happy I got involved with her. It's truly a life-saving experience. During my fights, I was aggressive, I was a maniac.

I can't believe now I have a life with a woman, now I'm a pacifist. I don't want to fight any more.'

His public image began to soften after a cameo appearance in the two *Hangover* movies. Then after watching Chazz Palminteri's stage version of *A Bronx Tale* at the Venetian Hotel in 2010, Tyson was confident he could also entertain audiences with his life story. Kiki Tyson helped write the play that ultimately premiered in Las Vegas and landed on Broadway. By then Tyson had lost 130 lb on a vegan diet and was looking fit, trim and happy. He's living the 'courageous life'. That's what Tyson calls it.

'It's something he always wanted but could never commit to,' Kiki Tyson said.

Carrying the stain of being convicted felons has strengthened their bond. They've rescued themselves together. 'I think I needed to go through that to understand how it feels to be constantly judged for something that I didn't do, the way that Mike had to go through that,' Kiki says of Tyson's rape conviction. 'It's having that stigma that as soon as someone knows you've been to prison and that you're a felon, they automatically have an opinion of you before you walk in the door. I always have that in my head ahead of time. I think that helped me in my relationship with him.'

The premiere of *Undisputed Truth* is a triumph for Tyson. He gives the audience a two-hour look into his life. He talks about growing up in Brownsville, Brooklyn, meeting Cus D'Amato, becoming the youngest heavyweight champion ever, Robin Givens, Don King, Buster Douglas, Evander Holyfield and 'the white bitch' he calls cocaine.

His sweat soaks through his pink shirt as Tyson uses large pictures on a screen to move into the different segments of his life. He mimics Don King's laugh, groans when he see the punches he absorbed against Buster Douglas and nearly comes to tears when he speaks about the deaths of his mother, sister Denise and Exodus.

After the show, the man once despised for what he did to

Holyfield is taking pictures with fans who paid $300 to meet the former heavyweight champion. They pay homage to their hero, balling their fists as they wait for the flash of the camera. Kiki sits just off the stage where Tyson can see her, the calming presence amid this new arena of celebrity. It's as if he doesn't want her to leave his sight for fear he could plunge back into the darkness.

'We're going to continue to persevere,' Tyson said of his marriage. 'It's not over yet. The enemy is still out there and we're going to deal with it. The fact that she and I respect one another makes it easier. Respect is more powerful than love. We just respect each other.'

Among those attending the show in Las Vegas was Evander Holyfield, who reconnected with Tyson when the two met on the *Oprah Show* on 16 October 2009. On the show, Tyson made a formal apology for biting him. Oprah, the daytime queen of television, seemed to relish brokering the reunion after Tyson appeared on her show alone and drew sympathetic reviews.

Until their nationally televised summit, there had been tension between them for more than a decade after the fight. Tyson says he always wanted to offer a personal apology but felt Holyfield would be leery of his motives. On *Oprah* they finally reconnected, understanding their careers and lives will be forever entwined.

'I think me and Evander are cool,' Tyson says now. 'We're fighters. He's a hard man, but I'm very sorry to have done something like that. It goes with the business. I was too crazy being a fighter. I had to be the toughest and the meanest. It was too much for me at that stage of my life. I'm so happy I let that go.'

Holyfield has not wanted to let go of boxing. As he approached age 50, he talked of fighting Wladimir or Vitali Klitschko, the tall, strong Ukrainian brothers who have dominated the heavyweight division since Lennox Lewis retired in 2003. 'I'm the only one that has the knowledge and the understanding of how to fight the Klitschkos,' Holyfield said in May 2012. He has clung to the intention of fighting until he captures the undisputed heavyweight championship again even though others cringe at the notion.

Out of the ring, Holyfield's life has endured its share of struggles. The 109-room mansion he built in suburban Georgia was sold for $7.5 million at a foreclosure auction in early 2012. He reportedly owed $14 million in taxes and liens. He was forced to move out of the 54,000-sq. ft home that June.

The house had been Holyfield's prized jewel. It had seventeen bathrooms, three kitchens, a bowling alley, a cinema and an Olympic-sized swimming pool. But after making nearly $200 million in the ring, Holyfield was having money troubles as the result of bad investments and child-support issues stemming from his 11 children.

Holyfield admits he was naive when he came to handling money. He once had $35 million in a regular bank account. 'I didn't want nobody to invest my money, because I ain't got no time to try to kill somebody because they lost my money,' he said.

Those that he trusted didn't always give him the best advice, he says. 'What kind of question is a person going to ask when they don't know what to ask?' Holyfield said. 'I'm the first one in my family to have what I have. I didn't have any brothers and sisters to help me. All at once I had $68 million in one year. When I started making all this money, I had accountants. I had the best of everything. But you can't keep money just by doing what people say. They'll get all your money.'

Investments that Holyfield had faith in but never prospered also hurt him financially. That included a recording company, Real Deal Records, that had only modest success, a restaurant that didn't work and a cable channel envisioned to be the Disney Channel for African Americans.

Jim Thomas tried to discourage Holyfield from assuming so much risk. He says he didn't learn about the cable channel until Holyfield was already fully committed. He recalled a conversation where Holyfield told him, 'I can't listen to you. You don't know anything about money. If you knew something about money, you wouldn't have to work.' Said Thomas, 'I told him, "Evander, there's a lot of people that go to work that know about money."'

Even those Holyfield thought knew about money didn't offer him the best advice, especially when it came to protecting his house and other assets. 'People tell me now you should have done this or did that so they couldn't put liens on your house. They have known that all their life and they tell me that stuff now,' he says. 'They left me wide open for all the things to happen to me.'

Athletes going broke is nothing new. In boxing, it's an epidemic. More house or houses than needed. More cars than two or three garages can hold, women at your beck and call, and dreams of being a billionaire without a business plan. It's a vicious cycle. Tyson calls it part of the metaphors of life in the black community. 'The gambling, the drinking, the drugs, the women, the clothes, the jewellery, the shit talking, the gangster walk, those are all the metaphors of life in the black community,' he said.

Holyfield accepts his share of blame for his financial struggles but says it wasn't all his foolishness. 'If an athlete comes from a generation where he didn't have any money, then he doesn't have any help,' Holyfield said. 'So the only way to get some is you have to believe somebody. When your parents didn't read and I'm the youngest of nine and everybody don't really know any more than I do, then you're just taking advice, and they're going by what somebody else said.'

His battles over child support have also been costly. Holyfield has deflected ridicule for his number of children out of wedlock by stressing, 'I take care of my kids.' But his name was once again in the headlines in June 2012 when he was sued for more than $300,000 in back child support for his 18-year-old daughter, Emani Holyfield.

'It's all in the headlines, but why don't they talk about from the time she was a baby to the time she was 15 years old, I never missed a payment,' Holyfield said. 'They talk about

Evander owes her $320,000. They never say Evander paid her $4 million in child support. How many kids get $4 million? Nobody has asked that.

'All of them are my kids,' he continued. 'But if somebody makes me pay them $20,000 a month and the rest of them $3,000 a month and they say the person in LA needs $20,000 a month and they make me do it, I say, "OK." But when I run out of money and I tell the person I run out of money, how does a person say, "You're still going to do this?"

'They write me up in the paper like you did that kid bad. But nobody said that kid had $4 million. Why didn't this money go into an account for her? Why would it go to the mother if it's for the kid? At least give the kid some of the money. Ultimately, I told the mother, you've got to understand all these other kids I have, I love them, too.'

In November 2012, an auction was held by Julien's Auctions in Beverly Hills to help pay towards Holyfield's debts. Among the 445 items sold were cars, clothing, furniture, photographs, jewellery and boxing memorabilia from his Olympic and professional boxing careers. The list included the boxing gloves he wore in Holyfield–Tyson II, which fetched $35,200.

'There's nothing that ever happened that I don't eventually overcome,' Holyfield said. 'You're not going to get me yelling and screaming and wanting to fight somebody. On this earth you're going to get tested. The only way you're going to get full peace is when you're in heaven. If you're on earth, you're going to be tested by your kids, your cousins, your aunts, everybody. You're going to get tested before you get out of the house every day.

'There ain't no way you're going to run on this earth and find all peace. I understand that and I tell my son that it's part of life. This is testing ground. If you've been put on this ground, you're here for the test.'

Tyson's boxing career passed a test when he was voted into the International Boxing Hall of Fame on his first year of eligibility. He was part of the Class of 2011 that included

Mexican legend Julio César Chávez, four-time light welterweight champion Kostya Tszyu, actor-director Sylvester Stallone, referee Joe Cortez and Mexican trainer Nacho Beristain.

On a cloudy day in Canastota, New York, Tyson was emotional when he accepted his place among boxing royalty. 'I have to be goofy so I don't get so emotional up here,' Tyson said when he took the podium to accept his honour. 'All of this started when I met Cus, well, Bobby Stewart in reform school, because I was always robbing people as a kid.

'All my life I watched these guys and I looked at them different than other people look at them. People would say, watch out for Carmen Basilio because he's always going to go in your pockets and punch you in the ribs like a silly old man. But I know him as a guy who will fight you to his death with every drop of blood in his body.

'Why would I want to be like these guys? When I met Cus we talked a little about money, but we wanted to be great fighters . . .'

He couldn't finish his speech. He was overcome by the emotion of knowing the talks and dreams that began when he met D'Amato when he was 12 years old had come true. He had been the youngest heavyweight champion of the world as Cus said he would be. Now he was in the boxing Hall of Fame, the fraternity of great fighters he had grown up idolising. It's their acceptance that means the most to him.

'When we're fighters, we like to hear from our peers,' Tyson said. 'The only thing that matters is what our peers say. When we hear somebody that's in our field that's trying to get where we were or got where we are, they understand what it took to get there. That's the biggest compliment I get – from my peers.'

From all appearances, it seems Tyson has found stability in his life, valuing sobriety and his role as a husband and father. He has distanced himself from the wild, reckless animal that millions saw in the Holyfield fight.

Ira Trocki, the plastic surgeon turned cut man, is still in Tyson's corner. 'He realises the hurt he's done to many people, mainly himself,' Trocki said. 'But he's really a nice guy and very intelligent. People underestimate him. We all have friends who are a little nutty. It doesn't make them bad. It just makes them nutty. But he loves his kids and he loves being married and he loves turning his life around. He's looking toward the future.'

Tyson says he often doesn't recognise the man he sees on television when replays of his fights are shown. 'When I look at myself on television, I think what was that all about? What was going through me? There was a lot of pain back then,' Tyson said. 'People were robbing you of your money. You don't have what you worked for. You work for everything you have, but you don't have everything you worked for. You're mad, you're frustrated. You're lonely. You feel like you've been betrayed. The dark side of love is betrayal. So you never really respect relationships because you never really respected the relationships you saw your mother in and the other adults you respected.'

He is now trying to be a role model his children can respect. 'I know I've had problems with women in my past and that's why I chose to be courageous and make a different name for myself and make them have a different image of myself in front of women,' Tyson said. 'I have daughters now that I want them to conduct themselves to where I'll be very proud of them. For that to happen I have to conduct myself in a way to show proudness.'

It is a daily battle to stay clean, sober, faithful and live contrary to the image millions saw on 28 June 1997. 'This is life on life's terms,' Tyson said. 'That's what I've learned in all my recovery programmes and recovering from being a self-destructive person. We're not going to be true as people unless we deal with life on life's terms. We deal with life and the situation that exists today, and we deal with the adversity of life today. Forget about the past and live in the present and the future.'

In one of his final interviews before his sudden death on 25 October 2012, the legendary trainer Emanuel Steward marvelled at Tyson's career. 'I never thought he was big enough physically to become the heavyweight champion of the world. But when he turned professional, he was just phenomenal,' Steward said. 'His speed compensated for his shortness and his size. What he accomplished was amazing.'

The admiration for Holyfield and what he accomplished in his career is just as strong. 'There's nothing not to love about Holyfield as a fighter,' HBO's Larry Merchant said. 'He's one of the best fighters ever, certainly one of the best fighters of his time. There are a lot of fighters, Sugar Ray Robinson among them, who fought well past their prime for whatever reason, money or how they define themselves. But to me athletes are measured on what they did in their primes. And he had a long and very successful prime. Nobody ever asked for their money back at one of his fights.'

Ronnie Shields calls Holyfield a 'shoo-in for the Hall of Fame', which goes without question. But that honour won't come until five years after his last fight and there remains uncertainty when that will be. 'Everybody knows the beginning, but nobody knows how it's going to end,' Shields said. 'I just hope and pray that if he does fight again that he doesn't get hurt. That's my only concern. I just hope one day he wakes up and says, "I've done more than any other fighter out there. I'm done." I think so many fans that really care about Evander will be so happy that he came to that decision, and it's a decision he made on his own.'

Jim Thomas summarised Holyfield's career by calling it 'one of the greatest stories of courage and perseverance. He overcame size and became one of the great champions of all time because of his mind and his will. The thing that made him great,' Thomas said, 'was ignoring what people told him his limitations were. He just stopped listening to that.'

Though his ideal dream is to retire as the undisputed heavyweight champion of the world, Holyfield seems at peace with his legacy. Fighters can lose the fortunes, their homes, their relationships and their artifacts, but their legacies as athletes are tied to what they accomplished in the ring and few compare to Evander Holyfield.

'I was able to get through a lot of things,' he said. 'When I really look back at my life, I was geared for boxing. I loved team sports, but in boxing it's not about skin colour. It ain't about nothing but you being able to outwork the other person. It's up to you to let somebody outwork you. They're in pain. You're in pain. But it's who is going to push a little bit farther.'

In many ways, the Bite Fight was not only a signature moment of the boxing careers of Mike Tyson and Evander Holyfield but continues to have a major impact on their current lives. Tyson regrets it happened. 'When I look back at my life and how it is now, to think back at how I could do something like that it's inconceivable,' he said. But he has learned to live with its reality. He complies with fans who ask if they can take a picture of him biting their ear, and in September of 2012 he helped promote Holyfield's new barbeque sauce by tweeting: 'A cookout just isn't a cookout without Real Deal BBQ sauce. Get some! It's ear-licking good!'

Clearly, his fans and friends have forgiven him for that night. When he attends boxing events and his face appears on the big screen, fans cheer wildly. He was especially touched on 20 October 2012, when the Barclays Center in Brooklyn held its first boxing event. Tyson travelled from Las Vegas to be in attendance. When he was introduced, the former hoodlum who once snatched purses and picked pockets in the same neighbourhood was treated to a hero's welcome. Thousands stood and applauded one of their own.

'I've had standing ovations all over the world, but I felt so whole when they were clapping for me in Brooklyn,' Tyson said. 'That was my finest moment in a weird way.'

Among those in attendance that night was Matt Blank, the CEO of Showtime who started his job by signing Tyson to a multi-million contact soon after he was released from prison. On this night in Brooklyn, they embraced and Tyson took pictures with his family. Blank said Tyson 'showed tremendous contrition after the ear-biting incident with Evander,' and doesn't regret the gamble he made signing the fighter.

'With Mike it was a combination of being incredibly mad at him, feeling sorry for him, wanting to help him and on the other hand wanting to earn our investment back,' Blank said. 'But if you asked what the most memorable part of my career was, I would say the signing of Mike Tyson and the ensuing half-dozen years of trying to get Mike in the ring and be successful. Good, bad or indifferent, Mike Tyson was important to boxing. Mike delivered some of the biggest pay-per-view events in boxing history. He was always an attraction. He was an attraction on pay-per-view. He was an attraction when he fought on the network. Mike really, really made the sport very commercial. From our standpoint, it was always interesting. Whenever you signed Mike for a fight, you didn't quite know what would happen. I'm just glad to see Mike seems to have more stability in his life these days. For all the pain and suffering, he was always personally gracious with me even in the toughest of times.'

Holyfield is also saluted when he is in public. He manoeuvres without an entourage and is often seen walking the casinos of Las Vegas by himself during a fight weekend. Every few steps he is stopped and asked for an autograph or a picture. He almost always complies but is never overly warm or friendly to strangers. Such is his nature.

His desire to continue his career in an age when most boxers are long retired has kept the public from fully saluting his legacy the way they have Tyson's. Fans admire what he has done but are concerned with what might lie ahead if he fights again. Holyfield is confident in his own plan.

'What drove me to the top,' he says, 'was so many people reminding me, "You ain't ever going nowhere. You started from the ghetto and you'll land back in the ghetto." I always said it's not going to be like that for me. My mama said she was poor so I would be rich. She said, "Son, everybody makes mistakes. Don't ever get mad for the mistakes you make. A good attitude gives you a second chance." When I go to schools and talk I tell people, "I've had more setbacks than anybody. But do you know how I got through all those setbacks? A good attitude. Treat people right and have a good attitude."'

Holyfield is among those happy Tyson has got his life together. They have both lived their highs and lows in public, bringing both acclaim and embarrassment. But they have survived by holding true to the vision they have of themselves. Both are relying on faith to get them through.

'It's a great thing,' Holyfield said. 'I tell people Mike can probably change more people than anybody because people will look at Mike and say, "If Mike can change, I can change."

'Mike didn't ask for all the things that happened to him as a kid. Then when he became a fighter, people were telling him how he needed to act and everybody liked him for how tough he was, but nobody liked him as a person. All of a sudden he's trying to be Iron Mike the whole time instead of being Iron Mike when you get in the ring and a different person when you're out of the ring.'

Their brief rivalry was an explosive confrontation that was inevitable since their childhood when both were told by their mentors they would be champions one day. Their battles in the ring made an indelible mark on boxing history in ways good and bad. Boxing hasn't been the same since. Today they understand they will be forever linked by what happened at the MGM Grand Garden Arena on 28 June 1997. And all that's happened since the bell sounded: *Ding, Ding*.

BIBLIOGRAPHY

BOOKS

Atlas, Teddy. *Atlas: From the Streets to the Ring: A Son's Struggle to Become a Man.* New York, N.Y., HarperCollins, 2006.

Garrison, J. Gregory and Roberts, Randy. *Heavy Justice: The Trial of Mike Tyson.* Fayetteville, Ark., The University of Arkansas Press, 2000.

Holyfield, Evander & Gruenfeld, Lee. *Becoming Holyfield: A Fighter's Journey.* New York, N.Y., Atria Books, 2008.

Illingworth, Montieth. *Mike Tyson: Money, Myth and Betrayal.* New York, N.Y.: Carol Publishing Group, 1991.

Lane, Mills. *Let's Get It On: Tough Talk From Boxing's Top Ref and Nevada's Most Outspoken Judge.* New York, N.Y., Crown Publishers Inc., 1998.

Layden, Joe. *The Last Great Fight.* New York, N.Y., St. Martin's Press, 2007.

Thomas, James. *The Holyfield Way: What I Learned about Courage, Perseverance and the Bizarre World of Boxing.* Champaign, Ill., Sports Publishing LLC, 2005.

Torres, José. *Fire & Fear: The Inside Story of Mike Tyson.* New York, N.Y.: Warner Books Inc., 1989.

FILMS

30 for 30: One Night in Vegas. ESPN, Air Date Sept. 7, 2010

SportsCentury. *Mike Tyson.* ESPN Classic. HBO

SportsCentury. *Evander Holyfield*. ESPN Classic. HBO
Fallen Champ: The Untold Story of Mike Tyson, Dir. Barbara Kopple, 1993
Tyson, Dir. James Toback, Sony Pictures, 2009

ARTICLES

'Text of Mike Tyson statement.' Associated Press. 1 July 1997.

'Holyfield bit fighter during amateur match.' Associated Press, Boca Raton, Fl., 2 July 1997.

Berns, Dave. 'Fight may have KO'd casino action.' *Las Vegas Review-Journal*. Las Vegas, NV., 1 July 1997.

Carp, Steve. 'Stroke victim Mills Lane, family cope.' *Las Vegas Review-Journal*. Las Vegas, Nev., 9 November 2008.

Feour, Royce. 'Tyson loses license, fined $3 million.' *Las Vegas Review-Journal*, Las Vegas, Nev. 10 July 1997.

Feour, Royce. 'Referee Halpern takes his own life.' *Las Vegas Review-Journal*, Las Vegas, Nev., 22 August 2000.

Gargano, Anthony. 'Iron Mike's team demand new ref.' *New York Post*, New York, N.Y., 26 June 1997, p. 75.

Gargano, Anthony. 'Mike's camp loses ref decision.' *New York Post*, New York, N.Y, 27 June 1997, p. 110.

Gilbert John. 'Ousted referee watches fight at home.' *Las Vegas Review-Journal*, Las Vegas, Nev., 29 June 1997.

Iole, Kevin. 'Champion stunned by Tyson tactics.' *Las Vegas Review-Journal*. Las Vegas, Nev., 29 June 1997.

Keown, Tim. 'Ref wouldn't change Garcia fight.' *San Francisco Chronicle*. San Francisco, Calif., 27 May 1995.

LaBelle, Fran. 'This stockbroker has some fight left in him.' Sun-Sentinel.com, Fort Lauderdale, Florida., 15 March 1988.

Logan, Greg. 'Matter of heart condition ends career of Holyfield.' *Newsday*, Melville, N.Y., 27 April 1994.

Logan, Greg. 'Tyson return a family affair.' *Newsday*, Melville, N.Y., 27 March 1995.

Logan, Greg. 'He's king at getting his man: Promoter tops at closing a deal.' *Newsday*, Melville, N.Y., 1 April 1995.

Matthews, Wallace. 'It's Holyfield, big KOs Douglas in 3rd

round to take title.' *Newsday*, Melville, N.Y., 26 October 1990.

Pope, Bobby. 'Macon boxer Winters had link to Holyfield.' *Macon Telegraph*, Macon, Georgia, 22 October 2012.

Powell, Jeff. 'Lewis will fall in third round says Holyfield.' DailyMail Online, London, 25 February 1999.

Sandomire, Richard. 'Tyson apologizes for bites, saying he "snapped".' *New York Times*, New York, N.Y., 1 July 1997.

Saraceno, Jon. '"I want to tell my story": Mike Tyson's tumultuous life becomes a raw one-man act in Vegas.' *USA Today*, Washington, D.C., 21 March 2012, Sec. C, p. 1–2.

Smith, Timothy W. 'Tyson distances himself from King.' *New York Times*, New York, N.Y., 5 February 1998.

Smith, Timothy W. 'Tyson alleges massive fraud in suit against King.' *New York Times*, New York, N.Y., 6 March 1998.

Smith, Timothy W. 'Report says Tyson has mental woes, but is fit.' *New York Times*, New York, N.Y, 14 October 1998.